DEFENSE POLICY CHOICES
for the Bush Administration

Library of Congress Cataloging-in-Publication data
O'Hanlon, Michael E.
Defense policy choices for the Bush administration 2001–05/
Michael E. O'Hanlon.
   p.   cm.
Includes bibliographical references and index.
ISBN 0-8157-6437-5 (paper)
1. United States—Military policy. 2. United States—Armed Forces.
3. United States—Armed Forces—Appropriations and expenditures.
I. Title.
  UA23 .O33 2001   2001000440
  355'.033573'090511—dc21   CIP

9 8 7 6 5 4 3 2

The paper used in this publication meets minimum requirements of the
American National Standard for Information Sciences—Permanence of Paper for
Printed Library Materials: ANSI Z39.48-1992.

Typeset in Sabon

Composition by R. Lynn Rivenbark
Macon, Georgia

Printed by R. R. Donnelley
Harrisonburg, Virginia

DEFENSE POLICY CHOICES

for the Bush Administration

Second Edition

Michael E. O'Hanlon

BROOKINGS INSTITUTION PRESS
Washington, D.C.

₿ THE BROOKINGS INSTITUTION

The Brookings Institution is an independent organization devoted to nonpartisan research, education, and publication in economics, government, foreign policy, and the social sciences generally. Its principal purposes are to aid in the development of sound public policies and to promote public understanding of issues of national importance.

The Institution was founded on December 8, 1927, to merge the activities of the Institute for Government Research, founded in 1916, the Institute of Economics, founded in 1922, and the Robert Brookings Graduate School of Economics and Government, founded in 1924.

The general administration of the Institution is the responsibility of a Board of Trustees charged with safeguarding the independence of the staff and fostering the most favorable conditions for scientific research and publication. The immediate direction of the policies, program, and staff is vested in the president, assisted by an advisory committee of the officers and staff.

In publishing a study, the Institution presents it as a competent treatment of a subject worthy of public consideration. The interpretations or conclusions in such publications are those of the author or authors and do not necessarily reflect the views of the other staff members, officers, or trustees of the Brookings Institution.

To

Ray Della,
Jack Lamb, James Lynch,
and the memory of
Steve Austin and Al Briskey

Foreword

In this 2002 revision to his 2001 book, Michael O'Hanlon describes and assesses the Bush administration's defense policy and proposes a somewhat different and less expensive defense plan for the United States. He is grateful to Aaron Moburg-Jones for research assistance and to James Steinberg for his guidance and suggestions.

As in the previous edition of this book, O'Hanlon is further grateful to his former research assistants, Jason Forrester and Micah Zenko, as well as Todd DeLelle, for tireless work in helping him prepare the study. He also thanks Richard Haass, David Mosher, David Ochmanek, and Tom Stefanick, who provided invaluable comments, as well as Brookings military fellows Lansen Conley, Terry Lockard, and Bernard Zipp for their suggestions. Jeffrey Caspers, Shuhfan Ding, David Fidler, Brian Finlay, Bates Gill, Sean Lynn-Jones, Dennis Stokowski, Robert Suettinger, John Wissler, and I Yuan helped considerably with the analysis of Taiwan-China scenarios. Thanks are also owed to Dana Allin, Richard Betts, Stephen Biddle, Ivo Daalder, Michele Flournoy, Richard Garwin, Candice Geouge, Philip Gordon, Jeffrey Hunker, James Lindsay, Andrew Marshall, Ellen McHugh, Tara Miller, Mike Mochizuki, Monique Principi, Frank von Hippel, and a number of officials at the Department of Defense.

The author would like to thank the Department of Defense for its support of this effort.

The views expressed here are solely those of the author and should not be ascribed to the persons whose assistance is acknowledged above or to the trustees, officers, or other staff members of the Brookings Institution.

MICHAEL H. ARMACOST
President

April 2002
Washington, D.C

Contents

DEFENSE POLICY CHOICES

for the Bush Administration

ONE Introduction

A decade after the end of the cold war, the process of cutting United States defense forces and defense spending is over. The United States has chosen to retain a substantial global military capability, making it the only country on the world scene that does so and rightfully earning it the moniker of the sole surviving superpower. Moreover, it has managed to trim its military by one-third, without imperiling the basic quality and cohesion of the armed forces. Without reversing those cuts in forces and personnel, it is now planning on a major defense spending increase that would return resources to Reagan-like levels (see tables 1-1 and 1-2).

Why is this the case? September 11 provides some of the answer, but there are other factors at work as well. Although the U.S. military remains excellent, there are numerous strains and shortfalls in its combat readiness. Personnel are being worked to the limit of their endurance; many are voting with their feet and leaving the services, though fewer than in the late 1990s. Equipment purchased largely during the Reagan buildup of the 1980s is beginning to wear out in large blocs, necessitating prompt replacement. New security challenges require attention—most notably defending America against various forms of attack, as well as being ready to face clever potential adversaries who would likely identify and exploit American military vulnerabilities more effectively than Saddam Hussein did in 1991. Possible conflicts against Iran, Iraq, and

Table 1-1. *National Security Spending, Various Years, Historical Perspective*

Billions of constant 2002 dollars

Year	Outlays
Planned, 2007	406
Planned, 2003	372
2002	348
2000	295
Cold war average	335
1980s peak (1989)	410
1990	390
1982–91, ten-year average	370
1992–2001, ten-year average	310

Source: Office of the Under Secretary of Defense (Comptroller), *National Defense Budget Estimates for FY 2003*, March 2002; and Executive Office of the President, *Budget of the United States Government Fiscal Year 2001* (GPO, 2000), p. 118.

Note: Includes spending for Department of Energy nuclear weapons programs. National security budget authority would be $420 billion in 2007 (or $470 billion in nominal dollars).

North Korea remain serious concerns, and the specter of conflict with China over Taiwan has become more worrisome.

This book considers how to address these new challenges and how to do so within realistic fiscal limits. The war on terrorism and the Bush administration's budget plans make it reasonable to anticipate that real defense spending will increase. However, increases are unlikely to be as great as the Pentagon now expects. The Congressional Budget Office (CBO) forecasts deficits through 2009 (not counting Social Security surpluses); in these circumstances, year-after-year defense budget jumps may prove politically unsustainable. Moreover, the homeland security budget

Table 1-2. *Defense Personnel, 1990–2000*

Thousands unless otherwise specified

Component	1990	2000	Percent change, 1990–2000
Active	2,069	1,408	32
Reserve	1,128	865	23
Civilian	1,070	700	35

Source: For active component, as of June 30, 2000, Office of the Secretary of Defense, http://web1.whs.osd.mil/mmid/military/ms0.pdf (September 14, 2000). For reserve and civilian component, as of September 30, 1999, William Cohen, *Annual Report to the President and Congress* (Department of Defense, February 2000), appendix C-1.

may be more important than many defense needs in this new era, making it important on national security grounds to restrain Pentagon spending (a summary of that budget is presented later in this chapter). To respect fiscal realities and to relieve the heavy burdens being placed on the men and women of the armed forces, difficult decisions will need to be made on subjects ranging from overseas deployments to force structure to weapons modernization goals.

Some observers believe that U.S. defense spending should be drastically reduced. Noting that it now constitutes more than one-third of global defense outlays, roughly as much as the world's next eighteen military powers combined, about five times more than either China's or Russia's defense spending, and about thirty times the sum of Iranian, Iraqi, and North Korean military spending, they question why America's annual defense budget remains at around $350 billion today (see tables 1-3 and 1-4).

However, such broad arguments are unpersuasive. There are good reasons why the United States should spend far more than any other country on its military. The United States has unique global interests and multiple military commitments far from its national territory. It maintains worldwide military deployments to keep alliances credible. It rightly desires a military so unambiguously strong that it can generally deter war and, failing that, win decisive victories with minimal casualties. Finally, given that its armed forces are not particularly large (constituting only about 6 percent of global military manpower), it relies on high-quality and thus expensive equipment and manpower rather than sheer size for its war-fighting edge.

Even if the United States cut its defense spending in half, it would still outspend Iran, Iraq, and North Korea by a factor of fifteen, and China by more than 2 to 1. Yet it would then have far too small a military to maintain its global commitments. As a result, potential foes might be tempted to attack U.S. allies in key regions such as the Persian Gulf and Northeast Asia. Recognizing the potential danger, these U.S. allies would be likely to embark on military buildups, perhaps even pursuing nuclear weapons capabilities, in a manner that could be destabilizing. So broad defense budget comparisons resolve little, especially when made between countries with different types of global military responsibilities, economies, and political systems.

Finally, although U.S. defense spending remains high in absolute terms, it is far smaller as a percent of the nation's economic output than

Table 1-3. *Global Distribution of Military Spending, 1999*

Countries	Defense spending (billions of 1999 dollars)	Percent of global total	Running total (percent)
United States and its major security partners			
United States	283.1	35.0	35
NATO (not including the United States)	186.1	23.0	58
Major Asian allies[a]	60.3	7.4	65
Other allies[b]	39.7	4.9	70
Other friends[c]	66.4	8.2	79
Others			
Russia	56.8	6.9	85
China	39.9	4.9	90
"Rogue states"[d]	11.4	1.4	92
Remaining Asian countries	34.7	4.3	96
Remaining European countries	9.5	1.2	97
Remaining Middle Eastern countries	10.8	1.3	98
Others[e]	9.8	1.9	100
Total	808.5	100	100

Source: International Institute for Strategic Studies, *The Military Balance 2000/2001* (Oxford University Press, 2000), pp. 297–302.

a. Japan, South Korea, and Australia.

b. New Zealand, Thailand, Philippines, and the Rio Pact countries minus Cuba.

c. Austria, Belize, Egypt, Guyana, Israel, Ireland, Jordan, Kuwait, Oman, Qatar, Saudi Arabia, Suriname, Sweden, Switzerland, and Taiwan.

d. Cuba, North Korea, Iran, Iraq, and Libya.

e. Principally African and Caribbean countries.

at any time during the cold war. In fact, the 3 percent of gross domestic product (GDP) currently devoted to the armed forces is about half that of the Reagan era and about one-third that of the early cold war decades (see figure 1-1). Even the planned Bush administration increases will not push defense spending beyond 3.5 percent of GDP. Some use this historical perspective to argue, rather unconvincingly, that current U.S. defense spending should increase to perhaps 4 percent of GDP. But the real point is that such broad, sweeping arguments can be marshaled to suggest that U.S. military spending is either very high or very low, and hence prove

Table 1-4. *Defense Spending by NATO and Major Formal U.S. Allies, 1999*

Country	Defense expenditures (billions of 1999 dollars)	Percent of GDP	Size of armed forces (thousands)
NATO			
United States	283.1	3.1	1,371.5
France	37.9	2.7	317.3
United Kingdom	36.9	2.6	212.4
Germany	31.1	1.6	332.8
Italy	22.0	2.0	265.5
Turkey	10.2	5.5	639
Canada	7.5	1.2	60.6
Spain	7.3	1.3	186.5
Netherlands	7.0	1.8	56.4
Greece	5.2	5.0	165.6
Belgium	3.4	1.5	41.8
Poland	3.2	2.1	240.7
Norway	3.1	2.2	30.7
Denmark	2.7	1.6	24.3
Portugal	2.3	2.2	49.7
Czech Republic	1.2	2.3	58.2
Hungary	0.7	1.6	43.4
Luxembourg	0.1	0.8	0.8
Iceland	...	...	...
Total, non-U.S. NATO	186.1	2.2	2,725.6
Total, NATO	469.2	2.2	4,097.1
Other major formal U.S. allies			
Japan	40.4	0.9	242.6
South Korea	12.1	3.0	672.0
Australia	7.8	1.9	55.2
Total, other major U.S. allies	60.3	1.9	969.8
Grand total	529.5	2.1	5,066.9

Source: International Institute for Strategic Studies, *The Military Balance 2000/2001*, pp. 297, 299.

Figure 1-1. *U.S. Defense Spending Relative to Gross Domestic Product, Fiscal Years 1947–2007*

Percentage of GDP

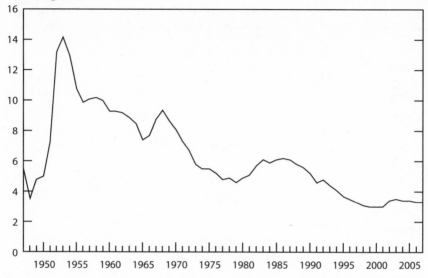

Source: *Budget of the United States Government, Fiscal Year 2001* (February 2000), pp. 103–09; *Budget of the United States Government, Fiscal Year 2003* (February 2002), p. 126.

little by themselves. A more detailed strategic and military assessment is needed to reach a thoughtful conclusion about whether military spending is adequate, and about how U.S. defense resources should be spent. This book offers such an assessment.

A Successful Defense Drawdown

Along with cuts in annual defense spending and troop strength, the combat force structure of the U.S. military has also declined considerably over the last decade. Most types of units—such as Army divisions and Air Force fighter wings—have been reduced by 20 to 40 percent (see table 1-5).

Nevertheless, the past decade has hardly been a story of cuts alone. The defense budget has not dropped below 85 percent of its overall cold war average and has recently returned to that average. Three consecutive

Table 1-5. *Major Elements of Force Structure, 1990 and 2000*

Service unit	1990	2000
Army		
Active divisions	18	10
Reserve brigades	57	42
Navy		
Aircraft carriers (active/reserve)	15 (1)	11 (1)
Air wings (active/reserve)	13 (2)	10 (1)
Attack submarines	91	55
Surface combatants	206	116
Air Force		
Active fighter wings	24	12+
Reserve fighter wings	12	7+
Reserve air defense squadrons	14	4
Bombers (total)	277	190[a]
Marine Corps		
Marine expeditionary forces	3	3

Source: Cohen, *Annual Report to the President and Congress,* chapter 5, table 2.
a. Reflects the planned reduction of eighteen B-52 aircraft.

presidents and five defense secretaries, while differing on details, have agreed to sustain a U.S. military prepared for two nearly simultaneous major regional conflicts, at least one of them akin to Operation Desert Storm. They have maintained all preexisting U.S. security commitments in Europe, the Middle East, East Asia, and Latin America. In fact, they have increased the overall number of allies that the United States is committed to defend, notably by successfully promoting the membership of Poland, Hungary, and the Czech Republic in the North Atlantic Treaty Organization (NATO) alliance, and by helping protect the new government in Afghanistan.

As a result of these strategic interests and commitments, the United States has also decided to sustain overseas U.S. military presence in all the theaters where it was sustained before, albeit on a smaller scale in most cases. Roughly 100,000 U.S. military personnel are routinely found in East Asia, a comparable number in Europe, and lesser but nonetheless significant numbers in the Persian Gulf (see table 1-6). These overseas forces are intended to deter countries including Iraq, North Korea, and

Table 1-6. *U.S. Military Personnel in Foreign Areas, 1986–2001*

Thousands of troops

Country or region	1986	1996	2001
Germany	250	49	71
Other European countries	75	66	42
Europe, afloat	33	4	5
South Korea	43	37	38
Japan	48	43	40
Other Asia-Pacific countries	17	1	1
Afloat in East, South, and Southeast Asia, plus all forces in Persian Gulf/North Africa	36	30	40
Western Hemisphere	22	12	14
Miscellaneous	1	1	4
Global total	525	240	255
Percent of total active-duty strength	24	16	19

Source: Department of Defense, *Worldwide Manpower Distribution by Geographical Area*, September 30, 2001, September 30, 1996, and September 30, 1986. All available at http://web1.whs.osd.mil/mid/military/miltop/htm. Numbers may not add up to totals due to rounding.

China from attacking their neighbors, to prevent friendly states from feeling the need to build undesirably large conventional forces or to pursue nuclear weapons to ensure their security unilaterally, to give credibility to key alliances, and to promote American values in saving lives and promoting democracy. In addition, about 30,000 U.S. military personnel have been deployed to Central Asia in recent months, roughly a third of them in and around Afghanistan and the remainder in the Arabian Sea.

Two presidents of different parties, and several Congresses led by both major U.S. political parties, carried out the 1990s U.S. defense drawdown. They have much to be proud of. Never before has the United States adapted to a major change in geostrategic circumstances so carefully and so prudently, neither letting down its guard nor hollowing out its military in the process. Mistakes have been made over the past decade, and some of them have exacted a heavy toll on the men and women of the armed forces in terms of their workload, their time away from home, and their general morale. Nevertheless, the problems can easily be exaggerated and the accomplishment taken for granted. U.S. military forces remain remarkably capable and ready today, as the war in Afghanistan has again demonstrated, just as the Kosovo war did in 1999 and as other operations have done throughout the past several years.

The 2001 Quadrennial Defense Review

Even though the 1990s defense drawdown was unquestionably the most successful in the nation's history, the Bush administration came into office bent on major change in defense policy. In the end, it settled on a defense strategy that departed from the previous Bush and Clinton policies only modestly, in terms of broad concepts, forces, and requirements. However, in the aftermath of September 11, it proposed a major defense budget increase that had more in common with Ronald Reagan's presidency than the administration's immediate predecessors.[1]

Donald Rumsfeld's Quadrennial Defense Review (QDR) was originally expected to emphasize ideas that had their antecedents in a speech given by then-governor George Bush in September 1999 at the Citadel in South Carolina. In that message, Bush promised a radically transformed U.S. military if elected president. He promised to "skip a generation" of weapons purchases in order to create a military featuring advanced systems. Major increases in research and development spending would help usher in such new capabilities. Cutbacks in overseas military presence, especially peacekeeping operations, would help provide some of the financial and human resources needed to make such a revolution feasible within affordable defense budgets (which, according to candidate Bush, would grow by only about $5 billion relative to the annual levels planned by the outgoing Clinton administration).[2]

Once in office, Mr. Bush continued to promise a radical overhaul, as did his new secretary of defense, Donald Rumsfeld. Word from the Pentagon suggested a new emphasis on long-range strike systems and more focus on possible future competition with a rising China. European commitments were reportedly seen as less important; Iraq and North Korea were seen as nagging problems from yesterday, not major concerns for the future; unconventional or "asymmetric" military tactics were

1. This section draws in part on Michael O'Hanlon, "Rumsfeld's Defence Vision," *Survival* (Summer 2002).

2. Governor George W. Bush, "A Period of Consequences," speech at the Citadel, South Carolina, September 23, 1999 (www.citadel.edu/pao/addresses/pres_bush.html).

expected from enemies (though there was at least as much emphasis on asymmetric attacks by countries as on terrorists). In addition, Rumsfeld brought a great concern with the ballistic-missile threat and a conviction that warfare would soon move into space.[3]

Ultimately, however, the Bush administration chose not to cut existing weapons programs, streamline the combat force structure, or reduce overseas deployments of the American armed forces.[4] In fact, the absence of almost any change in any of these areas was striking. The 2001 QDR contained the fewest programmatic and force structure initiatives of any of the four major U.S. defense reviews since the end of the cold war (as it contained virtually none). Before September 11, Secretary Rumsfeld had essentially settled on a conservative Quadrennial Defense Review document.

There were changes and initiatives, to be sure. At the rhetorical and conceptual levels, Rumsfeld placed homeland security at the top of the Pentagon's agenda.[5] He also emphasized the need to accelerate the process of defense innovation—or transformation, as it is increasingly known by those who sense the opportunity for a major change in U.S. combat forces in the years ahead and wish to accelerate that change.[6]

But at the practical level, Rumsfeld essentially reaffirmed the core elements of Clinton administration defense policy—in terms of forces, weapons modernization plans, overseas troop commitments, and most other concrete matters. Given that this was the fourth major defense review of the post–cold war era, including the first Bush administration's base force concept, as well as the Clinton administration's 1993 Bottom-Up Review and 1997 Quadrennial Defense Review, there was perhaps less pressing need for a radical rethinking. But given the administration's early rhetoric, the continuity with Clinton policy was nonetheless surprising.

Secretary Rumsfeld promised that his QDR, released on schedule on September 30, 2001, would hardly be his last word on defense reform. Numerous panels were created to continue reviews of overseas military presence. (General language about increasing carrier presence in the western Pacific while also eventually moving some medium-weight ground

---

3. See for example, Thomas E. Ricks, "Rumsfeld Outlines Defense Overhaul: Reorganization May Alter, Kill Weapons Systems," *Washington Post*, March 23, 2001, p. A1.

4. See Secretary of Defense Donald H. Rumsfeld, *Quadrennial Defense Review Report* (Department of Defense, September 30, 2001), available at (www.defenselink.mil).

5. Rumsfeld, *Quadrennial Defense Review Report*, pp. 17–20.

6. Rumsfeld, *Quadrennial Defense Review Report*, pp. 29–32.

forces into Europe and more Army capability into the Persian Gulf was included in the report.)[7] A commitment was made to use the annual budget cycle to review plans for purchasing weaponry, since the QDR had not done so (in contrast to the previous defense reviews of the Clinton and first Bush administrations). Obviously, in the aftermath of the tragic September 11 attacks, a whole new agenda concerning home-land security rapidly became paramount in Pentagon thinking as well; until then, Secretary Rumsfeld's primary concern in this area had been ballistic missiles. So in that sense, the QDR is more of a starting point than a definitive study. In fact, Secretary Rumsfeld later argued that defense reviews should be conducted in the second year of a new admin-istration, essentially acknowledging that he had not had enough time to fully digest all the issues before him in time for the September 30, 2001, deadline imposed on him and implying that he would come up with fur-ther policy proposals in the months ahead.

Secretary Rumsfeld's QDR retained the planned Clinton administra-tion force structure with only the smallest of modifications. He stated an intention to retain, at least for the foreseeable future, ten active-duty Army divisions, roughly twenty Air Force fighter wings (specifically, forty-six active squadrons and thirty-eight reserve squadrons, with four squadrons in the typical wing), three Marine Corps divisions and associ-ated air wings, twelve Navy aircraft carriers and eleven associated air wings, 116 additional surface combatants, fifty-five attack submarines, and over 100 bombers.[8] These numbers are all virtually identical to those in the Clinton administration's 1997 QDR. In fact, they differ only slightly from the numbers in the 1993 Bottom-Up Review, though they are often 10 to 25 percent less than what was proposed by the first Bush administration in its "base force" concept. Similarly, while the base force envisioned active-duty troop levels of more than 1.6 million, the 2001 QDR reaffirms Clinton administration levels of just under 1.4 million.

Implicitly, Rumsfeld retained the Clinton weapons modernization agenda as well, since he indicated no new plans. He repeated the Clinton administration's intention to ask Congress for the authority to close more military bases, ultimately convincing Congress to approve another round in 2005 (two years later than he would have liked, but better than noth-ing). He also added other efficiency initiatives, such as a desire to further

---

7. Rumsfeld, *Quadrennial Defense Review Report*, p. 27.
8. Rumsfeld, *Quadrennial Defense Review Report*, pp. 22–23.

privatize defense support functions and to streamline headquarters staffs by 15 percent.[9]

Perhaps the most notable nuts-and-bolts decision made by Rumsfeld in these early months, as codified in the QDR, was to increase funding for the military simply to improve immediate combat readiness. Arguing, just as candidate Bush had done, that the Clinton administration had neglected the basic needs of the military, he continued a trend, begun in the late 1990s, of adding money to readiness accounts. Specifically, he added nearly $6 billion to the 2001 defense budget through a supplemental appropriation request, and then nearly another $20 billion above what the Clinton administration had envisioned for the 2002 budget, all before September 11. Previous initiatives of the Republican Congress and the Clinton administration had focused on military pay, equipment spare parts, and resources for training. Rumsfeld added yet more money to these accounts, while also increasing funding for improving military health care and the Department of Defense's infrastructure—that is, facilities such as housing and bases.[10]

Backing away from the campaign rhetoric about reducing U.S. deployments abroad, Rumsfeld decided that U.S. forces should essentially remain in their current configurations overseas. Indeed, his desire that forward forces should, in conjunction with regional allies, be able to defeat attacks quickly without requiring large reinforcements pointed, if anything, in the direction of increasing capabilities based abroad (though the QDR indicates a hope that improved technologies, rather than increased troop numbers, would provide these enhanced capabilities).[11] Rumsfeld also conceded that smaller operations, including but not limited to peacekeeping missions, might sometimes be necessary and made explicit allowance for that possibility in sizing the force structure.[12]

At a more strategic level, Rumsfeld argued for a shift in thinking about the scenarios that should guide U.S. force planning. Claiming that a fixation on replays of Desert Storm against Iraq and North Korea was harming the armed forces' abilities to prepare for other threats, he shifted force planning away from a requirement that two all-out regional wars could

---

9. Rumsfeld, *Quadrennial Defense Review Report*, pp. 49–53.
10. Rumsfeld, *Quadrennial Defense Review Report*, pp. 7–10.
11. Rumsfeld, *Quadrennial Defense Review Report*, p. 20.
12. Rumsfeld, *Quadrennial Defense Review Report*, p. 21.

be won almost simultaneously. Instead, he held out a slightly less demanding standard: a requirement that one such war be won in absolute terms—including an overthrow of the enemy government and occupation of its territory—while a second war was prosecuted vigorously enough to stop an enemy and begin some offensive operations against it. In other words, Rumsfeld retained the requirement for a two-front warfighting capability, but adjusted Pentagon expectations about the likely nature of that two-front worst-case scenario. Undoubtedly thinking that one future adversary might be a country such as China, instead of Iraq or North Korea, he also avoided specifying who the likely foes would be. His QDR described such generic defense planning as a "capabilities-based" approach, in contrast with the Clinton administration's scenario-oriented or "threat-based" framework that more explicitly designated likely future foes.[13] But this change seemed more semantic than real, since capabilities ultimately must be sized to specific scenarios and to likely foes if they are to be adequate for the potential tasks at hand. At most, the resulting change was one of nuance.

In keeping with the desire to avoid fixation on Iraq and North Korea, Rumsfeld also advocated the idea of standing joint task forces. Today's U.S. military does, of course, have standing units within the individual armed services—divisions and wings and so on—as well as permanent headquarters for handling specific theaters and specific trouble spots, such as Korea. But it does not have permanent formations involving units from numerous services that train together frequently and that would essentially be on call for unexpected contingencies. Rumsfeld would remedy that shortfall.

The QDR was notable for several other changes as well. In contrast to the Clinton administration's emphasis on "shaping" the international environment through "engagement" with neutral countries such as China, Rumsfeld talked only of reassuring allies and of dissuading, deterring, or if necessary defeating enemies. The concept of devising proper U.S. policies toward a genuinely neutral country was not given much attention—though Rumsfeld has been busily doing just that since September 11 in his dealing with the likes of Pakistan, Uzbekistan, Tajikistan, and Russia.

Continuing a desire to foster military innovation—even if no longer using the radical rhetoric and compressed time horizons of many enthusiastic proponents of a revolution in military affairs—Rumsfeld and the

13. Rumsfeld, *Quadrennial Defense Review Report*, p. 21.

Table 1-7. *Department of Defense Discretionary Budget Authority*

Billions of dollars

Category	2002 estimate	2003 estimate
Military personnel	82.0	94.3
Operations and maintenance	127.7	150.4
Procurement	61.1	68.7
RDT&E	48.4	53.9
Military construction	6.5	4.8
Family housing	4.1	4.2
Other	4.5	3.0
Total discretionary budget authority (not including Department of Energy)	334.3	379.3

Source: Department of Defense,"FY 2003 Defense Budget," February 2002.

Bush administration made several key decisions. They advocated significant increases in research and development funding, a greater emphasis on joint-service experiments (most innovation takes place within, not between, the individual military services today), and support for new ideas, such as the Army's desire to create lighter, more deployable units.

The September review was silent on the question of costs; only with its February 2002 budget proposal for 2003 did the Bush administration attach dollars to its plan. And that is where the biggest changes from the Clinton administration arise. The Clinton administration's national security budget had grown to about $300 billion a year by 2001 (including about $15 billion in annual funding for nuclear weapons activities at the Department of Energy). Incorporating the effects of September 11 and Operation Enduring Freedom in Afghanistan, President Bush's budgets are now as follows: $329 billion in 2001, $351 billion in 2002, and $396 billion proposed for 2003 (see table 1-7 for the Pentagon's share of these budgets).

Equally striking are the price tags envisioned for the years ahead: $405 billion (2004), $426 billion (2005), $447 billion (2006), and $470 billion (2007). Congress will not act on those budget plans immediately, but the plans show where the Bush administration's budgets are headed if they are approved by Congress: toward a period of very high defense spending.

In a sense, the increases are not quite as great as they seem. The figures for 2001–03 include the costs of the antiterrorism war; all the figures include funding for the Department of Defense's heightened vigilance and contributions to homeland security after September 11. All of these combined costs were running about $30 billion a year in 2002. Moreover, due to the effects of inflation, the $470 billion budget for 2007 represents about $425 billion when expressed in 2002 dollars. And compared to the size of the U.S. economy, defense spending would still reflect a smaller fraction of GDP—about 3.5 percent—than at any time during the cold war.

Still, despite these factors, the increases are remarkable. The Pentagon's budget in 2007 would be a full $100 billion greater than what the Clinton administration had envisioned for that year in its own long-term plan. And these figures would approach the peak levels of the Reagan years, as well as those of the Vietnam era.

Why does President Bush wish to restore defense spending to such high levels? He does not plan to increase the size of the military, which remains one-third smaller than in cold war times. Moreover, with the exception of missile defense, Bush administration officials have not yet added any major weapons systems to the modernization plan they inherited from their predecessors. Instead, the Bush administration claims that in general it is only fully funding the force structure and weapons procurement agenda that was laid out in Secretary of Defense William Cohen's 1997 Quadrennial Defense Review, as well as the immediate exigencies of the war on terrorism. This argument can be seen explicitly in the Pentagon's breakdown of the proposed increase in the 2003 defense budget, as shown in table 1-8.

The main point that the Bush administration wishes to make with this table is that most of the $48 billion added between 2002 and 2003 follows almost automatically from the policies and plans the administration inherited as well as the demands of war. The Bush administration is essentially arguing that $36.6 billion of the increase is necessary, given preexisting policy, and another $10 billion is simply a conservative estimate of what military operations will entail in 2003. Indeed, were it not for the $9.3 billion in program cuts, postponements, and accounting changes the Bush administration managed to make, virtually no money would be left for other purposes, such as increased weapons acquisition. Even the $9.8 billion added for weapons will fund a plan for fighter jets, ships, Army transformation, and other advanced systems that was primarily inherited from Clinton administration.

Table 1-8. *Understanding the Increases in the 2003 Defense Budget Proposal (Department of Defense Funding Only)*

Billions of dollars of budget authority

Item	Amount
Enacted budget for 2002	331.2
Upward adjustment for inflation	6.7
"Must-pay" bills	
Over-65 health care	8.1
Civilian retirement/health care	3.3
Military and civilian pay raises	2.7
Subtotal	14.1
Realistic costing	
Realistic weapons costing	3.7
Readiness funding	3.1
Depot maintenance	0.6
Subtotal	7.4
Cost of war (including $10 billion contingency fund)	19.4
All other requirements[a]	9.8
Savings from transfers and program cuts or delays	–9.3
Total 2003 budget request	379.3

Source: Department of Defense, "FY 2003 Defense Budget," February 2002.
a. For example, weapons acquisition.

For those who doubt the need for added defense spending, it is further true that a military of a given size costs more to maintain each year. Whether it is the price of weaponry, the burden of providing military health care to active-duty troops and their families, as well as to retirees, or the price of paying good people enough to retain them, most defense costs rise faster than inflation. Moreover, the U.S. military took a "procurement holiday" of sorts during the 1990s, since money was tight and it had so much modern weaponry on hand after the Reagan buildup. That holiday must now end, as systems age and require refurbishing or replacement.

In addition, it is necessary to build on the lessons of Operation Enduring Freedom. That conflict has demonstrated, more than any other before, the importance of unmanned aerial vehicles, real-time information networks, certain precision munitions, and good equipment for special

Table 1-9. *Desirable "Transformation" Initiatives in 2003 Budget Proposal*

Millions of dollars

Initiative	Amount
Convert 4 ballistic-missile submarines to cruise missiles	1,018
Add funding for new satellite communication system	826
Add funding for space-based radar	43
Add funding for Global Hawk unmanned aerial vehicles (UAVs)	629
Accelerate development of new UAVs	141
Upgrade, arm, and purchase more Predator UAVs	158
Develop small-diameter bomb	54
Initiate Navy unmanned underwater vehicle	83
Start new program for advanced surface combatant technologies	961
Expand wideband, secure global communications network	1,300
Upgrade data links to combat platforms and troops	3,300

Source: Department of Defense, "FY 2003 Defense Budget," February 2002.

operations forces. These and most other "transformation" initiatives proposed by the Bush administration merit support (see table 1-9).

Because of these various factors, real defense spending should indeed continue to increase, as it has been doing since 1999. It makes perfect sense that today's military, though only two-thirds the size of the cold war force, might cost nearly as much. It is surprising, however, that the Bush budget would not only reach but would easily exceed the cold war defense budget average, especially as expected spending in the war against terrorism declines substantially after 2003.

Critical Assessment of the Rumsfeld Plan

There are many sound elements to Rumsfeld's strategic plan, even if it is strikingly cautious for an administration that promised radical military transformation and a sharp break with the ways of the Clinton administration. The broad force structure it retains seems roughly right—anything larger would likely be unaffordable and dampen the services' incentives to find more efficient ways of doing business, anything much smaller would risk running ragged an already busy military. The adjustment in the two-war standard to a different and slightly less demanding type of two-front capability is prudent. After much early criticism by the Bush administration of peacekeeping operations and other such missions, capabilities for providing overseas presence and conducting smaller contingencies were retained as a core part of the force structure. Several of the review's new initiatives—standing joint task forces to prepare better for conflict outside the Persian Gulf and Korea, a greater emphasis on research and development as well as joint-service experimentation with new technologies and warfighting concepts—also make sense.

In its specific responses to the threat of terrorism, Rumsfeld's review also offers some sound thinking. Elevating the mission of homeland security to one of the top priorities in official defense strategy makes sense. Clearly, nothing could be more important for U.S. security than protecting the lives, property, and infrastructure of American society. At the same time, Rumsfeld was right not to make that mission the only top priority of the Pentagon, since doing so could logically have led to a reduced commitment to American overseas interests—and in effect, victory for the terrorists who seek such a result. To sustain a strong coalition effort against terrorism, the United States needs to remain committed to the security of its friends and allies; to deny terrorists safe havens in countries besides Afghanistan, it has even more reason to retain some form of a two-front warfighting capability; to prevent proliferation of dangerous weaponry, it has to keep a vigilant eye on countries such as North Korea and Iraq; to sustain its values, it must continue support for friends such as Israel, Taiwan, and other democracies; to keep its economy strong, it must continue to undergird global stability and commerce with its military forces. Thus counterterrorism and homeland security should indeed be a top priority for the Department of Defense and U.S. government more generally. But they should not become the exclusive top priority.

There are, however, several problems in Rumsfeld's review that could hinder the broader struggle against terrorism and the overall effort to enhance homeland security. The most basic problem is conceptual: the review actually downplays the importance of working with nonallied but nonhostile countries. Dropping the 1997 QDR's strategic pillars of "shape, prepare, and respond" (where the concept of shaping refers in part to the need to work with neutral countries) and the broader Clinton administration notion of engagement, it divides the world cleanly into those who are with us and those who are against. More specifically and formally, it lays out four goals for defense policy: to reassure allies, and to dissuade, deter, or if necessary defeat enemies. Where countries such as Russia, China, and India fit into this scheme is far from clear. Other elements of U.S. foreign policy may be able to compensate for the lack of an explicit emphasis on working with these states, and in fact many activities once described as engagement have been continued by Rumsfeld himself, especially since September 11. But dropping the idea of engagement is nonetheless a mistake, particularly in light of the obvious post–September 11 need to improve relations and work collaboratively with a number of countries that are neither treaty ally nor foe.

That said, the most important problem with Rumsfeld's review is probably budgetary. In light of shrinking federal surpluses, and competing national and international needs, spending increases of the type now implied by Rumsfeld's QDR are undesirable.

Rumsfeld is right to want to close unneeded military bases (as Congress now seems likely to do in 2005), streamline military headquarters, and find other economies in defense operations. But more must be done, given the country's fiscal situation and competing national priorities. Within a year or so the politics of the defense budget are likely to change, and the Pentagon may find it very difficult to sustain the new upward trend in defense budgets thereafter.

As a result, Secretary Rumsfeld will have to find less expensive ways to replenish the military's aging equipment stocks, perhaps by buying simpler fighter jets, ships, helicopters, and other weapons systems than now planned. He may have to find ways to make further small reductions in military personnel, even if he is surely right that the era of deep cuts is now over.

It is true that the 1997 QDR, developed during a period of fiscal restraint, did not provide enough funds for its own proposed plan. But Congress and the Clinton administration later added more than $20 billion to the annual real dollar budget, and Secretary Rumsfeld added another $20 billion for 2002, without counting added costs due to September 11. So the yearly baseline has already grown by $40 billion even as the plan for forces and weapons has remained mostly unchanged. Bush administration officials now tell us that is still not enough. Alleging a decade of neglect, they claim that further spending increases are needed for military pay, readiness, infrastructure, health care, research and development, and weapons procurement. Overall, the Bush administration proposes to add a total of more than $400 billion from 2002 to 2007. It is true that each of the main Pentagon budget accounts still needs more funding. But the needs are not sufficient to require such large increases.

Before examining each major defense account individually, there is the matter of war costs to address. The Bush administration has requested almost $20 billion for such costs in the 2003 budget—$10 billion as its best guess of the cost of military operations that year, and $9.4 billion primarily to replenish weaponry and spare parts inventories and otherwise recuperate from the effects of the war on terrorism to date. However, to ensure transparency and to protect Congress's role in the budget process, the latter costs should be added to the supplemental appropriations bill for 2002 rather than the overall defense budget for 2003. The $10 billion for 2003 should be appropriated if and when that becomes necessary. Making these additions supplemental appropriations will also avoid artificially inflating the defense budget for 2003 in a way that would make defense increases in future years look smaller than they really are.

Pay. After the largesse of the last few years, military pay (in inflation-adjusted dollars) has never been higher. Partly as a result, recruiting and retention have improved markedly in recent years.

Most additional increases should be targeted at those few technical specialties in which the Pentagon still has trouble attracting and keeping people, rather than the entire force. In that regard, the Bush administration's plan to add a total of $82 billion to military pay over the 2002–07 period is excessive. Since troops are receiving improved housing and health benefits at present, further pay raises should be held to the rate of inflation. Over the 2003–07 period, this approach would save about $30 billion relative to the Bush administration's plan (individuals would still get additional raises as they were promoted, of course).

In addition, another $5 billion could be saved through 2007 by modestly reducing the number of individuals in the military—primarily, ground combat troops and support personnel (see chapter 3 for more). Generally speaking, this should not be done by cutting the number of major combat units from current levels, but rather by making some of them slightly smaller, in recognition of the enhanced capabilities of modern weaponry—as well as the need for a lighter and more deployable force.

Operations and Maintenance. This part of the budget funds a wide array of defense activities related to so-called military readiness, including training, equipment repair, fuel, and other necessities for overseas deployments, and most spare parts purchases. It also funds the salaries and health care of civilian employees of the Department of Defense. Even though readiness funding per troop is at its highest real dollar level ever, the Bush administration proposes adding $146 billion to this budget over the 2002–07 period.

But reform in military health care could save $15 billion over that period, if ideas proposed in the past by the Congressional Budget Office—including merging the independent health institutions of each military service, employing market-based care wherever possible, and considering introduction of a small copay for military personnel—were adopted. At a time when Congress has legislated a huge increase in the defense health budget by mandating free lifetime care for retirees, reform is all the more important.

In addition, giving incentives to local base commanders to find efficiencies in their operations might help limit real cost growth to 2 percent rather than 2.5 to 3 percent a year in other parts of the budget, saving $10 billion more.

Research, Development, Testing, and Evaluation. President Bush has rightly emphasized research and development ever since he began running for president, but again, the 2002 budget added large sums to this area. Current real spending on research, development, testing, and evaluation already exceeds the levels of his father's administration and roughly equals those of the peak Reagan years.

No more than another $1 billion is needed for the 2003 budget and beyond. For example, economies should be possible by canceling one or two major weapons, postponing the army's future combat system until underlying technologies are more promising, and slowing at least one or two missile defense programs out of the eight now under way (while modestly increasing research and development on a national cruise missile defense). Rather than add $99 billion to the preexisting plan, about $55 billion should suffice for 2002–07 (primarily reflecting the increases in the 2002 budget that would be sustained thereafter).

Procurement. The Clinton administration spent an average of about $50 billion per year to buy equipment; the figure is now about $60 billion. According to CBO, however, the expensive modernization plans of the military services might imply an annual funding requirement of $90 billion or more. Accordingly, the Bush-Rumsfeld budget envisions procurement funding of $99 billion in 2007.

But Operation Enduring Freedom has underscored the potential of relatively low-cost systems, such as Global Positioning System (GPS) guidance kits added to "dumb bombs," unmanned aerial vehicles (at a fraction of the cost of manned fighters), and real-time data links between various sensors and weapons platforms.

To be sure, expensive weapons such as aircraft carriers have been used as well. Moreover, not every future foe will be as militarily unsophisticated as the Taliban and al-Qaida. That said, the services need to prioritize. They should recognize, as former vice chairman of the Joint Chiefs of Staff Bill Owens has argued, that the electronics and computer revolutions often promise major advances in military capability without inordinate expenditures of money.

The current procurement budget of about $60 billion does need to rise to the $70 billion level proposed for 2003; in fact, it probably needs to reach $75 billion or higher. But the $99 billion level envisioned for 2007 (about $90 billion in constant 2002 dollars) is greatly excessive.

For many critics, the problem with Rumsfeld and Bush's weapons plan is that it protects the traditional priorities of the military services without seeking a radical transformation of the U.S. armed forces. But this basic criticism is not quite right. Individual programs or omissions in the Bush plan can be debated, but it is beyond serious doubt that the Bush administration has an aggressive program for so-called defense transformation (see table 1-9). As is appropriate for such an effort, most of the emphasis is in the realms of research, development, and experimentation, where the administration envisions spending $99 billion more than the Clinton administration would have by 2007 (even though, as noted, these areas of the defense budget were not severely cut in the 1990s). The problem is a more classic one of unwillingness to set priorities. Despite the absence of a superpower challenger, the administration proposes replacing most major combat systems of the U.S. military with systems costing twice as much—and doing so throughout the force structure.

As discussed in more detail in chapter 4, a more prudent modernization agenda would begin by canceling at least one or two major weapons, such as the Army's Crusader artillery system. In addition, the Pentagon would only equip a modest fraction of the force with the most sophisticated and expensive weaponry. That high-end, or "silver bullet," force, as the Congressional Budget Office has described it, would be a hedge against possible developments such as a rapidly modernizing Chinese military. Otherwise, the rest of the force would be equipped primarily with relatively inexpensive upgrades of existing weaponry, carrying better sensors, munitions, computers, and communications systems. For example, rather than purchase some 3,000 joint strike fighters, the military would buy about 1,000, and otherwise purchase planes such as new

F-16 Block 60 aircraft (and perhaps even some unmanned combat aerial vehicles in a few years) to fill out its force structure.

After several initial months of rampant speculation that he would make major changes in the size, forward deployments, and basic nature of U.S. military forces, Secretary of Defense Donald Rumsfeld recognized that radical transformation was either unwarranted or infeasible in the short term. Indeed, in the end Secretary Rumsfeld has produced what is surely the most cautious major defense review of the four completed since the end of the cold war. In most cases, Rumsfeld was right not to follow the advice of those advocating military revolution, given the enduring importance of traditional defense missions and the technological impracticality of rapidly adopting a transformed force.

But there is a major problem with the Rumsfeld plan: its cost. He took the Clinton administration's forces and weapons plans, added a few initiatives of his own, made no notable program or personnel cuts, and then funded the entire package at a very robust level. This book explores ways in which the planned growth in U.S. defense spending, while necessary to a degree, can be held to more modest and fiscally sound levels.

The Bush Homeland Security Budget

Although it is not the focus of this book, a word is in order on the basics of the homeland security budget. On February 4, 2002, Director Tom Ridge of the White House Office of Homeland Security unveiled his plans for homeland security. He began by defining a homeland security budget for the first time. In recent years, budget categories were created to capture counterterrorist spending and the protection of critical infrastructure, but these categories did not include most efforts of agencies such as the Coast Guard and several others that have obvious homeland security ramifications.

The new homeland security budget concept reveals how quickly spending in this area has been rising. In 1995, the budget for homeland security was $9.0 billion; by 2000 it was $13.2 billion; in 2001, it was $16.9 billion ($0.9 billion being added after September 11).

For 2002, the federal government's planned homeland security budget would have been about $19.5 billion prior to the September 11 attacks; after the hijackings, about $9.8 billion more was added in a supplemental

Table 1-10. *Homeland Security Funding, by Initiative Area*

Millions of dollars

Initiative area	2002 enacted base	First FY 2002 supplemental	Bush administration FY 2003 proposal
Supporting first responder/ crisis management	291	651	3,500
Defending against biological terrorism	1,408	3,730	5,898
Securing America's borders	8,752	1,194	10,615
Using 21st-century technology to defend the homeland	155	75	722
Aviation security	1,543	1,035	4,800
Other non-DoD homeland security	3,186	2,384	5,352
DoD homeland security (outside initiatives)	4,201	689	6,815
Total	19,535	9,758	37,702

Source: Office of Homeland Security.

appropriation, making for a total of $29.3 billion. An additional $5.2 billion was requested in another supplemental. For 2003, Governor Ridge is proposing a total of $37.7 billion, or roughly four times what the government was spending on homeland security in the mid-1990s.

Director Ridge's budget plan for 2003 contained several priority areas that can be grouped into broad conceptual categories (see table 1-10 for the proposed increases in spending by category):

—supporting first responders,

—defending against biological terrorism,

—securing America's borders,

—using twenty-first-century technology to defend the homeland, and

—enhancing aviation security.

First Responders. The budget for supporting first responders would grow by $3.2 billion over the initial 2002 budget (or $2.5 billion over the actual 2002 budget, reflecting supplemental appropriations). It would primarily support equipment, training, and communications infrastructure for the nation's 2 million police, fire, and emergency medical personnel. In many ways, it is the logical successor to the much smaller Nunn-Lugar-Domenici program launched in the mid-1990s. These funds focus more on responses to chemical, conventional, or nuclear devices than on responses to biological agents, where victims would generally first show up in hospitals rather than at the site of an attack.

Biological Terrorism. The budget would increase by $4.5 billion relative to the initial 2002 budget plan. The increase would only be $800 million relative to the revised 2002 budget, but that budget included large one-time costs for purchasing smallpox vaccine and pharmaceuticals and decontaminating postal facilities. Those expenses are not expected to recur, so the 2003 budget in fact contains substantial funds for new initiatives. Most of the increase is in the area of research and development for defenses, medications, and detectors and will go toward work performed by the National Institutes of Health, the Centers for Disease Control, the Food and Drug Administration, and the Department of Defense. Smaller increases are proposed for medical surveillance and communications (about $300 million) and for public health and hospital infrastructure (about $200 million).

An increase of about $1.9 billion, relative to the original 2002 budget, is being requested for border security (an increase of $700 million over the post–September 11 budget for 2002). The major increases are for agencies such as the Department of Justice's Border Patrol agency, Treasury's Customs, and the Department of Transportation's Coast Guard.

Twenty-First-Century Technology. Most of the funding in this category is IT related. The increase would total $600 million over the original 2002 budget, and about $500 million over the post–September 11 budget. About $100 million is for cyberspace protection; the bulk of the funds (nearly $400 million) are proposed for an entry-exit visa system to keep better track of foreigners inside the United States.

Aviation Security. The proposed funding amounts to $4.8 billion in 2003, a tripling in funding relative to the initial 2002 budget and an increase of $2.2 billion even taking into account the post–September 11 supplemental appropriations. Most of the added spending on airports and airlines was made necessary by legislation passed in the fall of 2001; the 2003 budget would include large increases to fund measures that have already been widely debated and mandated.

Brookings is presently completing a study on homeland security, *Protecting the Homeland,* that provides more information on this issue and suggests an additional agenda for defending the United States against possible terrorist attack (see the Brookings homepage at www.brookings. edu). For the purposes of the present book, the main points from that study are that even more money, above the $38 billion requested by the Bush administration for 2003, may be needed for homeland security— and that most of those funds will not be devoted to the Pentagon. This message puts further pressure on the Pentagon to try to hold its own budgets in check, lest they compete with potentially even more pressing imperatives on the homeland security front.

Plan of the Book

The rest of this book considers competing defense requirements within a framework of fiscal constraints and on the basis of an assumption that U.S. military personnel are on average working as hard as is reasonable to expect—in some cases simply too hard. I argue that spending will have to increase for procurement of equipment, missile defense, other homeland defense efforts, and readiness. I propose some economies within the procurement plan, however, to keep increases within reasonable bounds, as well as some targeted streamlining of overseas U.S. military presence to ease burdens on the men and women of the armed forces. I also suggest an alternative and somewhat less demanding type of two-war framework, similar to that adopted by the Bush administration, that would further mitigate the pressures on the current force structure without fundamentally changing the nature or the credibility of U.S. global military engagement. My argument endorses an additional 10 percent cut in the U.S. domestic base structure and offers other suggestions to make the military more efficient.

As a result of the cumulative effect of these changes, active-duty military strength would decline slightly, to about 1.3 million from currently projected levels of 1.36 million. Cuts would be distributed roughly evenly among the services, though the Air Force would be largely spared given the importance of its rapid-response capabilities for regional war fighting (the Air Force's preferences for fighter modernization, however, would be curtailed significantly under my recommended approach). Army cuts would arise largely from making divisions somewhat smaller, reflecting the greater capabilities of modern weaponry; Navy cuts would derive largely from an end to quasi-continuous carrier deployments to the Mediterranean Sea; Marine Corps reductions would arise primarily from reducing that service's fixed-wing aviation force structure and scaling back planned purchases of the joint strike fighter. The Army would wind up with 450,000 active-duty soldiers, the Navy with 350,000 sailors, the Air Force with its existing end-strength of 340,000, and the Marine Corps with 160,000 Marines.

No service would be singled out for large or disproportionate cuts, however. It is too easy to imagine scenarios of strategic importance that could place heavy demands on each. Ground forces could be taxed by wars in Southwest or Northeast Asia, particularly if the United States and its allies elected to overthrow an extremist enemy regime, or by unexpected and nontraditional missions (for example, liberating a place such as Kosovo or helping a failing state with nuclear weapons—perhaps Pakistan—to restore order and central control). Naval forces in particular could be stressed by conflict in the Taiwan Strait or Persian Gulf. Air forces are of critical importance for waging high-technology warfare like that witnessed at the beginning of the 1990s during Operation Desert Storm and the end of the 1990s during Operation Allied Force.

What about spending levels? The defense budget would still need to go up. But with these economies, a defense spending level around $390 billion should be sufficient, as expressed in constant 2002 dollars. Combined with a homeland security budget approaching $50 billion, national security spending writ large would still remain under 4 percent of GDP, or half the typical cold war level. That price is affordable and sufficient.

TWO　　Military Readiness and
Overseas Commitments

Are U.S. armed forces ready? That is, can they handle the likely near-term missions that they are designed to handle? And, as a related issue, might their presence in specific overseas locales be reduced in order to mitigate the strains on personnel and equipment that increased in the last decade? To the extent that U.S. defense forces face serious readiness problems—and this chapter acknowledges that they do, even if the problems have often been overstated by Republican critics of the Clinton administration—reducing overseas operations might be one of the most effective ways to redress them.

Current and Future U.S. Military Readiness

The proper approach to evaluating military readiness is to inquire whether the U.S. armed forces have enough of the right types of skilled and adequately trained personnel and whether they own adequate stocks of equipment in good working order. Although a plethora of readiness statistics and stories exist, all ultimately bear on these two broad issues.

This formulation of the readiness question is intentionally somewhat narrow. It focuses on the nuts and bolts of well-understood military operations. It does not address the question of strategic readiness—whether the United States as a sovereign nation has prepared for the right types of threats and developed the right types of policy instruments to address them. Other chapters in this book address that broader question; this chapter simply focuses on the internal consistency of Pentagon plans. Given how the Department of Defense and, more generally, the U.S. government have assessed and described threats to the country's interests, have they also maintained military forces capable of handling those likely threats?

Even when the question of military readiness is put in these rather limited, technical terms, it is a difficult and contentious matter. Some readiness metrics make little sense and are confusing. For example, two Army divisions that had been deemed unready in 1999 were given that designation because they were involved in Balkans operations with the Stabilization Force (SFOR) and the Kosovo Force (KFOR). The fact that the Pentagon considered them unready because they were engaged in deterring Slobodan Milosevic and helping keep the peace in an area of key U.S. national interest in Europe, rather than training to fight in Iraq or North Korea, is an artifact of a strange and somewhat myopic readiness-measurement system that makes little strategic sense.[1]

A purported cruise missile shortage discussed during the 2000 presidential race still left the United States with an inventory of almost ten times as many cruise missiles as it used in Operation Desert Storm.[2] The shortage of a new weapon, the joint direct attack munition (JDAM), in Operation Allied Force in 1999 was due not to negligence in military planning but to JDAM's newness at the time; only a modest number had been produced by the time NATO went to war against Serbia.[3] In the war in Afghanistan thirty months later, thousands of JDAMs were available and played a decisive role in the conflict.

There are, however, enough signs of strain in the force to warrant additional remedial measures. By most readiness indicators, the U.S. military's condition was as good in 2000 as it had been, say, in 1985. Nonetheless, readiness in 2000 was not as good as it was in 1990 or 1992; readiness levels *did* decline during most of the Clinton-Gore era. That trend was beginning to be arrested by the time of the 2000 presidential campaign, but it remained—and remains—worrisome nonetheless.

1. See Steven Lee Myers, "What War-Ready Means, in Pentagon's Accounting," *New York Times*, September 4, 2000, p. A11.
2. David Von Drehle, "Cheney Steps Up Criticism of Military Readiness," *Washington Post*, August 31, 2000, p. A1.
3. For one point of view on some of the problems revealed in Operation Allied Force, see John Robinson, "Ready or Not?" *Washington Post*, September 7, 2000, p. A24.

Moreover, it may not be adequate for readiness levels to be comparable to their 1980s levels. That is counterintuitive, given how many resources Ronald Reagan devoted to the military. Nevertheless, the armed forces of the 1980s were focused at least as much on deterring a major war that never happened (and that was not, by then, particularly likely to happen) as on conducting various operations around the world. Today's armed forces have more immediate and frequent missions and are deterring conflicts in the Persian Gulf and Korea that loom more plausibly than did the prospect of world war between NATO and the Warsaw Pact during Reagan's time. Today's military ought, therefore, to be more ready than President Reagan's had to be.

The following assessment of readiness examines the issue from five perspectives. The first focuses on spending for readiness. The next two pertain to the near-term preparedness of the military—readiness in its most literal sense. One focuses on the condition of equipment and the other on the quality, preparedness, and availability of personnel. The Clinton-Gore administration deserves fairly high marks in these first three categories. However, its performance with respect to the next two categories—ensuring equipment readiness and personnel readiness for the decade to come—was less good. Because U.S. military equipment is aging rapidly and because many personnel feel overworked and overdeployed, a continuation of recent trends in hardware and in personnel could erode readiness over the years ahead. Fortunately, there are some indications that the recent negative trends are being reversed, but the country is hardly out of the woods yet.

Each of these issues is considered in turn below. My broad conclusions are twofold. First, targeted real spending increases will continue to be needed in operations and support accounts—funds paying for equipment maintenance, training, and personnel—during the years ahead. They need not be as large as those advocated by the Bush administration, but they are necessary. Second, it behooves the armed forces, and the new president, to find additional ways to mitigate the strain of deployments abroad, a strain that particularly affects the men and women of the U.S. armed forces. Doing so will not be easy and could be counterproductive if it leads to a careless downsizing or disengagement of the American military presence abroad. Thankfully, there appear to be sensible ways to reduce commitments. They are considered in the second half of the chapter, where I review major U.S. peacetime deployments and propose reductions in the continuous Marine Corps presence on

Okinawa, the nearly continuous Navy (and Marine Corps) presence in the waters of the Mediterranean Sea, the Air Force–led no-fly-zone operations over Iraq, and the Army presence in Bosnia. The Bush administration has only supported the last of these possible cuts to date, but reviews continue for other deployments.

Spending for Readiness

There is no clear single account for readiness, but the operations and maintenance budget is the best proxy. It funds everything from training to repairs to purchases of spare parts to deployments. (Funding for personnel is considered as part of a broader analysis in the following section.)

Per active-duty person, O&M resources have increased greatly in recent years—from around $57,000 in 1990, to $80,000 by 2000, to $85,000 in 2002 (measured in each case in constant 2002 dollars).[4] This is a very large increase, but it overstates actual funding for readiness, since increasingly large parts of the O&M budget do not fund readiness-related activities.

To fix this problem and make budget comparisons meaningful, spending for types of O&M activities that have increased significantly in recent years should be subtracted. These include environmental cleanup, frequent contingencies abroad, spare parts purchases formerly made out of the procurement budget, the added costs of maintaining older equipment (especially aircraft)—as well as more expensive health care and an excessively large base infrastructure. Accounting for such effects, adjusted resources for O&M remain more than $70,000 per person in constant dollars.[5] This would seem to suggest more than ample funding.

Historical trends over recent decades show a typical real-dollar increase in O&M spending per uniformed member of the armed forces of roughly 2 percent. Over a decade, therefore, one might expect costs that were $57,000 in 1990 to have grown to at least $65,000 in 2000. In other words, current funding for operations and maintenance appears adequate, but not as generous as raw dollar totals would suggest.

4. Office of the Under Secretary of Defense (Comptroller), *National Defense Budget Estimates for FY 2001* (Department of Defense, March 2000), pp. 131–33, 215.

5. See Michael O'Hanlon, *How to Be a Cheap Hawk: The 1999 and 2000 Defense Budgets* (Brookings, 1998), pp. 141–42; and Gregory T. Kiley, *The Effects of Aging on the Costs of Operating and Maintaining Military Equipment* (Congressional Budget Office, 2001), p. 2.

There are two points here. First, net O&M costs will probably keep rising, even if privatizations, base closures, and other economies are successfully achieved. They will go up faster than inflation, probably by at least 1 percent a year. Second, to gain real insight into the state of U.S. military readiness, one must look deeper and at more specific measures. The broad spending data, not surprisingly, are inconclusive.

Readiness of Personnel Today

Consider, therefore, the men and women of the military. On the whole they have never been better.[6] As measured by time in uniform, personnel are more experienced than they were during the Reagan and Bush years (see figure 2-1). Their scores on aptitude tests are higher than during most of the Reagan years, although lower than during the Bush and early Clinton years (see figure 2-2). By these latter metrics, conditions generally peaked in the mid-1990s but remain very strong today and near peak levels.

Training remains rigorous as well. Whether it is miles driven per tank crew per year, flight hours per fighter pilot per month, steaming days per ship per quarter, or some other metric of the intensity of training and exercises, today's levels compare favorably with those of the 1980s and early 1990s. In some cases they were 5 to 10 percent lower under President Clinton than under Presidents Reagan and Bush—though the benefits of improved simulators should not be ignored—but they are being increased in any case by the new administration.[7]

Anyone who doubts the abilities of U.S. troops need only review their outstanding performance in the Afghanistan and Kosovo wars, continuing peacekeeping missions in the Balkans, and the no-fly-zone operations over Iraq. They have suffered extremely low casualties, accomplished their missions effectively, and handled themselves with great professionalism and effectiveness in almost all circumstances. Even in the ill-fated Somalia mission of 1993, troops performed ably. It was the Clinton administration and top military officials who mishandled the mission, escalating the operation to a manhunt for one warlord without accepting—or preparing the country for—the associated risk of casualties.

6. See, for example, Anton Jareb and Matt Robinson, *Readiness Support for the Marines* (Alexandria, Va.: Center for Naval Analyses, 2000), p. 7.

7. See Department of Defense, "FY 2001 Defense Budget: Briefing Slides," February 2000; O'Hanlon, *How to Be a Cheap Hawk*, pp. 144–46.

Figure 2-1. *Age and Experience of U.S. Troops, 1973–2000*[a]

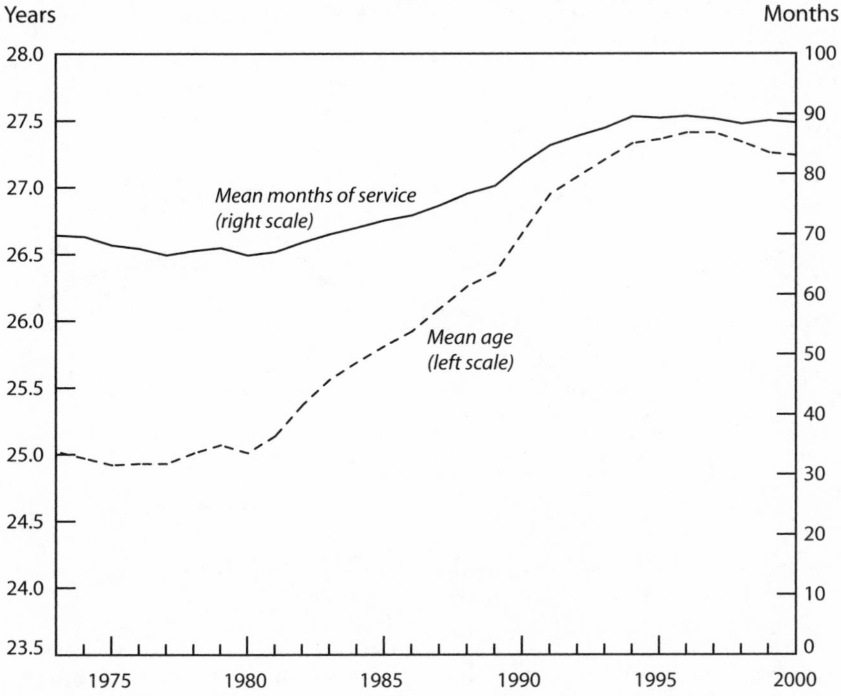

Years   Months

Source: Department of Defense, Office of the Assistant Secretary of Defense (Force Management Policy), *1998 Population Representation in the Military Services*, p. D-16 (http://dticaw.dtic.mil/prhome/poprep98/html/d16.html [May 16, 2000]).
    a. Through March 2000.

Personnel are being compensated reasonably well. Cumulative pay raises during the Clinton administration exceeded aggregate inflation over that same period substantially—something that did not happen during the first Bush administration (see figure 2-3).[8] In addition, retirement pay was restored to levels that prevailed until the second half of the Reagan era. Most of the real pay increases, as well as the restitution of earlier retirement benefits and an improvement in health care benefits for military retirees, occurred under pressure from a Republican Congress; pay raises in the first Clinton term were slightly below the inflation rate.

8. See Office of the Under Secretary of Defense (Comptroller), *National Defense Budget Estimates for FY 2001*, p. 56.

Figure 2-2. *Percentage of Enlisted Recruits Scoring above Average on the Armed Forces Qualification Test (AFQT), 1973–2000*[a]

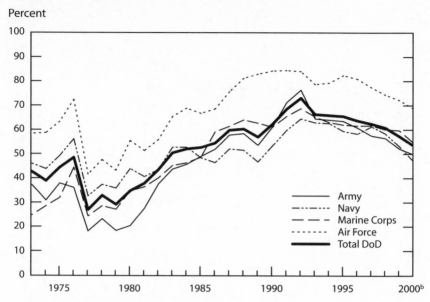

Percent

Source: Department of Defense, Office of the Assistant Secretary of Defense (Force Management Policy), *1998 Population Representation in the Military Services*, p. D-16 (http://dticaw.dtic.mil/prhome/poprep98/html/d13.html [May 16, 2000]); and Alphonso Maldon Jr., Assistant Secretary of Defense for Force Management Policy, "Prepared Testimony before the Senate Committee on Armed Services Personnel Subcommittee," February 24, 2000 (www.senate.gov/~armed_services/statemnt/2000/000224am.pdf [May 19, 2000]).

a. Many individuals taking the test ultimately do not join the military, but their scores constitute a database against which one can evaluate those who are enlisted.

b. 2000 data current as of March.

However one chooses to allocate the political credit for these policies, the overall record of the past eight years is nonetheless good, if not too generous in the case of health care. Increases have continued under President Bush as well. Reports of a 13 percent military-civilian pay gap have been inaccurate. In reality, military pay compares favorably with civilian pay for most types of specialties and most age and education categories in American society today.[9] The reality that about 5,000 troops and their

9. See Richard Fernandez, *What Does the Military "Pay Gap" Mean?* (Washington: Congressional Budget Office, June 1999).

Figure 2-3. *Military Pay Raises, 1974–2000*[a]

Percentage

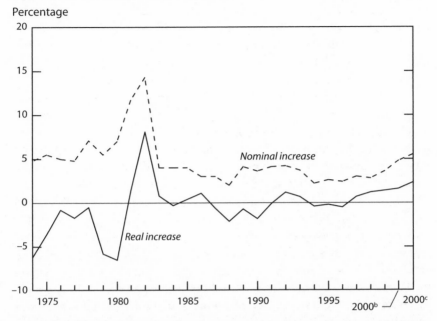

Sources: Office of the Under Secretary of Defense for Personnel and Readiness, *Defense Manpower Requirements Report, Fiscal Year 2001* (May 2000), table 6-2, "Percentage Pay Raises," p. 71 (http://dticaw.dtic.mil/prhome/docs/fy2001.pdf [June 12, 2000]); Minneapolis Federal Reserve, *Consumer Price Index, 1913–Present* (http://minneapolisfed.org/economy/calc/hist1913.html [June 12 2000]).

a. Overall average percentage increase in basic pay, basic allowance for quarters, and basic allowance for subsistence.

b. January 2000.

c. July 2000.

families remain on food stamps should be considered in light of the fact that 20,000 personnel were on food stamps in 1992.[10]

Recruitment proved difficult during the late 1990s, with shortfalls in both 1998 and 1999. Increases in advertising budgets and recruiting staffs, together with a large pay raise for all military personnel, however, helped all the services meet active-duty recruiting goals in 2000 and 2001. Some residual problems from previous years were ameliorated as well; for example, the Navy reduced a shortfall in key sailors, or "empty sea billets,"

10. Greg Jaffe, "Military Could Face Potential Problems with Modernization," *Wall Street Journal*, September 5, 2000, p. A36.

from 18,000 in 1998 to 6,000 in 2000.[11] Recruiting was still difficult in some parts of the reserve component, however.[12] Recent progress in recruiting is encouraging but is insufficient to alleviate concerns about the longer term. Similarly, reenlistment rates have improved but are still less than optimal in certain cases. (See figure 2-4 for historical context.)

As a consequence of recent challenges in retention and recruiting, personnel shortfalls remain in certain areas. Consider, for example, what the Army, Air Force, and Navy define as "critical billets"—personnel requiring particular specialization and skills. There are about sixty categories of such personnel. As of 2000, the three services maintained 90 percent or more of desired personnel in two-thirds of these categories, but fell below 90 percent in the remaining one-third. That may be a glass two-thirds full, but it is also a glass one-third empty. In notably short supply were Air Force pilots (1,200 below nominal need, though the shortfalls have at least stabilized in recent years), Army captains, several types of mechanics and electronics repair personnel, and a number of other specialties and grades. Not all shortfalls, many of which remain today, are of great concern; some could be addressed successfully simply by staffing the highest-priority positions first. Others are more serious and affect combat capability.[13] They may require further targeted pay raises or other inducements to attract and retain adequate numbers of personnel with the requisite abilities.

Readiness of Equipment Today

As for available weaponry, most U.S. military equipment is not in quite as good shape as it was a decade ago. It is still comparable, however, to the condition of weaponry during the early and middle years of the Reagan era.

The armed forces generally measure equipment readiness in terms of "mission-capable rates"—the percentage of weapons that are immediately available for major combat tasks and not awaiting repair or otherwise out of commission. Although actual rates vary greatly from one weapon to another, some "mission capable" rates were typically about

---

11. Jaffe, "Military Could Face Potential Problems with Modernization," p. A36.

12. Steven Lee Myers, "Military Reserves Are Falling Short in Finding Recruits," *New York Times*, August 28, 2000, p. A1.

13. Department of Defense, *Quarterly Readiness Report to the Congress, April–June 2000* (August 2000).

Figure 2-4. *Total Department of Defense Reenlistment Rates, 1981–97*[a]

Percentage

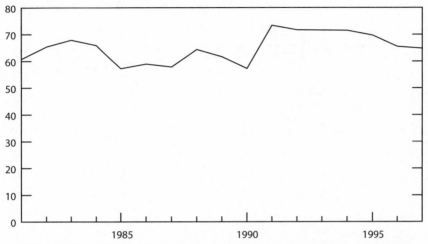

Source: Department of Defense, Washington Headquarters Services, Directorate for Information Operations and Reports, *Military Manpower Statistics,* 1996 & 1997, Table 2-21 (http://web1.whs.osd.mil/mmid/m01/sms221r.htm and http://web1.whs.osd.mil/mmid/m01/fy97/m01fy97.pdf [May 17, 2000]).

a. Adjusted rates, which exclude the effects of early separations and other discharges of eligibles under early release programs for strength control purposes.

75 percent during the mid-1980s and 85 percent during the early 1990s. They were generally back to around 75 percent in 2000. Historically, that is good, but not excellent and ultimately not quite good enough.

Equipment readiness within particular service branches varies greatly. Air Force mission-capable rates are down more than 10 percentage points over the past decade (see figure 2-5).[14] Navy ships continue to deploy dependably, and at rates similar to those of the past—but ships that are not on deployment are on average less ready, should they be needed in a crisis, than a decade ago. Army equipment, by contrast, remains every bit as ready as a decade ago (see figure 2-6). Marine Corps aircraft, despite

14. Air Force officials sometimes describe a drop of more than 20 percent, but that reflects a different, less transparent, and less useful way of measuring readiness—it refers to the C ratings of units, a complicated, subjective, and fickle indicator, rather than the more objective indicator of mission-capable rate. For recent information on such C ratings, see "Ryan Addresses Readiness Concerns before Congress," *U.S. Air Force Perspectives* (Washington: Air Force Office of Public Affairs, October 2000), p. 1.

Figure 2-5. *U.S. Air Force Mission-Capable Rates, 1991–2000*

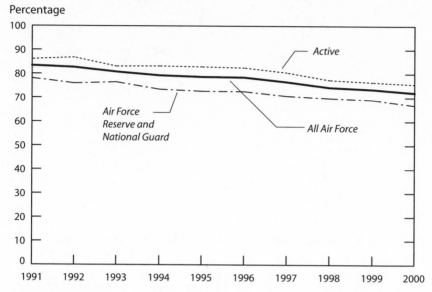

Source: Lt. Col. Dennis E. Daley, Aircraft/Missile Support Division, HQ USAF/Installations and Logistics (ILSY), June 5, 2000; personal communication.

a spate of temporary groundings for safety-related reasons in 2000, also remain just as mission-capable as they were during the early 1990s (see figure 2-7). Navy aviation readiness rates have dropped off a bit since the early 1990s, but not by nearly as much as those of the Air Force (see table 2-1). Marine Corps ground equipment appears to have declined in overall readiness since the early 1990s—though by no more than 1 or 2 percent, with recent trends positive.[15]

The military's overall readiness may not be captured, however, by the average condition of its equipment. Some systems may be more important than others. If a critical single system or type of system—such as a transport ship or plane, or electronic warfare aircraft—is not functional, an entire war plan can fall apart. Downturns in the readiness of specific systems must be watched carefully and where necessary addressed quickly

15. Anton Jareb and Matt Robinson, *Readiness Support for Marines* (Alexandria, Va.: Center for Naval Analyses, 2000), p. 8.

Figure 2-6. *Readiness of U.S. Army Equipment, 1987–99*[a]

Percentage

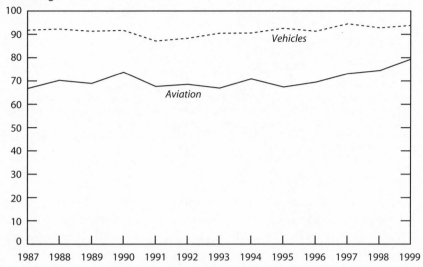

Source: U.S. Army communications to author, 2000.
a. Vehicles include M1A1, M1A2, M3, M109A6, M8, HEMTT, HMMWV, FMTV, MLRS, Patriot, Avenger. Aviation includes AH-64, OH-58D, UH-60, CH-47.

Figure 2-7. *Overall U.S. Marine Corps Aircraft Mission-Capable Rates, 1991–2000*

Percentage

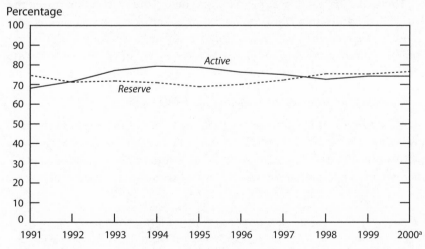

Source: MSgt David L. Davis, Aviation Analyst, Aviation Logistics Support Branch, Headquarters United States Marine Corps, Pentagon, July 5, 2000; personal communication.
a. Through May 2000.

Table 2-1. *Navy Aircraft Mission-Capable Rates, Selected Years, 1990–99*[a]

Percentage

Year	Rate
1990	70
1995	72
1999	69

Source: Capt. L. B. Callis, Director Fleet Support Department, Naval Air Systems Command, "Aviation Maintenance Supply Readiness (AMSR)," July 19, 2000 (http://www.nalda.navy.mil/amsr/19jul00.ppt); and Deborah Clay-Mendez, Richard L. Fernandez, and Amy Belasco, "Trends in Selected Indicators of Military Readiness, 1980 through 1993" (Congressional Budget Office, March 1994), p. 71.

a. Categories of aircraft covered by data may have changed slightly. Data indicate overall approximate readiness levels for all years.

regardless of the average caliber of equipment readiness. Moreover, given how frequently today's U.S. military is being used, and its smaller size relative to cold war levels, readiness levels equal to those of the Reagan era may not be good enough. The levels attained during the early 1990s should be viewed as the proper goals for today. Nevertheless, the broad message of these gauges, while not perfect and not a cause for complacency, is reassuring. The average fighter, ship, tank, or other major military system is as likely to be fit for combat today as it was halfway through Ronald Reagan's military buildup.

Altogether, the quality of people, equipment, and training has given the United States a military in very fine shape. In addition, it has produced a good safety record: despite occasional problems in certain parts of the force,[16] overall accident rates per person during training and deployments are as low as or lower than they have ever been (see figure 2-8).

Sustaining the Readiness of Personnel in the Coming Decade

Although things look generally good today, there are cracks in the U.S. armed forces that, if allowed to worsen, could change the basic readiness picture within a few years. Most notably, frequent and extended deployments have kept military personnel away from home and families and

16. A notable example of a problem in 2000 was the highest rate of Navy ship groundings and collisions since 1992. Thankfully, associated fatalities were few in number. See James W. Crawley, "Navy Calls for Safety Review by Whole Fleet," *San Diego Union-Tribune*, September 16, 2000, p. A1.

Figure 2-8. *Worldwide U.S. Active-Duty Military Deaths by Cause, 1980–98*[a]

Per 100,000 troops

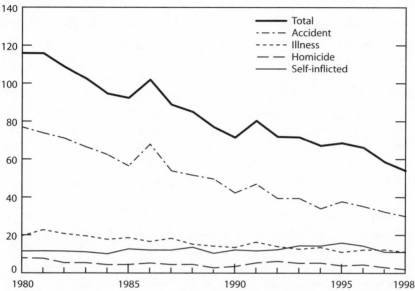

Source: Department of Defense, *Worldwide U.S. Active Duty Military Nonhostile Deaths by Manner: 1980–1998,* Washington Headquarters Services, Directorate for Information Operations and Reports, 1998 (http://web1.whs.osd.mil/mmid/casualty/manner.htm [May 18, 2000]).

a. Does not include deaths from hostile action, of which there were 563 over the period, including 256 in Lebanon, 18 in Grenada, 23 in Panama, 148 in Operation Desert Storm, 29 in Somalia, and 19 in Saudi Arabia.

caused many of them to work excessively long hours, whether on deployment or at home base. Selectively scaling back U.S. military deployments in some places would help considerably, as discussed below, but many other measures would be useful as well.

Recent pay increases and efforts to make overseas deployments more predictable have improved some of the downward trends in recruiting and retention. Nevertheless, the situation remains worrisome and requires further steps to reduce the strain on personnel and improve their well-being. These might include increasing the numbers of those types of specialized units that are frequently deployed today.

Army data show that 12,000 more personnel would be needed to relieve excessive burdens on existing "high demand/low density" units, such as military police units, Patriot defense battery staff, and nuclear, biological, and chemical weapons experts. (The Army also believes it should add some 25,000 additional troops to fully staff its entire force structure at desired levels—making for an aggregate increase of almost 40,000 more soldiers. However, these 25,000 are a less compelling requirement if the current two-war planning framework is revised, as the Bush administration has now decided to do, as discussed in chapter 3.) Generalizing this type of policy on high demand/low density units to the other services might make for a total increase of 20,000 to 30,000 active-duty personnel in certain types of specialties. (Since the Navy and Marine Corps are accustomed to deployments, needs are most pressing in the Army and Air Force. However, the Navy does not have enough electronic jamming aircraft.) Corresponding annual costs might be $1 billion to $1.5 billion for salaries, making for a total price tag of $2 billion or more once equipment is included.[17]

Adding these slots to the military should not increase overall end-strength and in fact would be consistent with a modest additional reduction of active-duty personnel from the 1.36 million recommended by the 1997 Quadrennial Defense Review to about 1.3 million. A revised two-war capability (see the next chapter) and new approaches to overseas deployments for the Navy (see below) would allow these cuts in existing personnel. All told, under the proposals detailed in this book, the Army would retain about 450,000 active-duty soldiers, the Navy about 350,000 sailors, the Air Force about 340,000 uniformed personnel, and the Marine Corps about 160,000 Marines. Those numbers would represent cuts relative to the 1997 QDR's proposed levels of 30,000 for the Army, 20,000 for the Navy, 0 for the Air Force, and 10,000 for the Marines.

The military services also should continue to find innovative ways to distribute deployment demands around more of the force structure. Doing so is admittedly difficult, for it can involve slightly reducing vigilance for regional war fighting. For example, the Army has been hesitant at times about allowing the 25th infantry division, based in Hawaii and intended for rapid deployment to Korea in the event of a war there, to conduct other missions—although ultimately part of the 25th did deploy to Haiti in the mid-1990s.

17. See General Accounting Office, *Contingency Operations: Providing Critical Capabilities Poses Challenges*, GAO/NSIAD-00-164 (July 2000); and Laurinda Zeman, *Making Peace While Staying Ready for War: The Challenges of U.S. Military Participation in Peace Operations* (Washington: Congressional Budget Office, 1999), p. xix.

The Army should also carry out its planned policy to fully staff whatever number of divisions it retains—even if that means cutting another division or shrinking the size of all of them—so that deploying one unit does not require "borrowing" personnel from another. This borrow-to-deploy policy has caused a harmful ripple effect throughout much of the force.

Other military services should make changes as well. Of the U.S. Air Force's forty airborne warning and control system (AWACS) crews, only twenty-seven are fully trained, and of those twenty-seven, commanders in the Pacific region do not approve of deployment outside of the region of the six they control. That leaves the remaining twenty-one to do a job in the rest of the world that requires close to twice their number.[18] Such policies are not prudent. To the extent that they have the effect of driving capable people out of the military, they can hurt readiness more than they help it. Solutions should involve increasing the numbers of these types of units and making full use of existing capabilities in order to handle ongoing operations.

Compensation for all troops should certainly keep up with inflation. Targeted pay raises in certain specialties in which the private sector pays particularly well may also be needed. They make more sense at this point than a general, large pay raise. Personnel shortfalls are far more significant in some parts of the force and in some areas of expertise than in others.

A pay raise well above the rate of inflation also makes less sense than fully reimbursing individuals for their costs of housing. Raising housing reimbursement from its existing level of 85 percent to 100 percent, as the Bush administration plans, would cost $1.5 billion a year, but it would alleviate demand for on-base housing. Renovation of existing military housing is proving burdensome for the Department of Defense, and it is to a large extent a waste of the department's time and energy, given that this function is outside of its core expertise.[19]

Sustaining the Readiness of Equipment in the Coming Decade

Remedies are also needed on the hardware front. Much of the equipment bought during the Reagan era is starting to wear out. Combat jets, for example, will soon average fifteen years in age. It is generally thought

---

18. General Accounting Office, *Contingency Operations*, pp. 15–16.
19. Congressional Budget Office, *Budget Options for National Defense* (Washington, March 2000), pp. 78–82.

prudent to retire these planes after about twenty years of service, meaning that average age should usually be around ten years. Combat helicopters currently average twenty-two years in age; the expected service lifetime for such equipment is a little less than thirty.[20]

Fighter jets are scheduled to be replaced, but the situation is not so fortunate for other types of systems. There are no plans to replace Army transport helicopters, nor maritime patrol aircraft, nor a number of support planes that carry out essential missions such as refueling and electronic warfare.[21]

Therefore, while near-term equipment readiness is good, the Bush administration will need to act fast to keep it that way in 2005 and 2010. Modest real spending increases will be necessary, focused particularly on the procurement account. This issue is discussed in more depth, and from a different perspective, in the chapter on military modernization, where it is linked most explicitly to the debate over a so-called revolution in military affairs. However, the procurement issue should also be viewed as a simple matter of ensuring readiness, and military safety, in the years ahead. Revolution or not, the U.S. military needs mission-worthy systems that have not drastically exceeded their reasonable service lifetimes. The civilian and uniformed leadership owe it to the men and women of the armed forces to provide them equipment that is safe and reliable.

At present, there is no assurance they will do so. The military services, in keeping their ambitious and probably unaffordable agendas for modernizing equipment, are putting sophisticated weaponry ahead of readiness and the well-being of their own personnel. They are not doing so intentionally, but that is the effect of holding onto an unrealistically expensive modernization agenda.

The effect of this policy is predictable, and lamentable. Future budgets may not suffice to buy new weapons—whose costs are certain to increase—in the numbers intended. As a result, weapons production schedules will be stretched out, leading to purchases of fewer new planes and ships and ground vehicles each year than now envisioned. Existing equipment will therefore have to be retained far beyond prudent retire-

20. See Statement of Lane Pierrot, Congressional Budget Office, on Aging Military Equipment, before the Subcommittee on Military Procurement, House Committee on Armed Services, February 24, 1999, p. 4.

21. Ibid., p. 4; and Frances Lussier, *An Analysis of U.S. Army Helicopter Programs* (Washington: Congressional Budget Office, 1995), p. 24.

ment dates. Mission-capable rates for key weapons will decline further. Accident and fatality rates for troops, which have declined continuously for many years, will at some point probably start growing again. Allowing that to happen, in order to purchase large numbers of expensive weapons, is unacceptable. Instead, the Pentagon must devise sound and practical weapons procurement plans, focusing on less expensive weaponry than it now prefers, and it must sustain those plans with little slippage in the years ahead.

Reducing Overseas Commitments

Unlike most countries in the world, the United States does not spend the majority of its defense budget defending its own territory. Instead, it attempts to protect its overseas interests and allies—a policy it came to the hard way, after two world wars finally persuaded it that an ounce of prevention is worth a pound of cure. To help deter conflicts, and to reassure and train with friends and allies, some 250,000 U.S. troops are based or deployed overseas at any given time. Roughly 45 percent of that total is in Europe, 37 percent in the western Pacific, 11 percent in the Middle East region, and most of the rest in Latin America (see table 2-2).[22] In late 2001 and 2002, an additional 30,000 have been in Afghanistan, neighboring countries, and the Arabian Sea.

During the presidential election campaign, then governor Bush talked about trying to reduce these numbers, particularly the numbers of troops deployed away from home base and their families. He also expressed a desire to reduce the number of missions that the U.S. armed forces are asked to address. Accomplishing these reductions will be tougher than it sounds, as Secretary of Defense Rumsfeld appears to have concluded himself, given the very modest cuts he has introduced to date. Consider where U.S. forces are found overseas today. Many anchor the U.S. commitment to NATO. Keeping 70,000 American military personnel in Germany may seem nonessential, but it is also inexpensive, since Berlin contributes financially to this modest additional burden. These troops are also deployed with their families. The same can be said of most of the U.S. forces in Japan—that is, the 20,000 to 25,000 or so who are not Marines on Okinawa. The situation is similar for the more than 10,000 uniformed

22. See also Michael O'Hanlon, "Come (Partially) Home, America," *Foreign Affairs,* vol. 80, no. 2 (March–April 2001).

Table 2-2. *Number of U.S. Troops Based in Foreign Countries,*
as of September 30, 2001[a]

Country or region	Number
Europe	
Belgium	1,578
Bosnia and Herzegovina	3,116
Germany	70,998
Iceland	1,743
Italy	11,704
Serbia (includes Kosovo)	5,679
Spain	1,990
Turkey	2,153
United Kingdom	11,318
Afloat	4,703
Other Europe	3,123
Total Europe (not including former Soviet Union)	118,105
Total former Soviet Union	151
East Asia and Pacific	
Japan	40,217
Korea, Republic of	37,605
Afloat	12,578
Other East Asia and Pacific	1,270
Total East Asia and Pacific	91,670
North Africa, Near East, South Asia	
Bahrain	2,065
Kuwait	4,208
Saudi Arabia	4,805
Afloat	13,546
Other North Africa, Near East, South Asia	2,254
Total North Africa, Near East, South Asia	26,878
Total sub-Saharan Africa	279
Total Western Hemisphere	14,015
Other	3,690
Total foreign countries[b]	254,788

Source: Department of Defense, Washington Headquarters Services, Directorate for Information Operations and Reports, Active Duty Military Personnel Strengths by Regional Area and by Country (309A), September 30, 2001 (http://web1.whs.osd.mil).

a. Only countries with more than 1,000 troops listed individually. The balance for each region can be found in the "other" row (for example, "Other Europe").

b. The military personnel in foreign countries break down according to service as follows: Army, 102,561 (40 percent of total); Air Force, 63,234 (25 percent of total); Navy, 60,315 (23 percent of total); and Marine Corps, 28,678 (11 percent of total).

personnel in Italy, a comparable number in the United Kingdom, and another 10,000 or so distributed among a range of other NATO member nations.[23] Of the total 250,000 troops away from the United States, therefore, at least half have a fairly good quality of life.

What about people deployed away from home base and families? Republicans often charged that the Clinton administration deployed forces to a new mission every nine weeks, or about six missions a year. That number was incorrect, however, since it counted several missions many times over (the database used to generate that figure erroneously considered a new mission to begin each time the president notified Congress that a given mission was being continued).[24] Most of the Clinton administration's missions were short term and involved only modest numbers of people. As a result, in dollar terms, costs have not been particularly onerous, averaging about $3 billion a year, or 1 percent of the defense budget.[25]

Longer missions generally took place only in regions of considerable importance to the United States. At the end of the Clinton administration, significant numbers of U.S. forces were deployed away from home in six regions: Korea, Okinawa, the waters of the western Pacific, the waters of the Mediterranean, the Persian Gulf, and the Balkans. Of the six deployments, five predated Clinton's tenure. The sixth was admittedly quite contentious, but it ultimately contributed to the end of the Bosnian civil war, provided protection for the ethnic Albanian population in the Kosovo war, and—at least indirectly—aided in the downfall of Yugoslav president Slobodan Milosevic. Moreover, the U.S. military role in the Balkans in the 1990s directly supported several U.S. treaty allies who had major national interests in stopping conflict on their borders: in other words, it helped protect important (if admittedly less than vital) U.S. security interests. One can disagree with this deployment, but it was hardly unimportant for American foreign policy and national security. The Clinton-Gore presidency did not use the military significantly more than its predecessors, frequently deploy U.S. forces to regions of peripheral importance for

23. Directorate for Information, Operations, and Reports, "Worldwide Manpower Distribution by Geographical Area," Dept. of Defense, Washington, December 31, 1999.

24. See Remarks of Senator Durbin, *Congressional Record,* October 30, 2000, S11353–58.

25. Zeman, *Making Peace While Staying Ready for War,* p. xii.

the United States, or spend a great deal of money on new missions. Most of the partisan sniping on the subject has been unfair.

President Bush nonetheless faces a problem. Missions abroad have clearly been hard on the uniformed personnel of the U.S. military over the past decade, and it is not going to be easy to end them. With more than 100,000 deployed continuously, nearly 8 percent of all U.S. military personnel are away from families and normal basing at any given time—not even counting those involved in Operation Enduring Freedom in central Asia and the Arabian Sea. During the last years of the cold war, the fraction was around 6 percent—130,000 to 140,000 personnel out of a total force of 2.2 million.

Today's figure of 8 percent may not sound large, but it is significant for two reasons. First, of the nearly 1.4 million active-duty troops in the U.S. military, only about 810,000 constitute the services' force structures.[26] Most deployments involve these 810,000, meaning that more than 10 percent of the total are generally deployed at a time. Second, many other demands on U.S. military personnel—most notably, training—take them away from home base as well. On balance, the typical soldier, sailor, airman, or Marine is away from home at least 15 to 20 percent of the time. If that is the average, many exceed it.

There are few easy answers about how to reduce these demands. U.S. interests in Persian Gulf oil, and in maintaining stability and impeding the proliferation of weapons of mass destruction there as well as in Northeast Asia, make it difficult to contemplate American military disengagement from those regions. Few in the U.S. foreign policy and defense debates would dispute these conclusions.

However, a careful survey of several of these key strategic regions suggests ways in which the United States may be able to reduce the extent of its presence in some cases without abandoning key strategic interests. Combined reductions in Okinawa, the Mediterranean, and the Persian Gulf might reduce the overall magnitude of U.S. deployments abroad by roughly 20 percent. More realistically, only a subset of these potential reductions in presence would be undertaken by a new administration, and even those would be phased in gradually—making for a reduction of perhaps 15,000 to 20,000 deployed U.S. troops after completion of a three- to five-year transition period. That would still be a big change from

26. Office of the Under Secretary of Defense for Personnel and Readiness, "Defense Manpower Requirements Reports" (Department of Defense, 2000), p. 9.

today, and it would make the pace of deployments per capita comparable to the sustainable levels of the late cold war period.

The Army in the Balkans—Reductions Already Have Been Large

U.S. military commitments in the Balkans, now totaling about 10,000 personnel, cannot be further reduced. The Bush administration, which has continued to streamline forces in Bosnia, just as the Clinton administration did, has gone as far as it should in this process for now.

Some Americans see U.S. commitments in the Balkans as an inherent distraction from the military's main missions and object to any and all such commitments on principle. Such a dismissive argument is ill advised, however. The alternative to engagement in the 1990s was to stand by and tolerate horrific civil conflict, the worst in Europe since the end of World War II, including many genocidal acts. That policy of disengagement was attempted and abandoned by the Bush administration in 1992, when it first kept the United States out of the war in Bosnia but then pledged U.S. military involvement in the event of a conflict in Kosovo. President Clinton got off to no better a start, failing to find a solution to the Bosnian civil war for more than two years. Finally, however, with the support and sometimes the prodding of Congress, his administration contributed to ending the Bosnian civil war.[27] From that point in 1995 on, the death toll from violence in that region was limited to about 10,000, including the Kosovo war—in contrast to the loss of 100,000 or more people in the three preceding years. The victory in Kosovo was an ugly one—attained only after a military campaign that began very poorly— but it did achieve a relatively good outcome compared with what might have been expected in the absence of NATO intervention.[28]

However one sees this track record, the United States now finds itself in two peace operations in the Balkans. Some have argued that the wealthy European allies should take principal responsibility for security on their own continent.[29] That policy may have some promise, but it needs to be adopted very selectively and carefully. First, U.S. abdication

---

27. See Ivo H. Daalder, *Getting to Dayton: The Making of America's Bosnia Policy* (Brookings, 2000).

28. See Ivo H. Daalder and Michael E. O'Hanlon, *Winning Ugly: NATO's War to Save Kosovo* (Brookings, 2000).

29. Michael R. Gordon, "Bush Would Stop U.S. Peacekeeping in Balkan Fights," *New York Times*, October 21, 2000, p. 1.

of dangerous security missions in Europe would violate the lesson learned not only in the world wars, but also in Bosnia from 1992 to 1995. Over that period, the United States stayed away from the Bosnian conflict, leaving its allies to founder—and to lose dozens of soldiers to snipers, mines, and accidents—in the UN's ill-fated UNPROFOR mission. Virtually all students of European security on both sides of the Atlantic have concluded that this type of situation needs to be avoided in the future: in other words, the United States must participate in future difficult and dangerous security missions in Europe, particularly if it wishes to maintain its leadership of the NATO alliance. Second, it would be unfortunate to codify a situation in which Europeans do little for security beyond Europe (though their contributions to Operation Enduring Freedom and the Afghan stability force have been very helpful to the United States). The United States should not condone such a division of labor, since most of the world's difficult future security tasks will probably be outside that continent. Encouraging Europe to remain militarily insular would not only be bad for the cause of equitable defense burden sharing; it could also reinforce existing differences in strategic perspectives between the United States and Europe on matters such as policy toward Iraq and Iran. Third, the proposed policy raises certain practical questions. For example, Russian troops in the Balkans serve under U.S. command, and a U.S. departure would put at risk an important collaborative effort between NATO and Russia.[30] Finally, one should not forget that the allies are already contributing most of the troops in the KFOR mission in Kosovo and the SFOR mission in Bosnia. U.S. troop contributions constitute less than 20 percent of the total in the Balkans (see table 2-3).[31]

These considerations lead to one conclusion: there may be ways to continue reducing U.S. troops in the Balkans, and possibly even to end American participation in one of the two ongoing missions there within a couple years—but only in the case of Bosnia, not of Kosovo. In Bosnia, a degree of stability has returned, facilitated by the division of territory in the 1995 Dayton Accords that all three major parties (Muslims, Croats, and Serbs) seem to accept as tolerable. Of course, the goals in Bosnia still

30. See Steven Erlanger, "Europeans Say Bush's Pledge to Pull Out of Balkans Could Split NATO," *New York Times,* October 25, 2000, p. A12.
31. Ivo H. Daalder and Michael E. O'Hanlon, "The United States in the Balkans: There to Stay," *Washington Quarterly,* vol. 23, no. 4 (Autumn 2000), pp. 157–70.

Table 2-3. *Total Number of Troops Participating in Kosovo KFOR Operations, Fall 2000*

Country	Troops	Country	Troops
NATO troops		*Non-NATO troops*	
Belgium	800	Argentina	113
Canada	800	Austria	480
Czech Republic	175	Azerbaijan	34
Denmark	900	Bulgaria	37
France	4,700	Finland	796
Germany	5,800	Georgia	34
Greece	0	Ireland	104
Hungary	324	Morocco	279
Italy	4,500	Russia	492
Netherlands	1,456	Slovakia	40
Norway	980	Slovenia	6
Poland	0	Sweden	765
Portugal	302	Switzerland	150
Spain	1,200	United Arab Emirates	1,240
Turkey	940	Non-NATO total	4,570
United Kingdom	3,900	KFOR headquarters	350
United States	7,000	KFOR total	38,697
NATO total	33,777		

Source: www.kforonline.com [December 7, 2000].

include reintegrating the Muslim-Croat and Serb sectors into a single functioning entity and allowing return of the displaced to their homes. Those goals may or may not be achieved. Even if they are not, however, the reasonably equitable territorial settlement reached at Dayton may help persuade Muslim, Croat, and Serb leaders and armies not to resume warfare. The new presidents in Croatia and Serbia, less nationalistic and far more upright than their predecessors, lend a further degree of stability to the situation. An outside stabilizing force certainly remains desirable, but it may not need to include Americans.

Kosovo, by contrast, remains a territory that both Serbs and ethnic Albanians consider their own. Moreover, there is no fallback position, as in Bosnia; no concept for partitioning the territory currently exists, except for the highly lopsided one that might accord to Serbs the tiny sector of Kosovo beginning at the city of Mitrovica and extending northward through the Trepca mine region to the border with Serbia proper. The fall of Slobodan Milosevic and his replacement by Vojislav Kostunica greatly improve the odds that peace will take hold, but a complete end to the conflict cannot be expected overnight. Milosevic was not alone among the Serb people in his willingness to use violence to reassert control over Kosovo. Furthermore, the ethnic Albanian population in Kosovo is fervently in favor of independence, and elements of the former Kosovo Liberation Army might well still be willing to fight for it—particularly if left unprotected and unchecked by a strong and credible NATO force. In this situation, U.S. forces remain highly desirable, if not essential.[32]

For these reasons, cuts in American forces in the Balkans have properly focused on Bosnia. The total U.S. military presence there numbered about 5,000 to 6,000 troops when Mr. Bush took office and is now closer to 3,000. With time, it may become possible to make deeper cuts, but doing so immediately would be a mistake.

The Marines on Okinawa

The United States typically stations nearly 20,000 Marines on Okinawa at any given time. They are an important component of the 100,000 total U.S. military personnel based or deployed in the western Pacific region. Since 1995, when the Pentagon released a document entitled *United States Security Strategy for the East Asia-Pacific Region* (more commonly referred to as the Nye report, after Assistant Secretary of Defense Joseph Nye), maintaining that number of troops in the Asia-Pacific has been held up as an important symbol of sustained U.S. commitment to the region. In light of unsettled security conditions in the Taiwan Strait and on the Korean peninsula, the Clinton administration felt it important to establish a floor below which U.S. military strength in the region would not drop, and the Bush administration has essentially retained this policy to date.

Of the nearly 20,000 Marines stationed on Okinawa, about half are deployed there without dependents for several months rather than based there for extended stays. That makes Okinawa by far the largest regular Marine Corps deployment in the world; in fact, forces there typically exceed all other Marine Corps deployments worldwide combined. The Marine Corps itself does not tend to complain about these demands; in fact, preparing for and conducting such deployments, be they on

32. See Daalder and O'Hanlon, *Winning Ugly.*

Okinawa or at sea, are at the heart of the service's definition of its raison d'être. In addition, the Marine Corps presence there is cost-effective, given that Japan foots much of the bill for operations and base needs; were the Marine Corps to leave, it would probably forfeit Japanese assistance with its annual operating costs (though Tokyo would likely help fund the one-time costs associated with establishing bases elsewhere).

Despite these advantages, the continuous presence on Okinawa has more downsides than are commonly recognized. It effectively consumes operational tempo, or available deployment capacity, that could be used elsewhere—be it for peace operations in the Balkans (for example, to give the Army a spell), a humanitarian intervention elsewhere (for example, should another major genocide occur in Africa), training missions or exercises with foreign militaries, or crisis response activities. The Marines, with their expeditionary philosophy, provide too valuable a resource to squander on a deployment that is not militarily or strategically essential—and that is on balance harmful to the U.S.-Japanese alliance (through no particular fault of the Marine Corps). Indeed, the strains that the current Marine Corps presence places on the U.S.-Japanese alliance are being recognized by an increasingly broad swath of the American defense policy community.[33]

The Marine presence on Okinawa has only a limited military logic. Just three amphibious ships are based in Japan, enough to transport the 2,000 Marines of the 31st Marine Expeditionary Unit with their equipment, but no more than that. The other Marines could not quickly deploy with their equipment. Okinawa itself is not at risk, and Japanese forces have the capacity to defend it even if it were. The Marines on Okinawa could be flown, without their heavy equipment, to Korea in the event of a war there, to help in noncombatant evacuations or similar missions. However, quickly airlifting infantry soldiers in wartime is not a major logistical challenge for the United States, even if troops are based in the United States. Furthermore, South Korea does not suffer for lack of infantry troops. The same is true for Taiwan, where critical U.S. contributions in any war would be in the areas of air and naval forces.

33. Kurt M. Campbell, "Energizing the U.S.-Japan Security Partnership," *Washington Quarterly*, vol. 23, no. 4 (Autumn 2000), pp. 133–34; National Defense University Study Group on the U.S.-Japan Partnership, "The United States and Japan: Advancing toward a Mature Partnership," Institute for National Strategic Studies, National Defense University, October 11, 2000.

Not only is the continuous Okinawa presence a major consumer of scarce U.S. military operational tempo; it is also a major strain on the U.S.-Japan alliance. Three-fourths of the acreage of U.S. bases in Japan is on the small island of Okinawa, which is home to more than a million people, making it densely populated even by Japanese standards. Those bases take up almost 20 percent of Okinawa's land area. Changes to the base structure agreed to in the 1990s will reduce the size of the U.S. presence on Okinawa by only about 15 percent, if indeed they are even carried out in full. Local resistance to moving the Marines' Futenma air base has stymied efforts to carry out much of the plan. Meanwhile, Marine flights continue in and out of Futenma—located right in the middle of Ginowan City—with associated risks of accidents. Polls in recent years showed that more than 80 percent of all Japanese consider the Okinawa arrangement undesirable and unfair to local citizens.[34] By trying to hang onto all of its bases in Japan, the United States risks causing a backlash and ultimately losing everything, including those facilities with greatest military benefit—the Kadena air base on Okinawa, as well as U.S. Navy and Air Force facilities on the main islands.

Given all these arguments, it would appear wisest to scale back the Marines on Okinawa from their present number of about 18,000 to 5,000 or so. Most Marine Corps facilities and training ranges would be returned to Japan, but access to storage and staging facilities would be retained for emergency use in the event of war, and facilities needed by the 31st Marine Expeditionary Unit (MEU) would be retained as well. The reduction could be carried out gradually, largely to allow compensating military steps to be taken. Such steps might include increased prestationing of U.S. military supplies on Okinawa or on ships in Japanese ports, to facilitate rapid deployments in the region (Tokyo might well pay for the necessary equipment and many of the Marine redeployment costs). Time would also be needed to coordinate the action with Tokyo and Seoul and, if possible, to find a new home for several thousand of those Marines in the region; likely candidates would include Australia and Korea. Ideally, this action would also be coordinated with a new initiative by Japan to

34. Much of this material is drawn from Mike M. Mochizuki, "A New Bargain for a Stronger Alliance," and Michael O'Hanlon, "Restructuring U.S. Forces and Bases in Japan," in Mike M. Mochizuki, ed., *Toward a True Alliance: Restructuring U.S.-Japan Security Relations* (Brookings, 1997), pp. 5–40, 149–78.

contribute more militarily to the alliance.[35] It might also be linked to a future conventional arms control accord on the Korean peninsula, though it should not be postponed indefinitely if the latter developments do not occur.

Remaining U.S. forces would include the 2,000 Marines of the 31st MEU and a comparable number to maintain pre-positioned equipment and ensure access arrangements for the emergency use of Japanese military and civilian facilities if needed in a regional crisis. The United States would also retain the Kadena Air Force airfield on Okinawa. In addition, all other U.S. forces in Japan, and all of those in Korea, would remain where they are today, providing more than adequate testimony to the continuing American interest in the region's stability.

The Navy Presence in the Mediterranean

During peacetime, the U.S. Navy maintains continuous or nearly continuous aircraft carrier presence in the western Pacific Ocean and in the Persian Gulf. It also maintains a presence half to two-thirds of the time in the Mediterranean.

It is not hard to see why Washington has elected to keep a carrier in the Mediterranean as often as possible. That carrier presence reinforces the U.S. claim to leadership in NATO's southern command. It is the southern command that has handled various Balkans operations. NATO's greatest internal problems are in the southern command region (between Greece and Turkey). Moreover, NATO's southern command region borders the unstable Middle East and the Suez Canal. Nonetheless, despite these considerations, maintaining a U.S. aircraft carrier at least half of the time in the Mediterranean is excessive.

Consider first just how important, and irreplaceable, other U.S. carrier deployments really are. The continuous carrier deployment in the western Pacific makes sound geostrategic sense. Japan might not provide land bases, or at least not enough land bases, from which U.S. military forces could operate in a war between Taiwan and China (see chapter 7). Without U.S. Navy help, the Korean navy might not be capable of quickly neutralizing North Korean mines, submarines, and other maritime threats in any future war on the peninsula, thereby potentially delaying U.S. reinforcements and prolonging a bloody war. In addition, the United States

---

35. See Mochizuki, *Toward a True Alliance*.

does not have close allied relations with countries neighboring the important Indonesian Straits and South China Sea, meaning that military efforts to protect those key shipping lanes must generally be naval. Similarly, in the Persian Gulf, neighboring U.S. friends are skittish about allowing U.S. military deployments on their territories. Moreover, the waters of the Gulf as well as the Strait of Hormuz themselves need protection against possible threats from ships, submarines, mines, and cruise missiles.

The situation used to be similar in the Mediterranean, a region that constitutes NATO's southern flank and Israel's western flank. During the cold war, Soviet naval forces posed a potential threat in those waters, perhaps most notably during Arab-Israeli crises and conflicts. Countries such as Greece and Turkey, somewhat isolated from the central NATO region, also benefited from the additional reassurance that proximate U.S. naval forces could provide.

These latter conditions have fundamentally changed, however. To be sure, there is still considerable volatility around the Mediterranean littorals, and many nations there welcome the U.S. Navy presence for its psychological benefits. However, the U.S. Navy's priority should not be giving psychological comfort; it should be carrying out military missions. Seen from that perspective, the purposes of the Mediterranean carrier presence today are far less clear. NATO's southern flank and Israel's western flank no longer constitute strategic vulnerabilities in the post–cold war era. Continuing problems with illicit migration into Europe from North Africa, which understandably concern many European countries, are not a proper focus for the U.S. Navy, but rather the responsibility of European coast guards and immigrations and customs agencies. U.S. influence over Greece and Turkey in preventing those two allies from entering into combat with one another has less to do with U.S. aircraft carriers—which would never plausibly be used against an ally in any event—than with the broader strategic and economic importance of the United States for both countries. A similar statement applies to U.S. influence over Israelis and Palestinians in the continuing effort to bring peace to the Middle East. All in all, U.S. naval presence in the region does not have the justification it once did.

In the event of a small crisis, some might still wish to have U.S. naval forces available for a quick action in the Mediterranean. However, the proximity of U.S. forces in much of Europe and the potential availability of land bases for fighter aircraft or other assets in a total of half a dozen friendly countries along the Mediterranean rim mean that alternatives would generally be available. That is even more the case today, given the stationing of various types of combat aircraft at Aviano in Italy and at Incirlik in Turkey.

To be sure, European friends and allies have not and will not always see crises the same way as Washington. In 1986 only Britain permitted its bases to be used by U.S. forces in the strike on Libya. Only Portugal allowed the United States to use its facilities for supplying Israel during the 1973 Yom Kippur War. For situations in which American lives were at direct risk, however, or in situations of great consequence to general western security, base access could generally be presumed. For missions like the strike on Libya, moreover, carriers could always be surged and deployed to the Mediterranean if necessary.[36]

Trying to maintain a quasi-permanent naval presence in the Mediterranean can be counterproductive. Consider what happened just before the 1999 Kosovo war. A U.S. carrier had been in the region until ten days before the start of the NATO air operation, but it was sent to the Persian Gulf to relieve a carrier that had completed its standard six-month rotation there. This left the Mediterranean unattended when air strikes were initiated. Not only did that fact limit the intensity of NATO's campaign in the early going, but it may also have signaled to Milosevic that the United States and its alliance partners were not particularly serious about attacking him. Maintaining peacetime presence and ensuring that crews were not kept at sea longer than six months effectively became higher priorities than preventing or winning a war.

If the United States had had no carrier in the Mediterranean in the months before the conflict, it would have had fresh ships and crews available when they were truly needed. The Navy's argument that peacetime presence tends to foster stability and deterrence, while persuasive in many regions at most times, was thus not correct in this case.[37]

36. Robert E. Harkavy, *Bases Abroad: The Global Foreign Military Presence* (Oxford University Press, 1989), p. 77.

37. See Eric Schmitt, "NATO Dismisses a Milosevic Bid and Steps Up Raids," *New York Times*, April 7, 1999, p. A1; John Pike, "Where Are the Carriers?" Federation of American Scientists, December 27, 1999 (www.fas.org/man/dod-101/sys/ships/where.htm [January 5, 2001]); and Statement of Daniel Murphy, Hearings, Senate Armed Services Committee, Subcommittee on Sea Power, October 13, 1999, excerpted in "The Navy in the Balkans," *Air Force Magazine*, vol. 82 (December 1999), pp. 48–49.

This analysis suggests that the Navy reconsider its presence in the Mediterranean region. Doing so would allow the Navy to maintain and perhaps even occasionally bolster its presence in the three main regions where that is truly needed: the Persian Gulf and the western Pacific theaters, as well as the Arabian Sea. Such a disposition would still permit the Navy to make an occasional deployment to the Mediterranean, often while going to and from the Persian Gulf, to show the flag, to conduct exercises with allies, or to respond to a crisis.

Finally, this policy would reduce strain on sailors. In fact, it would do so even if the size of the carrier fleet were reduced by two, from twelve carriers to ten, once the war in and around Afghanistan is over. The Navy needs some six or seven ships in the fleet for every one deployed to the Persian Gulf, roughly four for the Mediterranean, and one or two for the western Pacific—stretching today's total fleet of eleven active carriers and one in reserve. (In fact, as noted, deployments to the Mediterranean are not continuous; gaps in coverage frequently occur there, and occasionally elsewhere too.)[38]

The main reasons for this unappealing deployment arithmetic are threefold. First, sailors need time to recover; in a best case, it would take three ships to sustain every deployment away from home base—one on station, one recovering from deployment, and a third working up for deployment. Second, ships sometimes need extended maintenance, taking them out of the deployment cycle for six months or more. Third, given the distance from U.S. ports to the Persian Gulf theater in particular, much deployment time is lost in transit, meaning that in any six-month tour, only three to four months are spent on station. For ships leaving the U.S. east coast for the Mediterranean, some five months are commonly spent on station out of six on deployment. For ships in the western Pacific, the math is different because a carrier battle group is permanently based in Japan—and considered to be deployed even when sitting in dock in Yokosuka. It only fails to be deployed in the region when it makes an occasional tour into the Indian Ocean or the Persian Gulf or when it needs maintenance.[39]

---

38. See Les Aspin, *Report on the Bottom-Up Review* (Department of Defense, October 1993), p. 50.

39. Ronald O'Rourke, "Naval Forward Deployments and the Size of the Navy," (Congressional Research Service, November 13, 1992), pp. 13–23.

Eliminating entirely a full-time presence in the Mediterranean would thus tend to reduce demands on the carrier fleet by four ships. Since today's presence there is not continuous, however, ending it would in fact reduce overall requirements by about three carriers. My proposal would eliminate only two carriers, however, since part of the purpose of this policy is to make remaining deployments less taxing on sailors and ships.

Corresponding savings and benefits would arise for the surface combatant fleet. In addition, other cost-cutting measures would be available there. For those combatants not escorting carriers, the practice of rotating crews by airlift while keeping ships forward deployed for a year or more should be adopted. Since ships of a given class are similar to one another, it should not be unduly difficult for a crew to train on one ship in home waters and then fly to an overseas theater to operate a similar ship; if necessary, a small cadre of sailors familiar with the ship in question could be on hand to help the new crew learn the idiosyncrasies of the ship for a few weeks. This idea should also work because surface combatants generally have crews of only three hundred sailors or so, thus limiting the practical logistical difficulties involved in transporting them around the world.[40] The benefit of this policy is that it would cut down greatly on time lost in transit. In theory, this approach could reduce the number of ships required to maintain a given deployment by nearly half. In practice, it would be more realistic to aspire to savings of 10 to 20 percent in fleet size for the foreseeable future—which would also allow a reduction in deployment tempo for crews.

The Air Force–Led Operation in the Persian Gulf

Since shortly after the end of Operation Desert Storm, the United States and Britain have maintained no-fly zones over Iraqi airspace. These zones were not authorized by the U.N. Security Council resolutions that ended the 1991 Gulf War. Rather, they were initiated in response to Iraq's post–Desert Storm abuses against its own minority populations, its unwillingness to comply with its obligations in regard to weapons inspections, and its other dangerous actions. Washington and London have hoped that these aerial interdiction operations would limit Saddam's ability to threaten his own populations, make him pay a price—in prestige, if

40. See William F. Morgan, *Rotate Crews, Not Ships* (Alexandria, Va.: Center for Naval Analyses, June 1994), pp. 1–9.

nothing else—for impeding the work of weapons inspectors, and possibly embolden internal Iraqi resistance forces to step up their efforts to unseat him. Carrying out these missions has been demanding. For example, in the fall of 2000, the U.S. military presence in the Persian Gulf region totaled more than 25,000 troops, largely devoted to carrying out operations in the no-fly zone. It featured about 60 land-based aircraft in Turkey, about 130 land-based aircraft on the Arabian Peninsula, and about 70 aircraft on an aircraft carrier in the Persian Gulf. (Of the total of 260 U.S. planes, about 65 were support aircraft and 190 combat jets. About 75 were Navy planes and nearly 200 Air Force aircraft.)[41]

As part of its policy review on Iraq, the Bush administration should consider a modification to the no-fly-zone operation over Iraq and a substantial reduction in the current U.S. military presence in the Persian Gulf. The costs of conducting the no-fly-zone operations, especially in strains and stresses on the U.S. and British militaries, now appear to be outweighing their benefits. Such a policy would of course only be put into effect once the debate over whether to overthrow Saddam had been completed.

Ideally, such a change in American and British policy would be linked to a resumption of some type of weapons inspections within Iraq and to an agreement by Saddam Hussein to show restraint in using force against minorities in Iraq's north and south. Domestic politics in the United States may make it difficult even to consider such an idea. The policy suggested here would, however, maintain robust deterrence and help the U.S. Air Force, while reducing pressure on Iraq in only a very limited way.

This proposal would keep U.S. fighter aircraft in the Persian Gulf region to deter Iraqi moves against its neighbors and minority groups. The numbers of those aircraft could be reduced, however, and their mission could be partially redefined, away from maintaining constant airborne patrols over Iraq and instead to carrying out robust air-to-ground attacks against any future large-scale Iraqi aggression or in response to any evidence of renewed Iraqi pursuit of weapons of mass destruction. It may also be possible to hand off some of this mission to bombers based in Europe or on Diego Garcia, with substantial numbers of autonomous all-weather homing munitions prestationed near Iraq, as soon as such

41. Federation of American Scientists, "U.S. Forces, Order of Battle, Saturday, October 14, 2000" (www.fas.org/man/dod-101/ops/iraq-orbat.htm [January 5, 2001].

munitions (such as the sensor-fused weapon) complete their development cycles and become widely available.

As a rough estimate, this proposal might cut U.S. military presence in the Persian Gulf region down to less than 20,000 troops from its recent levels. Effects would be greatest on the Air Force, the service that has suffered the most from the high operational tempo associated with the no-fly zone; its presence in the region would be reduced by nearly 50 percent. That single step would essentially solve the service's continuing problems with high operational tempo.

Although this change in policy might appear to be a tactical retreat in the U.S. policy of containing Iraq, it would in fact sacrifice little. Saddam does not need aircraft to oppress his own people, so the strategic benefits of the no-fly zones are limited in impact even today. The alternative policy would sustain robust deterrence against the most strategically significant potential Iraqi acts of aggression—attacks against Kuwait or Saudi Arabia, as well as possible large-scale internal repression of Kurds or Shiites—and visible resumption of Iraqi production of weapons of mass destruction.

Conclusion

Today's U.S. military readiness remains quite good, but at some risk. Aging equipment needs replacing, or it will gradually become less serviceable and less safe; chapter 4 treats this issue in greater depth. Most important of all, military personnel need—and deserve—a better lifestyle. Compensation is now in fairly good shape, but easing of the pace of deployments is definitely called for, even if difficult to achieve.

Reducing the long-standing U.S. military deployments of Marines on Okinawa, of carrier battle groups and other ships in the Mediterranean, and of Air Force aircraft over the skies of Iraq are the most promising ways to mitigate these pressures, and they should not harm U.S. security interests. The combination of these measures should greatly help all the services' operational tempo problems. Even adopting half of them, and phasing them in over a period of several years, would make an important difference.

Whatever happens on the deployment front, however, costs for ensuring readiness are likely to keep going up. Personnel costs may not grow greatly, but per capita operating and maintenance costs are likely to keep increasing at 1 to 2 percent a year in real terms. By 2010, ensuring readiness is likely to require another $10 billion to $20 billion more in annual real-dollar spending on operations and support than it does today—even if the next president and Congress do what they should, which is to close more military bases while also seeking other economies. U.S. military readiness may be good, but it is not to be taken for granted, and it does not come cheap.

THREE Modifying the
Two-War Framework

As noted in chapter 1, the Bush administration has changed the nature of the country's two-war requirement for waging simultaneous military operations in different geographic theaters. This policy change makes good sense.[1]

It is exceedingly unlikely that the United States would ever need to carry out overlapping all-out ground counteroffensives. Given South Korea's growing military strength vis-à-vis that of North Korea, a huge U.S. deployment to the Korean peninsula would probably only be needed if Washington and Seoul elected to overthrow the North Korean regime; a half million Americans would almost surely not be needed for strictly defensive purposes. Similarly, in the case of the Persian Gulf, Iraq is now so much weaker than it was in 1990—and U.S. military capabilities in the region are now so much greater (as they would remain even under my proposed restructuring of the U.S. military presence there)—that smaller forces would suffice for all operations short of a march on Baghdad, and perhaps even for that scenario as well. To be sure, the United States and its allies may well decide, once a future war is under way, that they should go to the root of the problem and overthrow the aggressive regime that

1. Similar proposals appear in Michael O'Hanlon, "Rethinking Two-War Strategies," *Joint Forces Quarterly,* no. 24 (Spring 2000), and O'Hanlon, "Prudent or Paranoid? The Pentagon's Two-War Plans," *Survival,* vol. 43, no. 1 (Spring 2001).

has caused the conflict. However, the likelihood of having to conduct two such operations—and to do so at virtually the same time—is quite modest. Finally, in a possible conflict between China and Taiwan, U.S. military contributions would be almost exclusively, if not entirely, aerial and naval.

Instead, it should suffice that the United States have the capability for a single all-out operation on the scale of Desert Storm that would include such an overthrow-and-occupy mission, together with a more limited capability for a nearly simultaneous but smaller war-fighting operation elsewhere. In addition, it should have a force structure adequate for a third mission on a modest scale, most likely a peace operation. This overall concept might be described as a "Desert Storm plus Desert Shield plus Bosnia/IFOR" posture (IFOR was the initial, relatively large NATO operation in Bosnia), in contrast to the current two–Desert Storm framework.

The Desert Shield operation would amount to much more than a simple defensive or "hold" capability. It would include roughly a quarter million U.S. troops, featuring significant ground-combat capabilities and very substantial airpower. There is a very high chance that, when teamed with local allies, it would be adequate to achieve victory—indeed, perhaps even an overthrow of the enemy regime and occupation of its territory—in Northeast or Southwest Asia, or any other place in which a major U.S. military operation can be imagined. For that reason, a Desert Shield force package should provide very robust deterrence of a second possible war, if and when the United States is primarily engaged in a major conflict elsewhere. In the highly unlikely event that deterrence failed in two places at once, the Desert-Shield force package would allow the United States to vigorously prosecute the second war, even if it might have to forgo some strategic options until its other conflict was completed.

Admittedly, there would be some risk associated with moving to a smaller capability for the second possible war. But there is also risk in overinsuring against regional conflict while overworking the U.S. armed forces and underinvesting in certain areas of military innovation, nontraditional defense activities, and weapons procurement—as the country has been doing in recent years. Moreover, the United States would still have recourses if it needed to carry out two nearly simultaneous overthrow-and-occupy operations, including using substantial numbers of reserve forces for the second or possibly swinging some forces from one theater to the other. These latter options are not ideal, but they do serve to remind us that the United States would not be without extreme responses to the extreme scenario of two all-out, large-scale wars at once.

If adopted, such an alternative to the two–Desert Storm posture would provide the Army in particular with considerable flexibility in its force structure. That might not lead to a substantially smaller U.S. Army, but it could allow the force to be reconfigured in a way that would greatly ease strains on military personnel while also ensuring funding for the Army's ongoing efforts to modernize weaponry and make itself more mobile and deployable.

The current two–Desert Storm war-fighting framework had its ancestry in the base force concept of Defense Secretary Richard Cheney and Chairman of the Joint Chiefs of Staff Colin Powell. It became truly prominent in the Pentagon's 1993 Bottom-Up Review under Secretary Les Aspin, and it was retained in similar form in the 1997 Quadrennial Defense Review (QDR).

Throughout this entire decade-long period, the framework has frequently had its critics. Notable among them was the congressionally mandated National Defense Panel (NDP). It produced its report in late 1997—about six months after the QDR was completed. In the report the National Defense Panel stated, "The two-theater war construct has been a useful mechanism for determining what forces to retain as the Cold War came to a close. . . . But, it is fast becoming an inhibitor to reaching the capabilities we will need in the 2010–2020 time frame."[2] The National Defense Panel appeared to view the two–Desert Storm concept as little more than a bureaucratic device with more relevance to the Department of Defense's internal politics and organizational requirements than to real-world threats. Similarly, the April 2000 (second) report of the congressionally mandated U.S. Commission on National Security/21st Century (USCNS/21) stated without further elaboration: "This Commission believes that the 'two major theater wars' yardstick for sizing U.S. forces is not producing the capabilities needed for the varied and complex contingencies now occurring and likely to increase in the years ahead."[3]

2. See National Defense Panel, *Transforming Defense: National Security in the 21st Century* (Arlington, Va.: Department of Defense, December 1997), p. 23.

3. Gary Hart, Warren B. Rudman, and others, *Seeking a National Strategy: A Concept for Preserving Security and Promoting Freedom* (Alexandria, Va.: United States Commission on National Security/21st Century, April 15, 2000), pp. 14–15.

Unfortunately, these criticisms have generally failed to advance the debate over the nation's war-fighting strategy. They have been too dismissive of the basic concept of a two-war capability; in fact, some type of two-theater capability does make strategic and military sense, even if the current version of the two-war strategy may not. In addition, the NDP and the Commission on National Security have been insufficiently specific or analytical about what should replace the current two–Desert Storm construct.

The fact of the matter is that Saddam Hussein and Kim Jong-Il still hold power in their respective countries, and their regimes, not to mention other actors, pose acute risks to important U.S. interests. The process of détente on the Korean peninsula offers the hope that one of these two major regional threats may soon diminish in severity, but it would be greatly premature to discount the North Korean threat at a time when the reconciliation process has led to virtually no reduction in the conventional military forces of the Democratic People's Republic of Korea (DPRK). We cannot drop the current two-war construct until we are convinced that its successor would provide adequate deterrent and defense capabilities vis-à-vis these and other threats. The vague musings of the NDP and the USCNS/21 on the subject of the two-war framework, while useful as political cover for those who wish to debate this subject, hardly form the basis for a new national military strategy.

Indeed, the sweeping way in which the NDP had dismissed the two-war notion gave Secretary of Defense William S. Cohen an easy response. As he poignantly noted, which bad guy did the NDP want him to forget about, Saddam Hussein or Kim Jong-Il?[4] Furthermore, which national interests did the panel want the United States to abandon, ensured access to Persian Gulf oil or commitment to South Korea's security—not to mention promotion of general stability and the nonproliferation of weapons of mass destruction in both theaters? Fortunately, Secretary Rumsfeld has found a careful way to replace the two–Desert Storm framework with a less demanding but still robust two-war capability, similar to that advocated in the rest of this chapter.

Given the need to pay attention to the North Korean and various possible Persian Gulf threats, this chapter emphasizes potential conflict in

4. Douglas Berenson and Roman Schweizer, "Cohen's Draft Response to NDP Reasserts Merits of Two-War Approach," *Inside the Pentagon*, vol. 13 (December 4, 1997), p. 1.

those theaters. However, its appendix adds several preliminary ideas about how one might think about force planning should one of the current major threats to U.S. and allied security—most likely North Korea—simply cease to be an acute military concern. Such a day may be a year off; it may also be a decade off. Nevertheless, it would be imprudent not to consider the possibility now, while there is ample time to mull over serious options. Even without acute threats from Iraq and North Korea, there is still a strong logic for a simultaneous two-theater war-fighting capability of some type, though its detailed nature may be different under such circumstances.

A New Two-War Concept: "Desert Storm plus Desert Shield plus Bosnia"

Even though their argumentation is unpersuasive, in a broader sense the National Defense Panel and Commission on National Security are right. Being able to handle overlapping crises or conflicts in two different places—if not more, allowing for a crisis in the Taiwan Strait, or the Balkans, or elsewhere as well—is indeed a sound strategic pillar on which to structure U.S. military forces. However, positing simultaneous replays of Desert Storm, most likely in Korea and the Persian Gulf, smacks of preparing to fight the last war.

Moreover, the current two–Desert Storm framework presupposes that in both cases the United States would use virtually identical types and numbers of forces—roughly six to seven active-duty ground-combat divisions, including Army and Marine Corps units, ten wings of Air Force aircraft, four to five Navy aircraft carrier battle groups, and various other assets. Whether the war was on the open desert of the Arabian peninsula or the Bosnia-like terrain of Korea, and whether U.S. armed forces were joined in combat only by relatively weak allies in the Gulf or by South Korea's fine military, official Pentagon documents suggest that roughly the same cookie-cutter U.S. force package would be deployed to the fight.[5]

This state of affairs would not be a major problem if the standard "major theater war" force package were ample for all possible scenarios

---

5. See Les Aspin, *Report on the Bottom-Up Review* (Department of Defense, October 1993), pp. 13–22; and William S. Cohen, *Report of the Quadrennial Defense Review* (Department of Defense, May 1997), pp. 12–13, 24–26, 30.

and if keeping two of them were easily affordable. Alas, the latter assumption is incorrect. Were there no opportunity costs to keeping the current two–Desert Storm planning framework, the Pentagon would suffer little harm in retaining it. Unfortunately, however, given the fiscal constraints likely to be in effect in coming years, keeping a high-priced insurance policy against regional conflict could leave the United States unable to afford other key military investments—and thus risk making it vulnerable on other fronts.

The Bush administration is right to revise current war-fighting strategy from the two–Desert Storm construct to a more realistic and less demanding type of two-war framework. That alternative framework might be described as a one and one-half Desert Storm capability. More descriptively, it might also be termed a "Desert Storm plus Desert Shield plus Bosnia/IFOR" framework. (The IFOR deployment was the large-scale U.S. commitment the first year after the Dayton peace accords were signed; it involved about twenty thousand U.S. troops in Bosnia, plus several thousand more in support roles in neighboring countries.) This construct would underscore the point that the United States need not plan to do the lion's share of the fighting in two overlapping large-scale ground counteroffensives.

The odds that two such counteroffensives would be needed at the same time are quite small. First, the outbreak of two wars at once is unlikely if the United States keeps a potent two-theater deterrent. Second, even if deterrence fails, the United States and local allies are unlikely to lose the initial battles, and to sacrifice territory, in both theaters at once. Third, although a major counteroffensive could still be needed to overthrow an enemy regime and occupy its country, such war aims are not necessarily the norm—as the Korean and Persian Gulf wars remind us. They might well not be adopted in two theaters simultaneously. Fourth and finally, even if two large counteroffensives were undertaken at once, the potential for allied help (particularly in Korea) is substantially greater than American war plans now postulate, and the potential for enemy forces to crumble (especially in Iraq) is considerable as well. This cascading line of logic does not rule out the potential need for enormous numbers of U.S. forces to conduct two nearly simultaneous major counteroffensives, but it is a reminder that the probability of such a scenario is quite low.

The "Desert Storm plus Desert Shield plus Bosnia/IFOR" slogan would also emphasize that if the two-war capability were scaled back, and its margin of insurance reduced, the United States would no longer be prudent to depend on forces that might be involved in peace operations for rapid response to regional conflicts. The demands of Bosnia-like operations should be seen as additional, not included.

More specifically, the alternative war-fighting construct would be based on the following key assumptions and judgments:

—Iraq, as was once feared, has not rearmed substantially since Operation Desert Storm and may not do so, depending on the future of sanctions regimes;

—North Korea's military has suffered from a decade of national economic decline and, while still formidable, is less battle ready than it once was;

—South Korea's military, the recent financial crisis notwithstanding, has continued to improve. It is now capable itself of holding off a North Korean invasion attempt with a high probability of success;

—A combination of improved precision-strike capabilities, more combat equipment prestationed near Iraq and North Korea, and improvements in strategic lift has increased the odds that the United States could make a highly effective rapid response to war in either theater, further reducing the odds that an enemy attack would be successful in its opening phases. Further improvements are desirable as well, for example in the realm of airlift, but a good deal has already been accomplished;

—South Korea's military would almost surely survive a North Korean onslaught well enough to play a major role in a combined U.S.–Republic of Korea (ROK) counteroffensive into North Korean territory, greatly reducing the probability that two separate corps structures and six to eight total ground combat divisions would be needed from the American side;

—British forces, now structured with a Persian Gulf scenario in mind, should be factored into U.S. war plans, reducing demands on U.S. forces there by roughly one division of ground troops and several squadrons of fighter aircraft (other NATO allies may be able to help as well, though perhaps not with enough aggregate capability or political reliability to factor into U.S. war plans significantly); and, finally,

—The Army National Guard's fifteen enhanced separate brigades, only a half a dozen of which factored into war plans in the 1997 Quadrennial Defense Review, provide additional capability for major theater wars that can serve as a hedge against the unexpected.[6] It is doubtful that all of

6. See Frances Lussier, *Structuring the Active and Reserve Army for the 21st Century* (Washington: Congressional Budget Office, December 1997), p. 11.

these brigades could be brought up to full war-fighting readiness within weeks or even several months of a decision to do so, but they should be able to perform some combat duties and contribute to tasks associated with military occupation. Since 1997 the Army has decided to try linking virtually all of its reserve combat force structure, including not only the enhanced brigades but also its Guard divisions, to concrete war plans. The military need for doing so, however, is suspect. The proposed new policy may really reflect a desire to give the Guard's units—many of which do not meet good standards today—specific goals and a clear focus rather than a need to use all of them in likely regional wars.[7]

This set of judgments and conclusions would allow a reduction in the total number of active-duty U.S. ground combat divisions required for regional war fighting from the current number of thirteen to roughly eleven. One might think that even deeper cuts should be possible, since most of the individual points described above would each reduce demands on U.S. forces by at least one division relative to current plans. However, some of them might not apply in the end; for example, it is at least theoretically possible that Iraq could rearm someday, and it is possible even if not likely that South Korea's offensive combat capabilities could be nearly decimated in resisting a North Korean assault, leaving little to wage a counteroffensive and invasion of the DPRK. In addition, the alternative approach would have to err on the side of caution, including a cushion of extra forces in case the United States and its allies encountered unexpectedly difficult conditions, such as widespread enemy use of weapons of mass destruction.

Specifically, the United States could retain three Marine and eight Army active-duty divisions under this proposal. Alternatively, the Army could retain ten divisions, but make them smaller and lighter than current plans suppose. Corresponding reductions in military personnel would be less than the 15 percent cut that would pertain to divisions, however, for two main reasons. First, most of today's units are short of troops. In moving to a war-fighting construct that is admittedly somewhat higher-risk in nature, it would be important not to compound the increase in risk by leaving units under strength. Second, while a good number of Army and

7. See Steven Lee Myers, "Army Weighs an Expanded Role for National Guard Combat Units," *New York Times*, August 4, 2000, p. A1; and General Accounting Office, *Army National Guard: Enhanced Brigade Readiness Improved but Personnel and Workload Are Problems*, GAO/NSIAD-00-114 (June 2000), pp. 5–6.

Marine Corps combat support structures could be reduced proportionately (including one corps, with its headquarters and associated logistical and combat assets), other personnel could not be. Individuals working in central direction or intelligence, officers involved in military education programs, individuals working in research and development programs, and others could not be easily reduced. In broad brush, Army and Marine Corps active-duty end strength might decline by only 6 percent or so under this proposal—perhaps from their current levels of 480,000 and 172,000 to 450,000 and 160,000. Even these modest troop reductions would exceed those planned by the Bush administration, which reduced the demands of U.S. war fighting strategy yet made no cuts in manpower or forces. The administration is right that large cuts are infeasible, but wrong not to look for any savings or efficiencies at all.

The Capabilities of Smaller, Rapidly Deployable U.S. Forces

A Desert Shield force of roughly 200,000 to 300,000 troops would be extremely effective. If deployed promptly, it could defend allied territory and key military infrastructure against virtually any threat the United States might face in the world today. It would also wield enough offensive firepower, primarily in the form of aircraft, to wreak significant damage on enemy forces even if its capability for an all-out ground offensive was limited. Furthermore, there are good reasons to think that it could be deployed quickly.

U.S. commanders felt confident that they could have defended Saudi Arabia with such a Desert Shield force once it was deployed in October of 1990. That should come as no great surprise. The high caliber of U.S. military personnel, combat equipment, and supporting capabilities such as advanced reconnaissance systems would make such a Desert Shield capability significantly superior to the notional regional aggressor force specified in the Bottom-Up Review, even though that aggressor force might be two to three times as large.[8]

The airpower component of a Desert Shield–like deployment, at least as large as that which participated in NATO's Operation Allied Force against Serbia in 1999, could devastate an enemy's defense and industrial

---

8. For one convincing analysis, see Lane Pierrot, *Planning for Defense: Affordability and Capability of the Administration's Program* (Washington: Congressional Budget Office, 1994), p. 22.

infrastructure while also striking at moving armor and other military vehicles. Its ground component could carry out certain types of offensives on land too, even if an all-out counteroffensive might be beyond its reach. General Norman Schwarzkopf considered developing plans to evict Saddam from Kuwait with a force of this size before deciding to ask the president to double the deployment.[9]

Although it is not a certainty, the odds that such a Desert Shield–like force could be deployed in time to prevent significant loss of allied territory in a future conflict are now reasonably good. Since the end of the cold war, the U.S. military has stored more equipment in the Persian Gulf and Northeast Asian regions and purchased more fast sealift in the form of large, medium-speed, roll-on/roll-off ships. In addition to forces routinely based or deployed overseas, including about 37,000 in South Korea, more than 40,000 in Japan, and at least 25,000 in the Persian Gulf region, the United States has Army brigade sets of equipment in Korea and Kuwait, another set afloat at Diego Garcia in the Indian Ocean, and elements of a fourth in Qatar. Marine brigade-equivalent sets are at sea at Diego Garcia, at Guam, and in the Mediterranean. These units could be "married up" with troops airlifted from the States within one to two weeks. Modest additional improvements in pre-positioning and lift could improve response time further.[10] Just as important, significant stocks of Air Force precision-guided munitions are now located overseas.[11] Stopping an enemy quickly and then continuing to pound it from the air might make a major ground counteroffensive unnecessary, or at least reduce the urgency with which it would have to be conducted.

In the very unlikely event that two major counteroffensives were needed within the same year or so, this alternative force-sizing framework might well be up to the job, even without requiring the same units to fight first in one theater and then in another. To see why, consider the overall numbers. The Army estimated in 1997 that a total of nearly 200,000 combat soldiers could be needed in the event of two overlapping regional conflicts (together with even larger numbers of support person-

9. See Michael R. Gordon and Bernard E. Trainor, *The Generals' War: The Inside Story of the Conflict in the Gulf* (Boston: Little, Brown, 1995), pp. 123–41; Robert H. Scales Jr., *Certain Victory: The U.S. Army in the Gulf War* (Washington: Brassey's, 1994), pp. 121–28.

10. For one set of proposals, see Michael O'Hanlon, *Defense Planning for the Late 1990s: Beyond the Desert Storm Framework* (Brookings, 1995), pp. 33–34.

11. See Rachel Schmidt, *Moving U.S. Forces: Options for Strategic Mobility* (Washington: Congressional Budget Office, 1997), pp. 36, 40.

nel, mostly from the reserve component). Today's military comprises nearly 350,000 combat soldiers, including roughly half in the active force and the other half in the National Guard. The proposal advanced here would reduce active-duty combat soldiers by about 15,000, leaving almost 150,000. So about 50,000 would be needed from the reserve component. Such a number could be easily obtained from the Army's enhanced separate brigades, which comprise some 75,000 combat troops, and would not necessitate tapping into the less-ready National Guard divisions (which, if domestic politics ever allow it, should be substantially cut back in size, perhaps winding up as brigades).[12] Thus my proposal may well suffice for overlapping overthrow-and-occupy operations, even if they prove quite difficult.

The Hollowing Iraqi and North Korean Militaries

While they remain dangerous, the Iraqi and North Korean military machines are weaker than they were several years ago, and they have few prospects for getting much stronger soon. This increases the odds that a Desert Shield–like force, together with regional friends of the United States, could defend allied territory in a future war. In fact, it might not require much more U.S. capability to conduct a large-scale counteroffensive, regime overthrow, and occupation.

Saddam's conventional military forces remain only about half the size and strength they were in 1990. Before Desert Storm Iraq had an inventory of 5,500 tanks; it now has some 2,200. Its total number of light tanks and armored personnel carriers is down from 7,500 to 3,500; troop levels have declined from 1,000,000 to just over 400,000.[13] Nor has the decline in raw numbers been counterbalanced by any improvement in equipment quality, troop training, or other intangibles.

In 1997 the Defense Intelligence Agency reported that, while North Korea's military remains dangerously poised near Seoul, its "capability to conduct large-scale combat operations continues to deteriorate as worsening internal economic conditions undermine training, readiness, and

---

12. See Lussier, *Structuring the Active and Reserve Army for the 21st Century*, p. 11.

13. International Institute for Strategic Studies (IISS), *The Military Balance 1990–1991* (Oxford, England: Brassey's, 1990), p. 105; IISS, *The Military Balance 2000–2001* (Oxford: Oxford University Press, 2000), pp. 140–41. For measures of capability that factor in equipment quality as well as quantity, see O'Hanlon, *Defense Planning for the Late 1990s,* p. 43.

sustainment."[14] The decline continued thereafter. North Korea did reverse the decline significantly in 1999, but its ability to restore its combat capabilities to earlier levels is in serious doubt. It continues to have a weakening economy, with a GDP that has declined by roughly half in the past decade and now totals only about $12 billion.[15] Moreover, as is also the case with Iraq, virtually all DPRK equipment is now a decade older than it was in 1990. Over the past decade most weapons have been produced at modest rates, and arms imports have been quite limited. The U.S. intelligence community cannot easily determine the implications for force readiness, including the reliability of the equipment, the degree to which some weapons must be cannibalized for parts to keep others running, and so forth. However, it would be surprising indeed if the mission-capable rates of North Korean equipment had not declined significantly—probably by considerably more than the 10 percentage-point drop experienced by U.S. aircraft over the past decade.

The South Korean capital does remain vulnerable to North Korean artillery, missiles, and special forces. North Korea now has about five hundred long-range artillery tubes within range of Seoul at all times, roughly a doubling from levels of a few years ago.[16] The DPRK unquestionably possesses, therefore, what amounts to a massive terrorist capability against the South Korean capital. As a result, any war on the peninsula would be tragic, causing untold civilian deaths as well as large numbers of military casualties.

Most of the military casualties of such a conflict would be North Korea's, however. Its armored forces are even more obsolescent than Iraq's. In any invasion attempt, those weak armored forces would have to cross the most militarized swath of land on the planet—in fact, the density of ROK/US troops forward-deployed near the demilitarized zone (DMZ) in Korea is greater than NATO's were along the intra-German

14. "Global Threats and Challenges to the United States and Its Interests Abroad," Statement of Lieutenant General Patrick Hughes, Director, Defense Intelligence Agency, before the Senate Select Committee on Intelligence, 105 Cong., 1 sess., February 5, 1997, p. 6; Tim Weiner, "U.S. Spy Agencies Find Scant Peril on Horizon," *New York Times,* January 29, 1998, p. A3.

15. Kongdan Oh and Ralph C. Hassig, *North Korea through the Looking Glass* (Brookings, 2000), p. 42; Statement of General Thomas A. Schwartz, Commander in Chief, United Nations Command/Combined Forces Command, and Commander, U.S. Forces in Korea, before the Senate Armed Services Committee, 106 Cong., 2 sess., March 7, 2000, pp. 1–8.

16. Statement of General Thomas A. Schwartz, pp. 5–6.

border during the cold war (see table 3-1 below).[17] North Korea would have to conduct this thrust without using roads and bridges that would surely be destroyed in the early minutes of any attempted invasion. If DPRK forces were attacking near Seoul through the Chorwon or Munsan corridors, they would need to cross the Han or Imjin rivers. Those rivers routinely freeze in the winter, but their ice might not prove strong enough to support a large armored force, especially under bombardment by allied aircraft and pounding by artillery. North Korean chemical weapons, commandos deploying through tunnels, and forward-deployed, dug-in artillery would complicate the battle and cause many casualties, to be sure. Nevertheless, North Korean armored forces would have great difficulty breaking through allied lines and marching on Seoul.[18]

Indeed, as observed above, the Iraqi and North Korean threats have diminished enough that 200,000 to 300,000 U.S. troops might even prove sufficient for many types of counterattack. A single, robust Desert Storm–like capability should be retained just in case, as argued above, for an all-out war to overthrow an enemy's government or to conduct other difficult missions. But there is less and less reason to think that such a large force would be needed, even for a march on Baghdad or Pyongyang.

South Korea's Strong Military

The country's recent economic troubles notwithstanding, South Korea's armed forces are much improved and still getting better. Together with the modest U.S. forces in place on the peninsula, they could quite likely hold off a North Korean invasion attempt. South Korea, together with the U.S. Army's 2nd Infantry Division and forward-based American airpower, could cause great damage to North Korean forces, stopping an assault well north of Seoul with very good confidence of success.

South Korea possesses less armor than North Korea. However, the Republic of Korea's technological edge evens out the overall military balance

17. On NATO, see William P. Mako, *U.S. Ground Forces and the Defense of Central Europe* (Brookings, 1983), p. 54; on Korea, see Ministry of National Defense, Republic of Korea, *Defense White Paper 1997–1998* (Seoul: 1998), p. 223; Michael O'Hanlon, "Stopping a North Korean Invasion: Why Defending South Korea Is Easier than the Pentagon Thinks," *International Security*, vol. 22, no. 4 (Spring 1998), p. 149.

18. For what little is publicly available about the Pentagon's expectations for a future Korean war and its operations plan 5027, see Don Oberdorfer, *The Two Koreas* (Reading, Mass.: Addison-Wesley, 1997), pp. 313–25. For a more detailed assessment of the Korean military balance, see O'Hanlon, "Stopping a North Korean Invasion."

of tanks, artillery, airplanes, and other heavy equipment between the two countries. For example, on a per weapon basis South Korea's tanks are nearly the equal of the U.S. inventory; the Korean K1 is based on the U.S. M1 and in fact shares a number of important components with it.

Factoring in South Korea's superior readiness as well, the ROK undoubtedly possesses net superiority over the North. By examining a wide body of historical battle outcomes, Colonel Trevor Dupuy estimated that such readiness factors can at least double combat capability. Yet, as Lawrence Korb has pointed out, in the 1990s the Pentagon's models appeared to assume, unjustifiably, that South Korean soldiers would in fact fight *less well* than North Koreans.[19]

The Republic of Korea also fields a force that is in an excellent posture to stop any invasion attempt. Attackers attempting to penetrate directly through such densely prepared positions have usually advanced at most a few kilometers a day historically—even when they were not technologically outclassed by their opponent, as the North Koreans certainly are in this case. Given the lethality of modern airpower, and the ability of the United States to quickly fly combat jet reinforcements to the region, such a slow pace of advance would be a recipe for disaster for Pyongyang within days of the start of a war. The United States and the Republic of Korea have potent airpower in the region at all times, but if North Korea chose a heavily overcast day to attack, that airpower might not be very effective at first. It would once the weather broke, however.

Nor could North Korea pull off a "left hook" or bypass the equivalent of the allies' Korean Maginot Line. Defenses extend across the peninsula, and, as noted, they are even denser than NATO's were in Germany during the cold war (see table 3-1). In addition, the allies enjoy overwhelming dominance in all-weather day-night reconnaissance systems that keep watch over all significant troop movements.[20]

Chemical and biological weapons do pose a special hazard in Korea, given the limited confines in which a battle would be fought. U.S. forces have wisely increased their attention to such threats in recent years, Secretary Cohen's initiatives in the 1997 Quadrennial Defense Review

19. Trevor N. Dupuy, *Attrition: Forecasting Battle Casualties and Equipment Losses in Modern War* (Fairfax, Va.: HERO Books, 1990), pp. 105–10, 148; Lawrence J. Korb, "Our Overstuffed Armed Forces," *Foreign Affairs*, vol. 74, no. 6 (November/December 1995), p. 25.

20. Barry R. Posen, "Measuring the European Conventional Balance: Coping with Complexity in Threat Assessment," *International Security*, vol. 9, no. 3 (Winter 1984/85).

Table 3-1. *Comparative Strength of South Korean Military*

Country	Military strength
Active-duty military personnel	
South Korea[a]	670,000
Kuwait + Saudi Arabia	120,000
All Gulf "GCC" countries combined	250,000
Active-duty forward defense posture	
South Korea	1,500 troops per kilometer along DMZ
NATO during cold war	950 troops per kilometer along intra-German border

Source: International Institute for Strategic Studies (IISS), *The Military Balance: 1999/2000* (London: Oxford University Press, 1999), pp. 129–50, 195. For cold war troop levels see IISS, *The Military Balance: 1989/1990* (London: Brassey's, 1989), p. 232.

a. Ninety percent of all active South Korean divisions are stationed north of Seoul, but to be conservative the table assumes that only two-thirds of all active-duty South Korean manpower is north of Seoul. See Andrea Matles Savda and William Shaw, eds., *South Korea: A Country Study* (Government Printing Office, 1992), p. 283.

being especially noteworthy, and South Korea should do more as well.[21] However, it is more difficult to use chemical weapons effectively on the battlefield than commonly is asserted, especially for an infantry army like North Korea's.[22] It is extremely challenging for a foot soldier, suited up in bulky and probably rather mediocre protective gear, to cover many kilometers on foot in an effort to take advantage of possible holes in enemy lines created by chemical attack.

Nor should North Korea blithely assume that such an attack, particularly if it proved highly lethal, would not be met with U.S. nuclear retaliation, a possibility that has become even more plausible after the Bush administration's nuclear posture review, which reportedly stated explicitly that U.S. nuclear weapons might be used against an enemy that employed chemical or biological arms. Airbursts in invasion corridors just north of the DMZ would cause little harm to the allies, while having

21. William S. Cohen, *Report of the Quadrennial Defense Review* (Department of Defense, 1997), pp. 24, 49.

22. See Victor A. Utgoff, *The Challenge of Chemical Weapons: An American Perspective* (St. Martin's Press, 1991), pp. 6–7, 148–88; Anthony H. Cordesman and Abraham R. Wagner, *Lessons of Modern War, Volume 2: The Iran-Iraq War* (Boulder, Colo.: Westview Press, 1990), p. 518; O'Hanlon, "Stopping a North Korean Invasion," pp. 161–66.

a very considerable tactical effect on DPRK forces. They would also send a powerful message that the United States will not tolerate the use of weapons of mass destruction against its military or its allies. That is a message that Washington and Seoul might want to send under such circumstances regardless of military need—and despite long-standing U.S. policy not to use nuclear weapons against nonnuclear countries unless they are themselves allied with nuclear powers.[23] The DPRK chemical threat, while real, does not change the basic military balance fundamentally.

Conclusion

The U.S. Department of Defense's two-war framework of the 1990s, while hardly the obsolescent and outmoded concept that its critics often alleged, was not optimal for the United States. It overinsured the country against the risk of regional conflict, meaning that it caused other defense investments and priorities to be shortchanged. This was increasingly the case throughout the last decade, given the continued deterioration of Iraqi and North Korean capabilities, as well as ongoing improvements in the South Korean armed forces and in the rapid response capabilities and high-technology assets of the U.S. military.

The previous emphasis on fighting two nearly simultaneous Desert Storm–like conflicts should be replaced with a framework that would envision a single all-out Desert Storm in one theater together with a smaller wartime operation elsewhere and a modest peacekeeping mission in yet a third theater. Indeed, the Bush administration has just adopted a similar force posture. Modest force reductions should be made possible by this alternative framework (though the Bush administration did not propose any). More important, the Pentagon could modestly restructure the military to make it capable of handling the current broad panoply of overseas deployments with less strain on the U.S. armed forces.

These arguments should not be pushed too far. If an enemy pulled off a massive coordinated surprise attack or used weapons of mass destruction, Desert Shield–like forces could prove insufficient. Most responses to possible enemy use of weapons of mass destruction should focus on bet-

---

23. On the effects of nuclear weapons, see Samuel Glasstone and Philip J. Dolan, *The Effects of Nuclear Weapons*, 3d ed. (Department of Defense, 1977), pp. 28–36, 543–70.

ter protective gear and on war-fighting concepts that minimize vulnerabilities. There could be an old-fashioned need for more manpower as well, however, if an enemy attack caused large numbers of U.S. casualties or detracted from the U.S. ability to fully exploit its high-technology capabilities. And if, in a future war, the United States and its allies decided to overthrow the Iraqi or North Korean regimes—as seems quite plausible—large U.S. forces could be needed to mount a major ground counteroffensive. Even if a U.S. president decided to negotiate an asylum arrangement for leaders of the regime it wanted out of power, rather than risk the large numbers of U.S. casualties that could result from a march on Baghdad or Pyongyang, it would probably need to be able to credibly threaten an all-out counterinvasion in order to convince enemy leadership to step down. Making that threat credible could in itself require deploying significant numbers of the troops who might be needed for an actual all-out counteroffensive.

In addition, war could occur in a place where the United States has important interests yet is less prepared to respond quickly. Plausible military scenarios in that category include war against China over Taiwan, efforts to help a disintegrating Pakistan put down internal revolts and secure its nuclear materials, war against Iran over access to the Persian Gulf and the Arabian peninsula's oilfields, aid to Israel in a future Mideast war, and a large-scale multilateral peace operation on the Indian subcontinent to reduce the chances that an Indo-Pakistani conflict could escalate to the nuclear level. These would not require 500,000 American troops, including two full corps of ground units, but some could involve several divisions nonetheless. For these and other reasons, keeping the capability for a single Desert Storm–like war, as well as a Desert Shield–like capability and a smaller deployment elsewhere, is critical. Planning for two overlapping Desert Storms is excessive, however.

Some will surely see the similarity between such ideas and those of a plan put forth as a trial balloon by Les Aspin, then secretary of defense, in 1993. Known as a "win-hold-win" strategy, it envisioned completing an all-out war in one theater while simply holding the line in a second. Once the first war was won, troops were to be redeployed to reinforce the U.S. position in the second theater and to permit a major counteroffensive operation there too. However, the win-hold-win caricature of that approach understated its actual military capabilities and doomed it to rejection. Subsequently derided as "win-hold-oops" for the excessive risk it allegedly introduced into war plans, it never stood a real chance bureaucratically or politically.[24]

The important point to recognize is that a Desert Shield capability, with its overwhelming airpower and other long-range strike systems, can do far more than hold a defensive line. Operation Allied Force against Serbia in 1999, in which NATO won a war with only 50,000 troops, showed how much is sometimes possible when modern airpower works in tandem with a modest ground force. Operation Enduring Freedom, involving about 60,000 U.S. troops, was even more striking in this regard. So was the coalition air campaign against Iraq in 1991, which severely weakened Iraq's forces before the coalition ground counter-offensive. This concept has its limits, to be sure, but a Desert Shield force package—defined here essentially as the airpower for a major theater war, plus roughly one corps of ground combat units—constitutes far more than a "hold" capability. It could even suffice as the U.S. contribution to an overthrow-and-occupy operation in some scenarios.

In addition, South Korea is among the best and most capable military allies of the United States, and Pentagon war plans should stop underrating its strength. In fact, when Aspin was still chairman of the House Armed Services Committee, he had emphasized the differences between the Korean and Persian Gulf theaters in a defense white paper—but regrettably that analysis never seemed to make it to the Pentagon with him.[25]

Appendix: Beyond the Korean and Iraqi Threats

Today's U.S. military posture in Asia is still focused largely on a relic of the cold war—the Korean peninsula and the threat posed there by the DPRK regime. At some point, that threat could come to an end, with major implications for the strategic environment and for U.S. force planning.

By contrast, the eventual unseating of Saddam Hussein in Iraq, while almost surely a desirable development for the United States, would probably not change the fact that that important economic region would remain unstable. Saddam's departure would make it easier to reduce the

24. Barton Gellman and John Lancaster, "U.S. May Drop Two-War Capability; Aspin Envisions Smaller, High-Tech Military to 'Win-Hold-Win,'" *Washington Post*, June 17, 1993, p. A1.

25. Les Aspin, "Aspin Shows Defense Alternatives," News Release, U.S. House of Representatives Armed Services Committee, February 25, 1992, pp. 23–24.

permanent stationing of U.S. forces in the region, but the United States would still need to keep enough military power to win a war in the region against a plausible foe or foes should that prove necessary. Thus changes in the Persian Gulf region are less likely to radically reshape the basic geostrategic backdrop against which U.S. military force posture is planned.

In all likelihood, improvements to the Korean security environment will come gradually. The most likely development is probably not the end of the North Korean regime, nor the complete end of military competition on the peninsula. More probable is a major drawdown in the conventional military competition and associated weapons levels. Deep cuts are certainly feasible. As Pedro Almeida and I argued in *Survival* in 1999, for example, even 50 percent reductions in the armored military holdings of all sides on the peninsula would appear to be stabilizing and desirable. They would leave North Korea with quantitative superiority in heavy weaponry, but would allow U.S. and South Korean forces to retain if not improve their impressive dominance in weapons quality and to maintain enough forces to preserve the basic viability of their forward-defense posture.[26] Should such cuts occur, the need for large-scale reinforcements from the United States in the event of any war on the peninsula would decline. They might not decline by 50 percent, because, for one thing, North Korean infantry forces would probably not decline proportionately under such a regime. They would probably drop by at least 10 to 20 percent, however.

If, by contrast, the Korean conflict does completely end, and the peninsula moves either gradually or immediately to reunification, the United States would need to consider more radical changes in its forward presence in East Asia and its overall military force posture.[27] Put in strategic terms, the central question reduces itself to three broad issues. The first is whether the United States should remain militarily committed to Korea's security. The second is how it should do so—with options ranging from a continued willingness to deploy large numbers of ground forces against any possible foreign threat, to a more limited American role focused primarily on

26. Pedro Almeida and Michael O'Hanlon, "Impasse in Korea: A Conventional Arms-Accord Solution?" *Survival*, vol. 41, no. 1 (Spring 1999), pp. 58–72.

27. Much of the discussion below is drawn from Michael O'Hanlon, "Keep US Forces in Korea after Reunification," *Korean Journal of Defense Analysis*, vol. X, no. 1 (Summer 1998), pp. 5–19.

air and naval capabilities. The final issue is how U.S.-Korean security cooperation might serve other American foreign policy goals in the region, beyond the peninsula itself.

First, a continuation of the U.S.-Korea alliance would be in American interests even after an end to conflict on the peninsula. The first rationale is the general principle that standing by allies is good policy in general, on the grounds that it reaffirms the U.S. commitment to its security partners in the eyes of friends and foes alike. That fact is good for deterrence and good for building trust and cooperation within alliances. Second, without a U.S. security commitment, Korea might well develop nuclear weapons and engage in military competition with both China and Japan. Third, Korea has fine security forces; even if they are significantly downsized after the end to the conflict on the peninsula, they will remain excellent. The United States benefits from having close security partners with excellent military forces willing to share with it some of the difficult missions of ensuring global stability, ranging from peacekeeping to counterterrorism, counterpiracy, and other efforts.

What form should the U.S. commitment to Korean security take—and on which potential threats should it focus? First of all, some permanent basing of American military forces in Korea would make sense. Doing so would produce a much more credible form of deterrence than simply retaining a formal alliance agreement on paper between the two countries. Only the presence of U.S. forces would guarantee that Americans would be immediately involved in any conflict, and demonstrate beyond a reasonable doubt the seriousness and military readiness of the alliance.

A U.S. force presence in Korea would also be beneficial for U.S.-Japanese and Korean-Japanese relations. It could reassure the Koreans, who would not have to wonder if they were a second-class ally of the United States in the event of a crisis with Japan over disputed territories or maritime resources. The Japanese government might prefer this arrangement as well. With U.S. military facilities also in Korea, Japan would avoid becoming what Richard Haass calls "singularized" as the only country in the region hosting U.S. forces, and Tokyo would probably find it easier to sustain the support of the Japanese people for the security alliance.[28] Both Japan and Korea are small, mountainous, and heavily populated countries where land, airspace, ports, and other neces-

28. See Robert Crumplar, "A Future U.S. Military Presence on a Unified Korean Peninsula," Paper presented at Brookings-IFANS Conference, Washington, D.C., July 1997,

sary ingredients for military bases and operations are at a premium. Although both countries recognize the importance of having a deterrent in place against instability in the region, both are also appropriately sensitive to the need to cultivate good relations with their neighbors and to avoid creating the perception that they are trying to contain China or any other specific country. Under these circumstances, asking either country to provide the United States with military bases while the other does not seems imprudent. Furthermore, keeping forces in the two countries would help Washington retain influence with both Korea and Japan, in much the same way the United States has ensured its influence with even more quarrelsome neighbors, such as Greece and Turkey or Israel and Egypt, by forging close military relations with both sides. In this way, the United States could also help facilitate tightening of a trilateral network of military officers and officials—complementing other steps to introduce confidence-building measures and to expand military-to-military exchanges in the region.

Determining the specific nature of a future U.S. military presence in a reunified Korea requires a more concrete threat assessment. In this regard, the major issue is clearly China. A major overland Chinese threat to Korea appears quite improbable. China seems less likely to put direct military pressure on Korea—a country whose long history of independence and clear ethnic, linguistic, and cultural identity make it a poor candidate for invasion—than to use force to gain resources or territory it considers its own. Taiwan and the South China Sea islands are the most notable examples of where China might use force. Disputes over overlapping economic zones could also arise with Korea and Japan, but would more likely focus on the sea and seabeds of the region. In other words, to the extent that it may pose a threat to its neighbors, China seems more likely to act as an irredentist power seeking to back up claims to specific localized regions, most of them at sea, than to pursue empire or regional hegemony.[29] This conclusion is reinforced by China's recent resolution of a number of territorial disputes with neighbors and its demilitarization of several borders.[30]

---

p. 3; Richard N. Haass, *The Reluctant Sheriff: The United States after the Cold War* (New York: Council on Foreign Relations, 1997), p. 85.

29. See Robert Ross, "Assessing the China Challenge" (Washington: Henry Stimson Center, May 14, 1997).

30. See David Shambaugh, "China's Security and Military Policy and the Potential for CBMs in the Region" (Washington: Henry Stimson Center, December 17, 1996).

Sovereign countries being what they are, it is not entirely out of the question that someday China could threaten Korea's core interests. Having U.S. forces in Korea would give future Chinese leaders who contemplated making any such threats further reason for pause. That does not mean, however, that U.S. forces need to be postured with a Chinese military threat in mind.[31]

The United States would best serve its own interests and those of Korea with mobile and deployable forces rather than large Army units. A combination of U.S. Navy, Marine Corps, and Air Force units in Korea would be best suited to operations around sea lanes, small islands, oil rigs in blue-water settings, and the like. They would also be most appropriate for addressing threats like piracy, which remains a problem in the region. Indeed, collaboratively addressing the piracy threat could provide a meaningful multilateral security mission for a wide range of Asia-Pacific countries. It could provide a first concrete step toward what might, in principle, eventually become a formalized regional security community, ultimately including even members such as China. Taking this step could help prove to Beijing the sincerity of the U.S., Japanese, and Korean position that their bilateral alliances might someday be broadened.[32]

Basing some U.S. ground forces in Korea would make sense as well—but again, their focus should be regional and expeditionary rather than peninsula-specific. For example, unless basing for them were available in a place like Australia, the Marines now on Okinawa might be moved in part to Korea. They could conduct routine patrols and other special missions from there. They could also train with Korean, Japanese, and perhaps someday also Russian and Chinese forces for peacekeeping, counterpiracy, or antiterrorist missions. U.S. Army forces might play a role in such joint training, too; they have the advantage of sharing doctrine and basic operational concepts with the militaries of other countries, which are generally dominated by ground forces.[33] But fewer U.S. Army forces than the 27,000 now in Korea would be needed for this purpose.

31. See Barry R. Posen and Andrew L. Ross, "Competing Visions for U.S. Grand Strategy," *International Security*, vol. 21, no. 3 (Winter 1996/97), pp. 15–16; Haass, *The Reluctant Sheriff*, p. 85.

32. See Russ Swinnerton, "Piracy Remains a Concern for Southeast Asian Nations," *Defense News*, August 25–31, 1997, p. 8.

33. William E. Odom, "Transforming the Military," *Foreign Affairs*, vol. 76, no. 4 (July/August 1997), p. 60. Odom makes the point in specific regard to Japan, but the point is valid more generally.

Finally, how would these strategic considerations affect broader U.S. military posture, including the overall size and shape of the American armed forces? This is the bigger question, with the answer having implications for hundreds of thousands of U.S. troops. The broad outlines of my answer follow from the above analysis. The United States should not plan to play a major ground combat role in any future Korean war against China or another regional power. Such a war is unlikely, and the need for U.S. ground forces in any such improbable conflict is even more unlikely. A reunified Korea with even one-third to one-half of its current aggregate military power would provide formidable capabilities for defense of territory, even against China. The United States could contribute air and naval power.

With this approach, U.S. ground forces would probably be sized beginning with the concept of a single Desert Storm–scale conflict, most likely in the Persian Gulf. Forces for such a contingency should err on the side of being large, since there would no longer be a second large pool of forces from which to draw reinforcements should the first group of forces encounter stiffer resistance or more difficult combat conditions than anticipated. In addition, the United States should have the capacity for at least one additional, modest-sized contingency. Plausible missions might include helping a failed Pakistani state secure or recover its nuclear arms, helping Russia deal with a renegade separatist group that got its hands on nuclear weapons, contributing to a large-scale multilateral peace implementation agreement in a difficult location such as Kashmir (with the local parties' permission), or carrying out a preventive and stabilizing deployment in, for instance, a Baltic state or a Central European country. Most such missions could entail one to three divisions. On balance, if this chapter's recommendation of a prompt 15 percent reduction in ground-combat capabilities had already been adopted, further reductions after an end to the Korean conflict might not be feasible.

FOUR   Modernizing the U.S. Military

In the current American defense debate, discussions of modernizing the armed forces' weapons, combat units, and war-fighting doctrine generally are motivated by the hypothesis that a revolution in military affairs of historical significance is attainable. Even for skeptics of this hypothesis, the debate is useful, for it helps organize discussions of military modernization conceptually. Otherwise they can quickly degenerate into a weapon-by-weapon assessment of the marginal value of this or that procurement program. Such analysis remains important, but it lacks thematic structure and makes it difficult to compare one type of proposed weapon system with another. This chapter begins with an assessment of the contemporary revolution in military affairs hypothesis and then considers several high-profile acquisition programs in more specific detail.

U.S. spending on military acquisition—that is, the sum of the procurement account and the research, development, testing, and evaluation (RDT&E) account—must increase in the years ahead. Equipment purchased primarily during the Reagan defense buildup is beginning to wear out en bloc and simply must be replaced. That said, there is a great deal of room for disagreement about which weapons should be purchased, the relative importance of RDT&E spending versus procurement spending, and the amount by which acquisition spending must increase.

The current U.S. military acquisition budget of roughly $110 billion would have to increase to $140 billion or so to fund the Pentagon's force and modernization agenda as outlined in the 1997 Quadrennial Defense Review (QDR) and essentially reaffirmed in the Bush administration's 2001 QDR.[1] That agenda is excessive. Nevertheless, a substantial real spending increase is still needed; the "procurement holiday" of the 1990s must be ended (see figure 4-1). According to the proposal advanced here, total acquisition spending should increase to about $120 billion annually (all figures are in constant 2002 dollars). In the steady state, procurement should be about $75 billion to $80 billion, and RDT&E about $45 billion, relative to 2001 levels of about $52 billion and $38 billion, respectively.

This proposal would follow the philosophy of purchasing "silver bullet" forces of advanced weaponry, rather than pursuing the Pentagon's current aspirations to replace most existing U.S. weaponry with next-generation and highly expensive systems. Aging equipment would otherwise be replaced by purchasing existing technologies—F-16s for F-16s, and so forth. This approach is partly motivated by cost considerations; even if the Pentagon's annual budget increases in the years ahead, it is unlikely to expand enough to fund the existing force and procurement program. Another motivation is the conviction that current trends in technology argue for a relative emphasis on electronics, sensors, advanced munitions, automation, and joint-service experimentation rather than traditional military platforms.

The Contemporary Debate on a Revolution in Military Affairs

Due to the excellent performance of American high-technology weapons in the 1991 Persian Gulf War, as well as the phenomenal pace of innovation in the modern computer industry, many defense analysts have posited that a revolution in military affairs (RMA) is either imminent or already under way. The RMA thesis holds that further advances in precision munitions, real-time data dissemination, and other modern technologies, together with associated changes in war-fighting organizations and doctrines, can help transform the nature of future war and with it the size and structure of the U.S. military. RMA proponents believe that military technology, and

---

1. See Lane Pierrot, *Budgeting for Defense: Maintaining Today's Forces* (Washington: Congressional Budget Office, 2000).

Figure 4-1. *Department of Defense Procurement Spending, Fiscal Years 1947–2007*
Billions of FY 2002 dollars

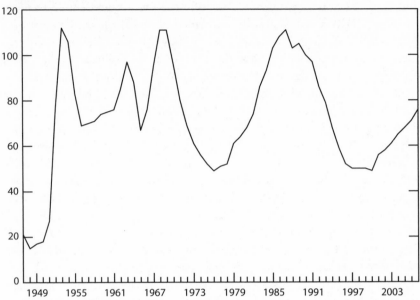

Source: Office of the Under Secretary of Defense (Comptroller), *National Defense Budget Estimates for FY 2001,* March 2000, pp. 128–33.

Note: The cold war annual average for procurement, 1951–90, was $82.4 billion. Budget authority levels for procurement are envisioned as follows: $64 billion (2001); $61 billion (2002); $67 billion (2003); $72 billion (2004); $75 billion (2005); $81 billion (2006); $90 billion (2007).

the resultant potential for radically new types of war-fighting tactics and strategies, is advancing at a rate unrivaled since the 1920s through the 1940s, when blitzkrieg, aircraft carriers, large-scale amphibious and airborne assault, ballistic missiles, strategic bombing, and nuclear weapons were developed.

In the abstract, it is unobjectionable to favor innovation, but the prescriptions of some RMA proponents would have major opportunity costs. RMA proponents tend to argue that more budgetary resources should be devoted to innovation—research and development (R&D), procurement of new hardware, frequent experiments with new technology—and, to the extent necessary, less money should go to military operations, training, and readiness. To free up funds for an RMA transformation strategy, some would reduce U.S. global engagement and weaken the military's deterrent posture.[2] For example, in its 1997 report, the National Defense Panel dismissed the current two-war framework as obsolete (without suggesting what should replace it, however). The NDP also suggested that U.S. military retrenchment from forward presence and peacekeeping operations might be needed simply to free up money to promote the so-called revolution in military affairs.[3] These suggestions, if adopted, would have important effects on U.S. security policy; they should not be accepted simply on the basis of vague impressions that an RMA may be achievable.

Some have argued that a radical transformation of the U.S. military will save money.[4] Nevertheless, that argument is unconvincing, at least for the short to medium term. Transformation means accelerating replacement of existing equipment, and while it is theoretically possible that doing so could produce smaller, less expensive units wielding highly advanced and effective weaponry, there is little practical evidence that such an outcome is achievable in the near term.

Given the budgetary and opportunity costs associated with rapidly pursuing a revolution in military affairs and the popularity of the RMA concept in the contemporary defense debate, some caution is in order. Before developing a modernization agenda, it is worth remembering what can go wrong with a rush to transform and what innovations can occur even if no RMA is formally declared or pursued.

Reasons Not to Rush an RMA

History provides ample grounds for caution about pursuing major defense transformation. Most contemporary RMA enthusiasts make

2. For an argument in favor of taking a large part of the active force structure "off line" so as to devote it to experimentation and acceleration of the RMA, see James R. Blaker, "The American RMA Force: An Alternative to the QDR," *Strategic Review,* vol. 25, no. 3 (Summer 1997), pp. 21–30; for a similar but more general argument, see also Richard K. Betts, *Military Readiness: Concepts, Choices, Consequences* (Brookings, 1995), pp. 35–84. For the view of a conservative critic of the RMA concept, see Frederick W. Kagan, "Wishful Thinking on War," *Weekly Standard,* December 15, 1997, pp. 27–29. Kagan argues that the country may need to spend more on technology—but must not do so at the expense of its present engagement and deterrence strategies.

3. National Defense Panel, *Transforming Defense: National Security in the 21st Century* (Department of Defense, December 1997), pp. vii, 2, 23, 49, 59, 79–86.

4. See, most notably, Admiral William A. Owens with Ed Offley, *Lifting the Fog of War* (New York: Farrar, Straus, and Giroux, 2000).

reference to the interwar years and claim that we are in another period of similar potential, promise, and peril today. However, military technology advanced steadily and impressively throughout the twentieth century, including its latter half. Helicopters radically reshaped many battlefield operations after World War II. ICBMs and space-launch vehicles followed. Satellite communications were first used militarily in 1965 in Vietnam, where precision-guided munitions delivered by aircraft also made their debut in the early 1970s. Air defense and antitank missiles played major roles in the 1973 Arab-Israeli War. Stealth fighters were designed in the late 1970s.[5] Infrared sensors and night-vision technologies made their debut in this period as well.

History also tells us that radical military transformations only make sense when technology and new concepts and tactics are ripe. At other times, targeted modernizations together with vigorous research, development, and experimentation make more sense. A good analogy is the period of the 1920s, when major military vehicles and systems such as the tank and the airplane were not yet ready for large-scale purchase. In addition, advanced operational concepts such as blitzkrieg and carrier aviation had not yet been developed to a degree that could guide hardware acquisition or the reshaping of military organizations. As a result, research, prototyping, and experimentation were the proper elements of a wise innovation and acquisition strategy. In the 1930s new operational concepts were better understood, technologies better developed, and geostrategic circumstances more foreboding. Under these circumstances, large-scale modernization made sense, and those countries that did not conduct it tended to perform badly in the early phases of World War II. Because most RMA proponents cannot clearly specify what a near-term transformation should encompass, today's situation should probably be likened to the 1920s rather than the 1930s.

It is far from obvious that military technology is now poised to advance even more quickly than it has in the past half century. Yet RMA proponents assert that it will when they call for a radical transformation strategy for current U.S. armed forces. No such DoD-wide transformation strategies were necessary to bring satellites, stealth, precision-guided

5. Lawrence Freedman, *The Revolution in Strategic Affairs*, Adelphi Paper 318 (New York: Oxford University Press, 1998), p. 21.

munitions, advanced jet engines, night-vision equipment, cruise missiles, or other remarkable new capabilities into the force in past decades.[6]

RMA proponents are certainly right to believe that a successful military must always be changing. The post–World War II U.S. military has already taken that adage to heart. The status quo in defense circles does not mean standing still; it means taking a balanced approach to modernization that has served the country remarkably well for decades. Indeed, it brought on the very technologies displayed in Desert Storm that have given rise to the belief that an RMA may be under way.[7] It is not clear that we need to accelerate the pace of innovation now.

Moreover, radical innovation is not always good. If the wrong ideas are adopted, transforming a force can make it worse. For example, in the world wars, militaries overestimated the likely effects of artillery as well as aerial and battleship bombardment against prepared defensive positions, meaning that their infantry forces proved much more vulnerable than expected when they assaulted enemy lines.[8] Britain's radically new all-tank units were inflexible, making them less successful than Germany's integrated mechanized divisions in World War II. Strategic aerial bombardment did not achieve nearly the results that had been expected of it; airpower was much more effective as close-air support for armored formations in blitzkrieg operations.[9] Later on, the U.S. Army's Pentomic

6. Martin Van Creveld, *Technology and War: From 2000 B.C. to the Present* (Free Press, 1989). Trevor Dupuy uses yet another categorization scheme, different from those of Krepinevich, Van Creveld, and others, to understand the history of military innovation. He groups all progress since 1800 together under the title "the age of technological change." See Trevor N. Dupuy, *The Evolution of Weapons and Warfare* (Fairfax, Va.: HERO Books, 1984).

7. For sound warnings about both dismissing the RMA and jumping on the bandwagon too enthusiastically, see Colin S. Gray, *The American Revolution in Military Affairs: An Interim Assessment* (Camberley, England: Strategic and Combat Studies Institute, 1997), pp. 5–7, 33–34; for a reminder that militaries must always be innovating and changing, see Jonathan Shimshoni, "Technology, Military Advantage, and World War I: A Case for Military Entrepreneurship," *International Security*, vol. 15, no. 3 (Winter 1990/91), pp. 213–15.

8. John Keegan, *The First World War* (Knopf, 1999), p. 20; Dan Goure, "Is There a Military-Technical Revolution in America's Future?" *Washington Quarterly* (Autumn 1993), p. 185; and Dupuy, *The Evolution of Weapons and Warfare*, pp. 218–20, 258–66.

9. Robert Pape, *Bombing to Win: Air Power and Coercion in War* (Cornell University Press, 1996), pp. 87–136, 254–313; and Brian Bond and Williamson Murray, "British Armed Forces, 1918–1939," in Allan R. Millet and Williamson Murray, eds., *Military Effectiveness*, vol. 2 (Boston: Unwin Hyman, 1988).

division concept, intended to employ tactical nuclear weapons, was adopted for a time and then abandoned in 1961.[10]

These are only historical arguments, uninformed by the realities of today's world. Current trends in defense technology and the potential for corresponding innovations in tactics and doctrine will be the real determinants of the prospects for a near-term RMA. These trends suggest that the technological case for a patient, targeted approach is much more compelling than that for a radical remaking of the U.S. armed forces more generally.

One type of evidence to support this argument is that, despite their haste to push the revolution along, radical RMA promoters tend to lack clear and specific proposals for how to do so. In that light, even if they are right that an RMA may be within reach sometime in the foreseeable future, they may be quite wrong about what should be done about it in the near future. In practical terms, there is a major distinction between the early stages of a possible RMA and the later stages. As Stephen Rosen writes:

> The general lesson for students or advocates of innovation may well be that it is wrong to focus on budgets when trying to understand or promote innovation. Bringing innovations to fruition will often be expensive. Aircraft carriers, fleets of helicopters, and ICBM forces were not cheap. But *initiating* an innovation and bringing it to the point where it provides a strategically useful option has been accomplished when money was tight. . . . Rather than money, talented military personnel, time, and information have been the key resources for innovation.[11]

Some individuals feel that the above arguments notwithstanding, the United States really has no choice but to rebuild its equipment inventories and combat units from first principles. They believe that future adversaries will make greater use of sea mines, cruise and ballistic missiles,

10. Stephen Biddle, "Assessing Theories of Future Warfare," Paper presented to the 1997 Annual Meeting of the American Political Science Association, Washington, D.C., August 1997, pp. 37–38; Andrew J. Bacevich, *The Pentomic Era: The U.S. Army between Korea and Vietnam* (National Defense University Press, 1986); John Keegan, *A History of Warfare* (Vintage, 1993), pp. 362–79; Van Creveld, *Technology and War*, pp. 193–95; and Stephen Peter Rosen, *Winning the Next War: Innovation and the Modern Military* (Cornell University Press, 1991), pp. 13–18, 37–38.

11. Rosen, *Winning the Next War*, p. 252.

chemical or biological weapons, and other means to attempt to deny the U.S. military the ability to build up forces and operate from large, fixed infrastructures, as it did in Desert Storm. As a result, they consider major changes in the way U.S. armed forces deploy and fight to be essential.

However, many of the solutions to these problems may not be in the realm of advanced weaponry. True, long-range strike platforms, missile defenses, short-takeoff aircraft, and other such advanced technologies may be part of the appropriate response. But so might more minesweepers, smaller roll-on/roll-off transport vessels useful in shallow ports, concrete bunkers for deployed aircraft, and other relatively low-tech approaches to hardening and dispersing supplies and infrastructure. The military services already are biased in favor of procuring advanced weaponry at the expense of equally important but less advanced hardware. By emphasizing modernistic and futuristic technology, the most ambitious RMA concepts could reinforce this existing tendency, quite possibly to the nation's detriment.

Most centrally, one should be skeptical about the RMA hypothesis because many of its key technical underpinnings have not been well established and may not be valid. Proponents of the RMA concept often make passing mention of "Moore's law"—the trend for the number of transistors that can fit on a semiconductor chip to double every eighteen to twenty-four months—and then extrapolate such a radical rate of progress to realms of technology of a very different nature. For example, in its 1997 report, the National Defense Panel wrote: "The rapid rate of new and improved technologies—a new cycle about every eighteen months— is a defining characteristic of this era of change and will have an indelible influence on new strategies, operational concepts, and tactics that our military employs."[12] However, conflating progress in computers with progress in other major areas of technology is unjustified. To the extent that RMA believers hinge most of their argument on advances in modern electronics and computers, they are at least proceeding from a solid foundation. When they expect comparably radical progress in land vehicles, ships, aircraft, rockets, explosives, and energy sources—as many do, either explicitly or implicitly—they are probably mistaken, at least in the early years of the twenty-first century.

A survey that I carried out in 1998 and 1999 suggested that progress in these latter areas of technology is, and will likely remain, modest in the

12. National Defense Panel, *Transforming Defense*, pp. 7–8.

years ahead (see figure 4-2). The case for aggressively modernizing electronics, munitions, sensors, and communications systems is thus much more compelling than that for replacing the main vehicles and large weaponry of the armed forces.

Promoting Innovation with the Defense Budget

What would it cost to adopt a defense modernization strategy that emphasized research, development, and experimentation, as well as advanced sensors, munitions, and other technologies that take maximum advantage of the modern electronics revolution? The strategy would correspondingly place less emphasis than the services now intend on expensive modernization of traditional weaponry such as large combat platforms.

A good starting point for answering this question is the Pentagon's existing acquisition agenda. Much of the Pentagon's plan consists of a traditional approach to procurement. Major platforms such as combat aircraft, helicopters, submarines, and surface ships constitute the core of the plan. If there is a greater relative emphasis on munitions, sensors, advanced communications, or other key defense technologies that are advancing most rapidly today, that fact is not obvious from an examination of standard Pentagon budget documents. The latter still tend to focus on major weapons platforms presenting no new categories of technology investment that allow the external observer to see the evidence of a shift in basic investment approach.[13]

In fairness to the Pentagon, it should also be noted that the current acquisition plan includes a large number of systems that, while frequently derided by critics as "legacy" capabilities, can be justified using the rhetoric of the RMA movement. Stealthy aircraft, for example, use advanced technology to evade defenses; tilt-rotor planes are intended to use speed and range to outflank prepared enemy positions; new destroyers will reduce their detectability while also reducing crew size and packing large numbers of smart munitions. The simple fact that the military services have invented most of these systems in traditional ways does not automatically make them bad ideas, even in a purported RMA era. Nevertheless, the longevity of traditional ways of doing business does raise warning flags about whether the services really have committed to the rhetoric of *Joint Vision 2010* and the 1997 QDR.

---

13. See for example, Lane Pierrot, *A Look at Tomorrow's Tactical Air Forces* (Washington: Congressional Budget Office, January 1997), pp. 31–35.

The Pentagon's current program, if truly implemented, would drive annual procurement spending to the vicinity of $90 billion a year or more. The reasons for this expected increase are essentially twofold. First, modern weapons systems, particularly larger platforms, continue to grow significantly in cost, and there is every reason to expect that their costs will keep climbing in the course of development programs and production runs. Recent evidence is provided by estimates that the Air Force's F-22 program will likely exceed budgeted costs.[14] Second, the so-called post–cold war procurement holiday must end. After a decade of having large stocks of new equipment that did not generally require immediate replacement, the Pentagon soon needs to begin procuring systems at sustainable rates.

An alternative acquisition strategy could provide fewer dollars for weapons platforms, while devoting top priority to R&D, experimentation, and technologies heavy in modern electronics—sensors, advanced munitions, advanced communications systems, and so on. The Bush administration had adopted this philosphy for R&D and experimentation, but not for procurement. Platforms would still have to be in good enough condition, and be sufficient in number, to fill out the needed force structure. In many cases, however, existing types of weaponry could be purchased rather than next-generation systems. This strategy would ensure adequate supplies of ready hardware at more modest cost. Small numbers of next-generation weapons, such as F-22s and joint strike fighters, could be purchased in modest, "silver bullet" quantities. Otherwise, modernization would depend largely on improvements in sensors, munitions, and real-time information networks—in other words, electronics-heavy and computer-heavy technologies that are advancing at prodigal rates today and that often provide greatly improved performance at modest cost.

Experimentation would be an important part of this philosophy as well. It would focus not only on new concepts for joint operations among the branches of the armed services, but also on concerted efforts to learn to cope with enemy countermeasures and possible enemy use of weapons of mass destruction—which are often not adequately incorporated into service training regimens today.[15] Budgets for joint-service experimentation

14. David Mulholland, "Cost Estimates Show F-22 Breaking Cost Caps," *Jane's Defence Weekly,* August 23, 2000, p. 3.

15. Ashton B. Carter and William J. Perry with David Aidekman, "Countering Asymmetric Threats," in Ashton B. Carter and John P. White, eds., *Keeping the Edge: Managing Defense for the Future* (MIT Press, 2001), p. 123.

Figure 4-2. Projected Degrees of Advance in Key Military Technologies, 2000–20

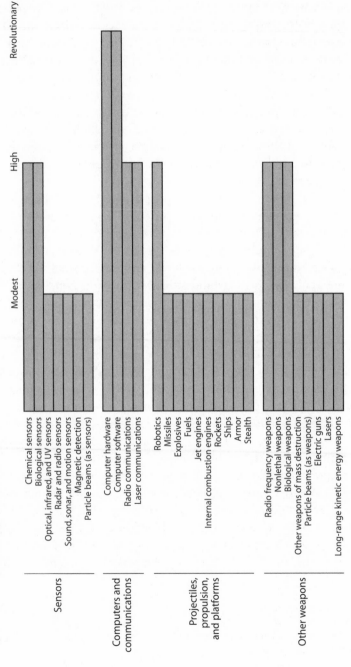

Source: Author's estimates.

Note: The terms *moderate*, *high*, and *revolutionary* are subjective and somewhat imprecise. In general terms, technologies showing moderate advances might improve their performance by a few percent or at most a couple of tens of percent—in terms of speed, range, lethality, or other defining characteristics—between 2000 and 2020. Those experiencing high advances will be able to accomplish tasks on the battlefield far better than before—perhaps by 50 to 100 percent; to the extent that improved performance can be so quantified. Finally, technology areas in which revolutionary advances occur will be able to accomplish important battlefield tasks that they cannot now even attempt.

would grow to several hundred million dollars a year and remain there. Costs of that magnitude would be comparable to current annual expenditures at each of the various training centers of the individual services. Over time, experimentation could grow even further to include the efforts of dedicated units not otherwise deployable—perhaps a fighter squadron, a brigade of ground forces, and a group of ships—with associated annual costs exceeding $1 billion.

This approach would be consistent with the changes in force structure that were discussed earlier, with modest reductions in ground forces. Those reductions would be in part a reflection of changing strategic circumstances (such as the weakening of the North Korean and Iraqi militaries since 1990) and in part a reflection of the new capacities of precision-strike weapons, which argue for a *modestly* larger role for airpower in the nation's military arsenal.

This approach to military innovation would not offer a clear endpoint. Transformation would be seen as a continuing process. The most likely immediate benefits would be in areas of C4ISR (command, control, communications, computers, intelligence, surveillance, and reconnaissance) and advanced munitions. Large weaponry such as ships, combat aircraft, and armored vehicles would be replaced only over time. The U.S. military would become lighter, more deployable, less vulnerable, and more lethal—but only gradually, in recognition of the simple fact that vehicles, engines, and large weapons are unlikely to experience radical rates of technological change in the immediate years ahead.[16]

There is considerable potential for improvement in areas of defense technology such as munitions and sensors. Consider, for example, precision-guided munitions. The sensor fuzed weapon (SFW), which has had substantial development problems in its past, has done better of late, achieving good results on the test ranges. It still has its limits, requiring delivery at low altitudes in a manner that leaves bomb-dropping aircraft vulnerable. It may or may not prove capable of identifying targets interspersed with civilian assets or purposefully designed to resemble such nonmilitary equipment.[17] Overall trends for these types of weapons are nonetheless clearly positive. Bombs depending on global positioning system

16. See Commander James R. Boorujy, "Network-Centric Concepts Can Guarantee Access," *Proceedings*, May 2000, pp. 60–63; and Robert Holzer, "U.S. Shifts Antimine Strategy," *Defense News*, March 13, 2000, p. 1.

17. David Mulholland, "Upgraded Sensor Fuzed Weapon Aces First Test," *Defense News*, April 24, 2000, p. 8.

(GPS) and inertial guidance are also showing growing promise. The joint direct attack munition (JDAM) performed very well in Operation Allied Force in 1999, with typical miss distances of several meters, and it performed brilliantly in Operation Enduring Freedom (see below). Other munitions in research and development are promising even greater accuracy.[18] New types of munitions in development promise greater lethality at lower weight; some analysts argue that in the future 250-pound bombs will be capable of destroying 85 percent of the targets that now require 2,000-pound weapons. That means a given plane will be able to effectively attack considerably more targets in the future than is the case today.[19]

Leaving aside new capabilities, there is also a strong argument for adding more of certain types of so-called high-demand–low-density assets. They include electronic warfare and reconnaissance assets, which the U.S. military appears not to have in sufficient numbers today. Notably, a restoration of the Joint Surveillance Target Attack Radar System (JSTARS) program to nineteen aircraft and an increase in the EA-6B electronic warfare aircraft fleet of at least one additional squadron are both sensible ideas.[20]

Potential adversaries can take steps to deny the United States intelligence on their operations and their capabilities. They can, for example, make use of the increasing availability of robust encryption technologies and of fiber-optic cable communications.[21] As serious as these problems are, however, they are of less concern for tactical war-fighting purposes, where mobile enemy forces would generally communicate by radio.

Lighter tanks, unmanned armed aerial vehicles, and perhaps arsenal ships would be bought in modest quantities to serve special purposes or to be thoroughly tested as prototypes. However, large numbers would not be purchased until the case for doing so was strong.[22]

18. Mark Hewish, "Smart and Smarter," *Jane's International Defence Review*, January 2000, pp. 49–55; on JDAM, see David Mosher, *Options for Enhancing the Bomber Force* (Washington: Congressional Budget Office, 1995), pp. 28–31.

19. David A. Fulghum and Robert Wall, "Mini-Bombs Dominate U.S. Weapons Plans," *Aviation Week and Space Technology*, September 25, 2000, pp. 86–87.

20. Robert P. Haffa Jr. and Barry D. Watts, "Brittle Swords: Low-Density, High-Demand Assets," *Strategic Review*, vol. 28, no. 4 (Fall 2000), pp. 42–48.

21. See Michael A. Caloyannides, "Encryption Wars: Early Battles," *IEEE Spectrum*, vol. 37 (April 2000), pp. 37–43.

22. For more specifics about one interpretation of what such a modernization/transformation agenda would entail, see Michael O'Hanlon, *Technological Change and the Future of Warfare* (Brookings, 2000), pp. 168–91.

Organizationally, this agenda would not necessitate fundamental changes in the Pentagon's main combat structures. It would, however, require improvement of their joint-service integration. Some new units would be established for experimentation and prototyping; others might be created to serve specific C4ISR roles. Otherwise, the Army might well retain divisions, the Air Force air expeditionary forces, and the Navy carrier battle groups under this approach.

The Lessons of Operation Enduring Freedom

These broad debates about a revolution in military affairs and defense transformation can be made more concrete by referring to the Afghanistan campaign of 2001–02. A number of important military innovations made their appearances in that war, commonly known as Operation Enduring Freedom. They occurred even though those who advocate rapid military transformation have generally felt frustrated in the U.S. defense debate over the past decade. Advocates of radical change have tended to underestimate the degree to which the U.S. military can and does innovate even without trying to transform in revolutionary style. (For a similar argument, see Michael O'Hanlon, "A Flawed Masterpiece," *Foreign Affairs* [May/June 2002].)

Several developments were particularly notable. One was the widespread deployment of special operations forces with laser rangefinders and GPS devices to call in extremely precise airstrikes.[23] Ground spotters have appeared in the annals of warfare as long as airplanes themselves, but this was the first time they were able to provide targeting information accurate to within several meters and do so quickly.

A second major development was the improvement in U.S. reconnaissance capabilities. Unmanned aerial vehicles (UAVs), together with assets such as imaging satellites and JSTARS, maintained frequent surveillance of much of the battlefield and continuous coverage of certain specific sites—providing a capability that Joint Chiefs' chairman General Richard Myers described as "persistence."[24]

Also notable were further advances in battlefield communications. The networks established between UAVs, satellites, combat aircraft, and command centers were faster than in any previous war, making Myers'

23. Eric Schmitt and James Dao, "Use of Pinpoint Air Power Comes of Age in New War," *New York Times,* December 24, 2001, p. 1.
24. Secretary Rumsfeld and General Myers, Department of Defense news briefing, December 11, 2001.

persistence so valuable.[25] The networks were not always fast, of course, especially when political leadership needed to intercede in specific targeting decisions.[26] Nor were they yet available for all combat aircraft in theater; for example, the Air Force's "Link 16" data links are not yet installed on many strike aircraft.[27] But they did make it physically possible to reduce the time between detection of a target by one platform or person and its destruction by another platform to less than twenty minutes in numerous cases and to less than ten in some.[28]

Perhaps most historic of all was the use of CIA-owned Predator UAVs to drop weapons on ground targets. Unless one counts cruise missiles, this was the first time an unmanned aircraft had effectively dropped ordnance in major warfare (in the form of "Hellfire" air-to-ground missiles).

There were also further milestones in the realm of precision weapons. For the first time in the history of major warfare these constituted the majority of all ordnance dropped. They were dropped from a wide range of aircraft, including carrier-based jets, ground-based aircraft, and B-52 as well as B-1 bombers. The bombers were effectively used as close-air support platforms, loitering over the battlefield for hours until targets could be identified. They delivered about 70 percent of the war's total ordnance.[29]

In addition to the old standby, the laser-guided bomb, the weapon of choice for the United States quickly became the JDAM. First used in Kosovo, this is a 2,000 pound dumb bomb enlightened by a $20,000 kit for steering it within 10 to 15 meters of its target using GPS and inertial guidance. That means it is not quite as accurate as a laser-guided bomb, but is much more resilient to the effects of weather. It can now be dropped by most American aircraft (in contrast to the Kosovo war, when only the B-2 could deliver it). In Afghanistan, the United States dropped at least 5,000 laser-guided bombs, and 5,000 JDAMs as well.[30]

25. See Vernon Loeb, "Technology Changes Air War Tactics," *Washington Post,* November 28, 2001, p. 16.

26. Thomas E. Ricks, "Target Approval Delays Cost Air Force Key Hits," *Washington Post,* November 18, 2001, p. A1.

27. David A. Fulghum and Robert Wall, "Heavy Bomber Attacks Dominate Afghan War," *Aviation Week and Space Technology,* December 3, 2001, p. 22.

28. Schmitt and Dao, "Use of Pinpoint Air Power Comes of Age in New War"; John T. Correll, "From Sensor to Shooter," *Air Force Magazine,* February 2002, p. 2.

29. Rumsfeld and Myers, DoD briefing; Fulghum and Wall, "Heavy Bomber Attacks Dominate Afghan War," pp. 22–23.

30. Eric Schmitt, "After January Raid, Gen. Franks Promises to Do Better," *New York Times,* February 8, 2002.

A number of special-purpose munitions were used in smaller numbers. They included cave-busting munitions equipped with nickel-cobalt steel alloy tips and special software and capable of penetrating up to 10 feet of rock (or 100 feet of soil). Prominent among these munitions were the 5,000-pound GBU-28 bomb and the AGM-86D cruise missile with the Advanced Unitary Penetrator warhead.[31]

What broad lessons emerge from this conflict? It is important not to overlearn from this war, since the next will surely be much different. But there are several key points to take note of nonetheless. First, military progress does not always depend heavily on highly expensive weapons platforms. Many of the most important contemporary trends in military technology and tactics concern information networks and munitions more than aircraft, ships, and ground vehicles. To take an extreme example, B-52 bombers carrying JDAMs were more useful in Operation Enduring Freedom than were B-2s.

Second, human skills remain very important in war, as perhaps was best demonstrated by special operations forces and CIA personnel. The basic infantry skills, foreign language abilities, competence and care in using and maintaining equipment, and physical and mental toughness of American troops contributed to victory every bit as much as did high-technology weaponry.

Third, military mobility and deployability should be improved further in the future. The U.S. Marine Corps executed an impressive ship-to-objective maneuver, forgoing the usual ship-to-shore operation and moving 400 miles inland directly, but most parts of the U.S. Army still cannot move so quickly and smoothly. Part of the solution may be the Army's long-term plans for new and lighter combat equipment (as well as Marine Corps plans for the V-22 Osprey, at least in modest numbers and once proven safe). But another part of the solution may be for the Army where possible to emulate the Marine Corps in organization, training, and logistics, and to do so soon.

And finally, as Secretary Rumsfeld has been arguing, more joint-service experimentation and innovation are highly desirable, given that the synergies between special operations forces on the ground and Air Force and Navy aircraft in the skies were perhaps the most important keys to victory in the entire war.

---

31. Vernon Loeb, "Concrete-Piercing Bombs Hammer Caves," *Washington Post*, December 13, 2001.

Rethinking the Pentagon's Modernization Agenda

How do these general arguments about a possible RMA relate to specific near-term modernization issues and individual weapons systems? The U.S. military has nearly a trillion dollars of major acquisition programs formally approved and under way (see table 4-1); some of the more prominent and expensive are considered here.

Fighter Aircraft

A good place to begin the discussion is with the F-22 Raptor fighter, the joint strike fighter, and the Navy's Super Hornet. Together, the U.S. armed forces plan to purchase some 3,500 of these three types of aircraft. They are likely to spend $350 billion in the process, for an average of about $15 billion annually through roughly 2020.

THE F-22 RAPTOR. As the Air Force rightly points out, control of the air has been a prerequisite to military victory in most wars of the past sixty years. The F-22 boasts speed, stealth, computer capabilities, and avionics more advanced than anything the United States has today—and anything the rest of the world will be able to build in the next couple of decades. Notably, enemy radars would have much more trouble picking up the F-22 than they would in detecting current fighters. Given these attributes, the Raptor's high production price tag—nearly $120 million per aircraft, in 2001 dollars, according to the latest Congressional Budget Office (CBO) estimate—is not unreasonable.[32]

Pentagon officials also are correct in saying that most of the money needed for F-22 research and development has already been spent. To cancel the program now would essentially throw away more than a $20 billion investment. The Air Force, moreover, has scaled back its intended number of F-22 purchases by more than half since the program was inaugurated in the 1980s, from 750 aircraft to about 300.

The Air Force tends to duck the question of the F-22's affordability, retorting that buying F-15s instead would save virtually no money. However, F-15s cost $50 million apiece, less than half the estimated price of an F-22. Improving the F-15 by adding more advanced capabilities could make it more expensive, it is true—but still nowhere near the cost of the F-22. More to the point, there is little need to add more advanced

---

32. Pierrot, *A Look at Tomorrow's Tactical Air Forces*, p. 5.

Table 4-1. *Selected Acquisition Report (SAR) Program, Acquisition Cost Summary*

Millions of current dollars

Weapon system	Cost	Quantity
Army		
Abrams upgrade	9,976.3	1,155
ATACMs-BAT	5,795.1	15,911
ATIRCM/CMWS	2,665.7	1,698
Bradley upgrade	3,859.8	926
CH-47F (ICH)	3,081.4	302
Chem Demil	13,183.6	15
Commanche (RAH-66)	48,134.3	1,213
Crusader	4,302.3	9
FBCB2	2,574.4	59,522
FMTV	17,789.4	83,185
IAV	7,039.4	2,131
Javelin	3,819.8	22,415
JSTARS CGS	1,845.9	135
Longbow Apache	8,755.7	850
Longbow Hellfire	2,524	12,905
MCS	1,278.8	5,665
MLRS Upgrade	4,891.6	63,005
Patriot PAC-3	10,669.4	1,092
SADARM	739.9	1,252
SMART-T	658.3	213
Subtotal	153,584.8	...
Navy/Marines		
AAAV	8,845.0	1,025
AIM-9X	2,822.8	10,146
AV-8B remanufacture	2,120.7	72
CEC	3,929.1	227
CVN-76	4,590.6	1
CVN-77	5,299.9	1
CVNX	3,587.6	...
DD 21	5,218.5	0
		(R&D for now)
DDG 51	55,807.6	58
E-2C remanufacture	3,193.2	36
F/A-18 E/F	46,825.7	548
JSOW	5,749.3	17,960
LHD 1	10,252.6	8
LPD 17	8,777.6	8
MH-60R	5,631.4	231
MH-60S	4,561.5	233
MIDS-LVT	1,527.6	2,721
Navy Area TMD	9,225.4	1,500
NESP	1,980.0	451
SSN 774 (NSSN)	65,677.5	30
STD MSL 2	9,616.9	11,665

(continued)

Table 4-1. *(Continued)*

Millions of current dollars

Weapon system	Cost	Quantity
Strategic sealift	6,113.1	20
T-45TS	5,242.1	171
Tactical Tomahawk	1,878.2	1,352
Trident II MSL	27,183.8	453
USMC H-1 upgrades	3,710.9	279
V-22	37,217.8	437
Subtotal	346,587.4	...
Air Force		
ABL	3,545.5	2
AEHF	2,385.9	2
AMRAAM	10,336.9	10,917
AWACS RSIP (E-3)	974.3	32
B1-CMUP	1,636.6	192
C-130J	2,633.2	32
C-17A	44,860.1	134
EELV	17,244.6	181
F-22	68,884.8	305
GBS	514.3	440
JASSM	2,101.4	2,482
JDAM	2,626.4	88,116
JPATS	3,974.6	712
JSTARS	8,597.1	16
Minuteman III GRP	2,324.4	652
Minuteman III PRP	2,503.8	607
NAS	1,001.6	88
NAVSTAR satellite	11,549.5	109
NAVSTAR user equipment	6,874.7	253,623
SBIRS	8,228.6	8
Titan IV	18,027.6	39
Subtotal	220,825.9	...
Department of Defense		
JSF	21,938.8	0
NMD	20,252.2	1
NPOESS	5,345.6	5
NTW TBMD	5,054.1	0
Patriot Pac-3	10,139.9	1,048
THAAD system	16,813.5	1,250
Subtotal	69,404.2	...
Grand total	790,402.3	...

Source: "Selected Acquisition Reports Summary from September 30, 2001" (www.defenselink.mil/news/dec2001/d20011207costsummary.pdf).

capabilities. Indeed, there are reasons to think that use of different materials and manufacturing techniques can reduce the costs of F-15s to less than their current price.[33] The Air Force also asserts that an F-22 will cost less to operate and maintain than an F-15. However, that would defy the historical trend for new fighters. In the specific case of the F-22, the Raptor's stealth coatings may well prove difficult—and expensive—to maintain.

If the F-22 were desperately needed, the Pentagon would be right to fight for it in large numbers even against the dictates of fiscal constraints. However, the U.S. military enjoys tremendous advantages in the air today, and no other country is in a position to catch up. The United States is the world's overwhelming aerospace power and will remain that way, with or without the F-22, for many years to come. U.S. armed forces enjoy at least a 50 to 1 advantage in modern fighter aircraft over Iran, Iraq, North Korea—and even China.

The Desert Storm operation against Iraq in 1991 graphically demonstrated the extent of American air dominance. The U.S.-led multinational coalition lost a total of thirty-eight fixed-wing aircraft in the Persian Gulf War—an extremely low toll by historical standards. Even more relevant to the F-22 debate is the fact that only one coalition plane was shot down in an air-to-air encounter. The Air Force's premier fighter, the F-15C, flew 6,000 missions without a single combat loss from air-to-air engagements or surface-to-air fire. Desert Storm was no fluke, as Operation Allied Force against Serbia recently reminded us. NATO lost only three planes in more than 35,000 combat missions (two of them shot down), a lower loss rate than even that for training missions.

Nevertheless, the Air Force suggests that whatever America's air dominance is today, it may not last long. The service points to impressive new aircraft like the Rafale, the Eurofighter EF-2000, the Su-35, and the Swedish Gripen, all of which rival F-15s and F-16s. It neglects, however, to acknowledge that these foreign fighters are also very expensive, and that virtually no country in the world outside the western alliance system has the resources to buy many, or to train pilots in their proper use.

U.S. Naval Intelligence projects that Iran, Iraq, North Korea, and China are all unlikely to acquire more than a few dozen additional

33. David Mulholland, "F-15 Costs Can Be Slashed," *Jane's Defence Weekly,* June 14, 2000; and James Talent, "Building the Affordable Fighter," *Defense News,* July 24, 2000, p. 37.

advanced fighters in the coming years. What is more, these countries are all far behind the United States in pilot training, electronic jamming aircraft, airborne warning and control system (AWACS) planes, and various other intangibles of air warfare.

At one time in 1999, the Air Force made the misleading argument that American casualties in a future war in a place like Korea might be reduced by 25 percent—several thousand lives—if the F-22 were available in place of the F-15. That is wrong under any reasonable set of assumptions. The United States could establish air supremacy very quickly in such a conflict, and it will remain able to do so well into the future, with or without the F-22. America would also surely begin to use its multipurpose aircraft to attack ground targets from the first day of combat—again, with or without the F-22. The mathematical models that give the Air Force its projection may be complicated, but that does not make them accurate. Remember, other Pentagon models forecast tens of thousands of American deaths in Desert Storm.

In fact, purchasing the F-22 could even hurt the United States in a future war. If U.S. defense budgets do not increase as much as the Pentagon hopes in the future, spending large sums of money on the Raptor might mean that the armed forces would spend too little on training, spare parts for tanks and airplanes, chemical protection gear, mine warfare vessels, or sufficient stockpiles of advanced munitions. The Air Force itself might wind up with fewer key capabilities, such as adequate stocks of precision weapons. In fact, there is already considerable analytical evidence that planned purchases of such munitions, even if fully completed, may prove insufficient. Such oversights would be likely to cost the United States far more in casualties than the F-22 could save.

The Air Force is closer to the mark in highlighting the threat to U.S. aircraft from improved air-to-air and surface-to-air missile (SAM) systems, such as Russia's AA-12 air-to-air missile and its SA-10 SAM (also known as the S-300). The AA-12 can be outfitted to older fighters that would not have a good chance of winning a classic dogfight against an American aircraft and pilot, but that could fire an advanced missile from standoff range. The advanced SAM systems have phased-array radars, which are capable of tracking several targets at once, and faster, longer-range interceptor missiles than the systems they supersede. Other countries will acquire these SAMs, even if they cannot afford or proficiently operate many top-line fighters. Against a future foe, moreover, the United States may not have the luxury of attacking from 15,000 feet for the first few weeks of the war, as it did in Operation Allied Force—meaning that the threats from SAMs could become even greater.[34]

These facts still do not translate into an overwhelming case for the F-22, however. Even without it, the United States would enjoy the benefits of aircraft that were at least somewhat stealthier than those of its opponents; it would generally field better radars capable of longer-range detection than those of its foes; and it would have the benefit of AWACS and other aircraft (not to mention unmanned aerial vehicles [UAVs], increasingly) with their long-range detection capabilities to warn U.S. fighter jets of the locations of enemy aircraft and radars. The F-22 would be useful for establishing air dominance quickly and safely, but it is not essential for achieving that dominance as a matter of principle.

The F-22 would also do relatively little to mitigate the SAM threat. It is not well equipped to attack SAM batteries; it will carry JDAMs, but not antiradiation missiles that home in on an enemy radar signal. Nor is the Raptor likely to be necessary to find enemy SAMs. Larger U.S. aircraft with sensitive radars flying at a distance from the immediate battle zone, coupled with inexpensive unmanned aerial vehicles able to fly low over enemy territory, can serve that purpose.

Instead of some 300 F-22s, the Air Force should purchase about 125 Raptors, enough for a single war. That was the number of F-15C air superiority fighters used in Desert Storm. Deploying 125 aircraft typically takes about 150 in the force structure, but the F-22 is designed to generate substantially higher sortie rates than the F-15, allowing some reduction in numbers. This number (125) of Raptors would provide a hedge against strategic and technological surprises—such as a rapidly strengthening and hostile China—at modest cost. Against a less sophisticated foe, it would allow the United States to establish air dominance with the Raptor in the early stages of a war if desired; follow-on operations could then be conducted quite safely by F-15s. This modest purchase of Raptors should be coupled with purchases of about 175 F-15s at some $50 million per plane to replace the rest of the aging air-to-air force structure. Total savings would be about $10 billion.

This discussion does not preclude consideration of an F-22 variant for replacing the F-117 and F-15E fleets eventually, as a deep-strike bomber. The stealth of the F-22—which would be more important in attacking

---

34. For a good summary of this Air Force view, see John A. Tirpak, "Can the Fighter Force Hold Its Edge?" *Air Force Magazine*, January 2000, pp. 25–31.

well-defended ground targets than in establishing air supremacy against most likely future foes—may place it in serious consideration for that task. It would hardly be necessary to replace all 250 F-15E and F-117 aircraft, given the improved capabilities of the F-22 (not to mention the attributes of new precision-strike munitions). The Air Force would be better served to make a pitch for the F-22 on these grounds than to argue for the program in its present configuration.

THE JOINT STRIKE FIGHTER. Although F/A-18E/F Super Hornets and F-22 Raptors have received most of the attention in recent years, the Pentagon plans to buy fewer than 1,000 of those two planes combined—and nearly 3,000 joint strike fighters. The first two aircraft programs are estimated by the CBO to cost a total of about $120 billion (in 2001 dollars), whereas the joint strike fighter (JSF) will likely approach $225 billion.

The Defense Department needs to find a way to make the JSF program less expensive. The solution is to buy a modest number of joint strike fighters, at a single production line—and to otherwise reequip most of the military's tactical fighter fleets by buying existing planes like the F-16.

First, a word on truth in advertising. The joint strike fighter gets better press than it deserves in the cost-containment category. Many describe it as a $29-million-a-copy aircraft, making it seem competitive even with existing F-16s. That is simply not realistic. The $29 million figure is expressed in 1994 dollars, and it represents "flyaway costs" rather than "unit procurement costs"—a distinction that seems arcane, but that is important here. Correcting for these two distortions in how the Pentagon describes the price of the plane, the unit procurement price (which includes some support costs and spare parts) is better estimated at $43 million for the Air Force version of the JSF, and at slightly more than $50 million for Marine Corps and Navy variants.

Not only that; these numbers also ignore likely cost growth. One must salute the Department of Defense for trying to keep the price of the JSF within bounds and commend its decision to view cost as an independent, important variable in the fighter's development program. But those facts will not ensure zero price growth. More likely, according to the CBO, are unit procurement costs of nearly $70 million for the version acquired by the Air Force, $75 million for the Marine Corps, and $90 million for the Navy. Compare those numbers to $25 million for the F-16, $37 million for the Harrier, and about $50 million for the F/A-18C/D Hornet (again, in 2001 dollars).

An alternative approach to fighter modernization would produce a significant, but much-reduced, number of JSF aircraft. Each service would reduce its program based on its own, individual rationale—but each such rationale is compelling.

The Navy might simply drop out of the JSF program, satisfying its future fighter needs with F/A-18C/D and F/A-18E/F aircraft rather than purchasing 480 joint strike fighters. The F/A-18E/F "Super Hornet" is already semi-stealthy. In addition, modifying the JSF for carrier operations is likely to be a major undertaking given the poor record of joint programs and the technical demands on planes operating off ships at sea.

The Marine Corps might scale back its planned purchase of 609 JSFs by 20 to 30 percent, on the grounds that the JSF is much more capable than the planes it is to replace. Indeed, one could even question the basic need for the Marine Corps to retain any fixed-wing aircraft, including the joint strike fighter. It is unlikely that the Marines would ever fight alone; in addition, they own combat helicopters for fire support. Nonetheless, the argument in favor of a vertical/short takeoff and landing aircraft for some part of the U.S. military, in an era when airfields are likely to become more vulnerable, is still strong. In addition, the Marines exercise with and use their aircraft in close coordination with their ground assets. In so doing, they help point the way to greater joint-service coordination among units for the military as a whole, and their efforts should be commended and continued. However, the need for what amounts to about five wing equivalents of airplanes for the Marines alone is not convincing.

The Air Force would scale back its JSF purchases dramatically. Rather than buy more than 1,700 JSF, it might purchase 500, largely to attack well-defended or mobile targets. The Air Force would buy more F-16s to make up the difference, and it would equip them with improved munitions, sensors, and command-control-communications-computers (C4) assets—the most promising part of the purported revolution in military affairs that many defense specialists anticipate today. Doing so would hardly amount to standing still technologically. Some would object that the F-16s would be too vulnerable, if not to advanced enemy fighters (which few potential foes can afford in significant numbers) then to advanced radar-guided surface-to-air missiles. However, improvements in antiradar missiles and the reconnaissance and information networks supporting them should make it possible to attack most such radars soon after they are turned on—perhaps using unmanned combat vehicles to carry the missiles to minimize risks to pilots. Moreover, JSF aircraft would be available for overflying the most heavily defended regions— allowing F-16s to be used where the threat to them was modest.[35]

Under this proposal, all JSFs would be produced by a single supplier. Lockheed Martin, the producer of the F-16, could drop out of the JSF competition, divest itself of the F-16 line if it won the JSF contract, or perhaps develop a firewall arrangement to keep two separate development and production teams under its single corporate roof.

A final benefit of this approach is that the nation's aging tactical aircraft inventory could begin to be replaced quickly. Rather than push its luck with the F-16, hoping that it will fly 8,000 hours, the Air Force could begin to replace it soon, and it could do so affordably. Under existing plans, fighter replacements would likely come too late. In fact, they could be further slowed due to JSF cost growth and Pentagon budget shortfalls in the years ahead, which would probably necessitate the Pentagon's stretching out its purchases of the new plane due to affordability concerns.

Revising the JSF program makes budgetary sense, conforms to most of the top priorities of enthusiasts for a revolution in military affairs, and ensures a healthy, safe, and reliable tactical fighter fleet into the future. The overall savings from this set of changes to the JSF program would total about $50 billion.

THE F/A-18E/F SUPER HORNET. The Navy is acquiring an expanded, enhanced, and stealthier version of its existing F/A-18 Hornet aircraft. In early 2000, after a somewhat difficult development program, the Super Hornet passed tests certifying its readiness for full-rate production.[36] It is to combine the roles of fighter and attack aircraft—just as today's A through D models can, but with greater payload and range for the attack role without sacrificing agility for the fighter role.

The F/A-18E/F was far cheaper to develop than the F-22,[37] but it will also represent a less significant improvement in technology. It will continue, for example, to carry weapons externally (making radar signatures high), to use avionics similar to those on current models, and to utilize

35. "USA Looks to Integrate Satellite Datalink on Tactical Missile," *Jane's Defence Weekly*, April 26, 2000, p. 6.

36. "Boeing Super Hornet Passes Key Tests," *Tacoma News Tribune*, March 24, 2000.

37. See George C. Wilson, "Wing Flaw Dogs Navy F/A-18E/F," *Defense News*, December 1–7, 1997, p. 3; and Elaine M. Grossman, "Navy Papers Cited Severity of F/A-18E/F 'Wing Drop' Prior to Milestone Approval," *Inside the Pentagon*, vol. 13, no. 49 (December 4, 1997), p. 1.

fairly traditional engine technology that will do little more than keep the larger F/A-18E/F as fast and maneuverable as A/B/C/D models.[38] It will have considerably greater weapons payload than the current Hornet; a somewhat smaller radar cross section, which may reduce the range at which it is readily detectable by nearly half; the ability to return to a carrier with more unused ordnance than current planes are permitted to land with; and other upgrades.[39] As a result, it is expected to cost significantly more than the A through D versions—at least $66 million a copy, expressed in constant 2001 dollars, in contrast to roughly $48 million for its predecessors. The Navy expects the F/A-18E/F to maintain the same technological edge over the Russian Su-35 that today's Hornet has over the Su-27 and to be at least the equal of next-generation European aircraft through 2015 and possibly beyond.[40] The 1997 QDR reduced the anticipated buy of E/F "Super Hornets" from 1,000 to 548, but it reserved the right to restore the planned buy to as many as 785 aircraft should problems develop in the JSF program as the year 2010 approaches.

Enhancing the Navy's power projection capabilities and standoff ranges makes sense. The Persian Gulf has the potential to be inhospitable to carriers in future battle, given increased Iranian acquisition of mines, submarines, and surface-to-surface antiship missiles, as well as other trends. Potential battle against China over Taiwan, for example to help the Taiwanese break an attempted Chinese blockade, could be joined more safely from greater distances. The A through D Hornets have a combat radius, depending on weapons loadings and other issues, of 500 to 1,000 kilometers; the E/F is intended to have 40 percent greater range, allowing it to patrol the Taiwan Strait while carriers remain well east of Taiwan.[41]

However, an increased buy of Super Hornets is not needed. Purchasing roughly 550 E/F aircraft should still be adequate, even in light of my recommendation to cancel the Navy variant of the joint strike fighter and

38. George C. Wilson, "Aircraft Dogfight Awaits Cohen at Pentagon," *Defense News,* January 27–February 2, 1997, p. 4.

39. Edward H. Phillips, "F/A-18E/F Meets Flight Test Goals," *Aviation Week and Space Technology,* vol. 147 (January 20, 1997), p. 58.

40. Office of Naval Intelligence, *Worldwide Challenges to Naval Strike Warfare* (1996), pp. 18, 35; Pierrot, *A Look at Tomorrow's Tactical Air Forces,* pp. 3–8; and Department of the Navy, *1997 Posture Statement,* p. VIII-10.

41. Timothy M. Laur, Steven L. Llanso, and Walter Boyne, *Encyclopedia of Modern U.S. Military Weapons* (New York: Berkley Books, 1998), p. 94.

scale back the size of the Navy carrier fleet by two ships (one active and one reserve). Remaining Navy force structure would be maintained with additional purchases of F/A-18C/D planes. For a nine-wing force, that translates into approximately two Super Hornet squadrons and one Hornet squadron per wing (alternatively, the Navy might deploy equal numbers of each). In addition to the savings noted above for the JSF program, buying some 250 C/D models instead of an equal number of Super Hornets would save more than $5 billion over the next decade.

Army Helicopters

The Army is modifying its existing AH-64 Apache attack helicopters, adding a sophisticated millimeter-wave radar to provide all-weather capability with the Hellfire antiarmor weapon (which is also capable against air defense radars and fixed targets). The Army plans to modify roughly 800 Apaches. In addition, it is slowly developing a next-generation scout and light-attack helicopter known as the RAH-66 or Comanche. It intends to build more than 1,200 of those Comanches eventually, with 700 for the light-attack role and more than 500 for the scout or reconnaissance role. Those two systems will be complemented by the aging Cobra and Kiowa fleets in the near term, but eventually will constitute the entire Army combat helicopter capability.[42]

Consistent with the philosophy embodied in the above F-22 and F/A-18E/F options, a reduced buy of Comanches makes sense. How many are enough? Two factors would allow roughly a halving of the current program size. In the Gulf War Apaches operated without scout helicopters, calling into doubt the basic need for the Comanche for that purpose. Improvements in UAVs and other sensors suggest that heavy attack helicopters may often be able to function independently in the future.[43] A sensible option could therefore eliminate the 500-plus Comanches intended for the scout mission. Consistent with the reduction of about 15 percent of the Army's combat strength suggested here, the remaining purchase of Comanche light-attack aircraft could be further reduced by at least 10 percent, as could the number of Apaches slated for upgrades to the Longbow configuration.

42. Fran Lussier, *An Analysis of U.S. Army Helicopter Programs* (Washington: Congressional Budget Office, 1995), pp. xv, 22.

43. Congressional Budget Office, *Reducing the Deficit: Spending and Revenue Options* (Washington, March 1997), pp. 53–54.

This approach would save the cost of buying some 600 of the helicopters at $20 million apiece, as well as the cost of refurbishing 80 Apaches at $9 million per aircraft. The resulting savings would be nearly $15 billion.[44]

Army Transformation

After its experience in the Kosovo war, when the Army needed several weeks to transport two dozen Apache helicopters and supporting weaponry to Albania, the Army leadership under General Eric Shinseki decided to undertake a modernization effort to improve its responsiveness in such austere combat theaters. The idea was to create an intermediate type of unit, medium-weight in protection and firepower, featuring a wheeled combat vehicle weighing about twenty tons. It would attempt to fill the gap between the undergunned light divisions and the too heavy armored and mechanized infantry divisions organized around the behemoth seventy-ton Abrams tank. The Army's goal is to transform two brigades by 2003, and a total of five to ten brigades within a decade, at an estimated cost of roughly $70 billion. Eventually, the Army hopes to be in a position to replace most of its heavy armored forces with medium-weight combat vehicles. Its ambitious goal is to be able ultimately to deploy a brigade anywhere in the world within 96 hours, a division within 120 hours, and five divisions within thirty days.[45]

There is good military logic to having units of intermediary weight. For example, had a quick ground invasion of Kosovo been needed in 1999 to stop a massive genocide (thankfully that was not needed), a force based around light tanks would have offered enormous advantages over either light units or Abrams-based heavy divisions. Similarly, light tanks might work well as the backbone of a peace implementation force in a place like the Balkans, where local forces possess substantial firepower but are not expected to use it in a concerted manner against western military

44. Increased spending would be needed for the Army's support helicopter fleet—but those costs are factored into CBO's $90 billion "baseline," which counts not only official Pentagon modernization programs but those that will be necessary to keep the force reliable into the future. Hence they are already factored into this analysis. Lussier, *An Analysis of U.S. Army Helicopter Programs,* pp. xv, 17–19, 40.

45. See Andrew Koch, "Transformation at a Price," *Jane's Defence Weekly,* March 22, 2000, p. 21; M. Thomas Davis, "U.S. Army Seeks Happy Medium," *Defense News,* May 29, 2000, p. 23; Rowan Scarborough, "Generals Not Fans of Lighter Army," *Washington Times,* May 30, 2000, p. A1; and Thomas E. Ricks, "Light Armored Vehicles Key to New Army Units," *Washington Post,* November 18, 2000, p. A8.

personnel—but where snipers, mines, and other such threats could be problems. Medium-weight forces could also be quite useful in a place like Afghanistan.

However, there are major reasons to doubt the Army's current plan in its more ambitious form. Even assuming that lighter tanks of comparable effectiveness to the Abrams can be developed, there is little reason to think that medium-weight forces could be deployed as fast as the Army postulates.[46] More fundamentally, the notion that armor, engine technology, and other key ingredients in modern mechanized infantry divisions are on the cusp of a revolution permitting a threefold reduction in total weight seems inconsistent with actual trends in technology.[47] At least the jury is still out and will remain out for many years. Advanced countermeasures and camouflage to make it easier for tanks to protect themselves from enemy fire without relying so heavily on their armor may or may not prove practical.

The Army's modernization plan seems an example of a good idea in danger of being taken too far, too fast—perhaps a result of the current conviction within the pro-RMA U.S. defense community that urgent military transformation is both necessary and possible. A slower, more patient pace of change, focused as much on experimentation and R&D as on near-term transformation, seems more advisable.

In addition, it is difficult to support the Army's continued interest in the Crusader artillery system, even in smaller numbers, and at lower weight, than once foreseen. Despite its interest in transformation, the Army still plans to build an artillery system weighing twice as much (forty tons) as the wheeled combat vehicle it soon hopes to develop. Yet it already has various forms of providing artillery fire, including the multiple launch rocket system (MLRS), not to mention air support from helicopters and the Air Force. Furthermore, the cost of redesigning Crusader will consume many if not most of the savings foreseen from reducing the total number of weapons purchased.[48]

It seems wiser for the Army to cancel the Crusader and to scale back its goals for transformation to a force of perhaps three to five brigades for

46. Sean D. Naylor, "Air Force Chief Says Vision's Airlift Might Not Be There," *Army Times*, May 8, 2000, p. 8.

47. Jason Sherman, "Dream Work," *Armed Forces Journal International* (May 2000), p. 26; and O'Hanlon, *Technological Change and the Future of Warfare*, pp. 81–85.

48. Ron Laurenzo, "Crusader Costs Rise Almost 50 Percent," *Defense Week*, April 24, 2000, p. 1.

the foreseeable future. Savings relative to the more ambitious plan would total around $25 billion.

B-2 Bombers and Other Bombers

The main argument for buying more B-2s than the twenty-one now authorized for the Air Force is to be able to search for, detect, attack, and destroy enemy armor while it is exposed early in a future war. Since a given bomber could carry about 1,000 submunitions, a lethality rate of 5 percent could theoretically allow a force of twenty bombers to destroy a heavy armored division in a single pass—assuming good targeting information and submunitions capable of distinguishing real targets from decoys and then penetrating their armor.

To be effective, however, the B-2 generally will need to be used early in a conflict, when enemy armor is isolated from allied and civilian vehicles and can therefore be attacked with homing munitions. At least for the foreseeable future, those munitions will be incapable of distinguishing between different types of vehicles, so using them in an urban environment or other complex terrain will be impractical. Even after munitions have been developed to distinguish one type of vehicle from another, enemies may respond by using standard civilian vehicles for as many military purposes as possible, using noise generators to fool acoustic detectors that identify vehicles based on engine noise, strapping superstructure onto tanks to disguise their silhouettes, and so on. Thus, if the United States failed to react quickly against aggression, when enemy forces were exposed, a larger B-2 fleet would do it little good. Furthermore, for hypothetical wars in many places, a prompt reaction would be politically difficult to generate out of the American political system. Even if the United States ultimately decided to oppose a major aggression in a place like south Asia, for example, it might need time to reach that determination politically—by which point the window of opportunity to respond with B-2s against exposed and isolated enemy armor could have passed.

Even taking into account the fact that B-2s are reusable and cruise missiles are not, the cost calculations would seem to come out decidedly to the advantage of the cruise missile. A B-2 can carry about thirty-six times as much ordnance as a Tomahawk cruise missile, which has a range of 2,000 kilometers. (In this example, Tomahawks would attack targets located by unmanned aerial vehicles or other assets.) Nevertheless, even when bought at reasonable production rates, the B-2 costs nearly 1,000 times as much as a Tomahawk (the latter costs just over $1 million apiece).[49] Even if the acute attack phase of a future war lasted ten days or so, and each B-2 could make half a dozen flights (as it might be able to if enough munitions, fuel, and spare parts were pre-positioned at places like Diego Garcia, Guam, or Okinawa),[50] it would in effect be carrying 200 times as much as a Tomahawk but still cost almost 1,000 times as much. Moreover, the upkeep costs of the Tomahawk are quite modest, whereas the operating and maintenance costs of the B-2 are at least $20 million per plane a year. That would add another 50 percent or so to the expected lifetime price tag of the bomber. So instead of being just five times as expensive a way to carry ordnance as cruise missiles, the B-2 bomber fleet could be seven or eight times as expensive.[51] A similar result would follow if one considered air-launched cruise missiles instead of Tomahawks. Either way, the conclusion is that B-2s would probably become economical only if a half-dozen high-intensity wars were fought over their service lives.[52]

The argument for the B-2 could also be weaker than suggested above, notably if the aircraft proved more vulnerable than now anticipated. Indeed, though details are classified, the B-2 has had considerable trouble in retaining its low observability during sustained testing and operations, apparently maintaining a mission-capable rate less than half the Air Force goal of about 80 percent.[53] It is perhaps partly for that reason that it was used so little in Operation Enduring Freedom.

Arsenal Ships and "Arsenal Bombers"

The case for arsenal ships is more compelling than for B-2 bombers, especially given that the former would be much less expensive. An arse-

49. David Mosher, "Options for Enhancing the Bomber Force" (Washington: Congressional Budget Office, 1995), pp. 24–25, 39; and Elizabeth Heeter and Steven Kosiak, "FY 1998 Defense Authorization and Appropriation Acts: Impact on Defense Programs and Industry" (Washington: Center for Strategic and Budgetary Assessments, November 19, 1997), p. 8.

50. David Mosher, "Options for Enhancing the Bomber Force," pp. 89–95.

51. "CBO Estimates on B-2 Production Costs," *Inside the Pentagon,* May 29, 1997, p. 4; and David Mosher with Raymond Hall, "Options for Enhancing the Bomber Force," CBO Paper (Washington: Congressional Budget Office, July 1995), p. 71.

52. For further explanation on why the assault phase is so different from other stages of battle, see Christopher Bowie and others, *The New Calculus* (Santa Monica, Calif.: RAND Corporation, 1993), p. 54.

53. Tony Capaccio, "Air Force Admits B-2 Maintenance Limits Overseas Deployments," *Defense Week,* August 11, 1997, p. 1; and William B. Scott, "Follow-On B-2 Flight Testing Planned," *Aviation Week and Space Technology,* vol. 147 (June 30, 1997), p. 48.

nal ship would have the advantage of being deployable in the waters surrounding a tense theater indefinitely, allowing even more rapid response than bombers based in the United States.

The major caveat to pushing this program is the uncertain potential of smart submunitions when encountering countermeasures and other real-world challenges.[54] The argument for buying arsenal ships today is also weakened by the existence of some seventy destroyers and cruisers that would be retained even under the smaller force posture advocated here. They wield considerable capacity for deploying missiles with homing submunitions to potential theaters of conflict. So will four submarines being converted to that mission.

Similar arguments are applicable to the nonstealthy bomber fleet. Such aircraft are, after all, "arsenal bombers," in that they are now valued largely for their ability to carry large numbers of autonomous weapons to the vicinity of a combat zone and then release them. Overall, the B-52 and B-1 bomber fleets seem big enough for now. These planes can each carry twenty to thirty advanced munitions, so one hundred such planes can carry a couple thousand medium-range munitions in a single sortie. A force of that size could carry as many precision munitions in four sorties as were dropped in the entire 1999 Operation Allied Force war against Serbia.[55]

All that said, the arsenal ship might be a technology worth trying out in a few years, particularly for the Persian Gulf region. To reduce the need for continuous deployments of Navy and Air Force fighter aircraft near Iraq, one or more arsenal ships might be stationed in the region, with the capacity to hit Iraqi armor fairly quickly and hard if Iraq attempted a march on a neighboring country or even on one of its own minority populations.

The V-22 Osprey

Having survived a tortured funding history that saw it ended by one secretary of defense, kept alive by the Congress, and then restored to life by the next administration and reasonably well protected by the QDR, the V-22 Osprey tilt-rotor program is now winding down the R&D phase and entering the production phase. The current plan is to purchase about 350

54. Laur, Llanso, and Boyne, *Encyclopedia of Modern U.S. Military Weapons,* pp. 422–36.

55. General Wesley K. Clark, "The United States and NATO: The Way Ahead," *Parameters,* vol. 29 (Winter 1999/2000), p. 10.

of the aircraft for troop and light-equipment transport for the Marine Corps, as well as roughly another 100 divided between special forces and the Navy.

The plane holds promise for certain types of missions, particularly because it is faster than other transport aircraft capable of operating from amphibious ships or other restricted spaces (all of which are helicopters). With a top speed of about 300 miles per hour (roughly 500 kilometers per hour), it is roughly twice as fast as most helicopters. With a normal mission radius of more than 200 miles (more than 300 kilometers), it has greater range than most current helicopters (though much less of an advantage than the Marine Corps routinely claims when comparing it against one particular shorter-range helicopter).[56] It also profits from improved systems designed to survive in a nuclear, chemical, or biological environment, to reduce the aircraft's infrared and acoustic signatures, and to absorb heavier fire than existing helicopters can take before catastrophic failure. Given that its R&D phase has been nearly completed, it makes sense to acquire at least a small fleet of the aircraft.

Caveats about the system abound, however, even if the serious safety issues that have plagued the program can be resolved. It is incapable of carrying heavy vehicles, meaning that CH-53 helicopters with all their vulnerabilities would still need to be part of any amphibious assault fleet even if V-22s were purchased in large numbers.[57] Its reduced vulnerability to enemy action has often been overstated; the aircraft is notably better only against small-arms fire (not surface-to-air missiles). Indeed, the well-known 1990 study of the V-22 by the Institute for Defense Analyses estimated that a V-22-equipped force would suffer only 5 to 25 percent fewer losses than the other options analyzed.[58] As a consequence, its major advantages over traditional rotary aircraft are most relevant to highly time-sensitive or longer-range operations and not as much to large-scale amphibious assault. Its technology remains promising yet untested under realistic circumstances; its operating costs may therefore prove

56. Marine Corps briefing on V-22 Osprey, June 13, 1997.
57. Congressional Budget Office, *Reducing the Deficit*, p. 37.
58. "Institute for Defense Analyses Study of V-22 Osprey," Hearings before Senate Subcommittee on Defense Appropriations 101-934, 101 Cong., 2 sess. (GPO, 1990), p. 5; and L. Dean Simmons, "Assessment of Alternatives for the V-22 Assault Aircraft Program" (Alexandria, Va.: Institute for Defense Analyses, June 1990).

higher than expected.[59] Its production costs are considerably greater than for helicopters with equivalent capability—specifically, about twice as great as for the CH-53E, which has a greater payload and an ability to carry heavy equipment that the V-22 cannot.[60]

In light of these various concerns, it would appear most sensible to buy a smaller number of V-22s than desired by the Marine Corps (as well as purchasing the planned numbers of Navy and special forces planes). Reducing the anticipated production run of some 350 Marine aircraft to about 150 would provide enough planes to transport more than a battalion equivalent unit, since the V-22 can carry about twenty troops. Perhaps more significantly, it would provide sufficient aircraft to use on routine Marine expeditionary unit patrols, which are often the nation's front-line reaction force for operations such as embassy evacuation. It would also provide aircraft for search and rescue and for antiterrorist or counterproliferation missions. A single Marine expeditionary unit force, of which two to three are deployed at a time, might include some thirty transport helicopters today.[61] Replacing those with V-22s in routine operations would be possible as long as the Osprey fleet numbered roughly one hundred or more. Using CBO assumptions that an Osprey unit would cost about $60 million to produce, and $35 million for the helicopter equivalent, net savings of $5 billion would be generated by downsizing the Osprey purchase and buying significant numbers of helicopters to compensate.[62]

Conclusion

A modernization strategy for the U.S. armed forces should be designed to focus principally on gaining maximum benefit from rapid progress in electronics and computers. That approach does not obviate the need to

59. Statement of David S. C. Chu, Assistant Secretary of Defense for Program Analysis and Evaluation, "Institute for Defense Analysis Study of V-22 Osprey," Hearings before Senate Subcommittee on Defense Appropriations 101-934, 101 Cong., 2 sess. (GPO, 1990), p. 47.

60. Congressional Budget Office, *Reducing the Deficit*, pp. 36–37; statement of David S. C. Chu, p. 47.

61. Vincent C. Thomas Jr., ed., *The Almanac of Seapower 1994* (Arlington, Va.: Navy League of the United States, 1994), pp. 144–48.

62. Congressional Budget Office, *Reducing the Deficit*, p. 36.

replace certain stocks of aging weapons platforms, or argue against limited purchases of next-generation fighters, ships, and armored vehicles. It does suggest, however, that fewer resources be devoted to comprehensively modernizing weapons platforms than the services now intend. It suggests instead that existing types of weapons can be purchased, complementing relatively small "silver-bullet" forces of high-cost and advanced platforms. This approach would keep costs in check and keep weapons inventories young, reliable, and safe. Additional measures should place greater emphasis on R&D and joint-service experimentation, as the Pentagon now intends.

Applying this modernization philosophy to various defense acquisition programs produces considerable savings. Just the major systems surveyed here—combat jets and helicopters, the V-22 Osprey, and the Army's transformation strategy—would yield savings of well over $100 billion, or nearly $10 billion a year. Extrapolating to other weapons systems, it is safe to conclude that this option would save more than $10 billion in annual acquisition costs—not enough to preclude the need for increases in procurement spending, but enough to close a large fraction of the projected defense spending shortfall in the years ahead.

FIVE

Building a Limited National Missile Defense and Cutting Nuclear Forces

Should the United States deploy a national missile defense (NMD)—and if so, on what schedule, with what technologies, and within what if any limits now that the United States will no longer be abiding by the 1972 Anti-Ballistic Missile (ABM) Treaty, which banned such defenses outright? The United States has never had a nation-wide defense against missile attack and still does not have one today. That fact raises questions about whether the United States will someday be deterred from projecting power abroad—or at least from considering certain military options, such as an overthrow of Saddam Hussein should he again start a war after having developed long-range missiles—out of fear of reprisal against its homeland.

Whatever President Bush decides about NMD, he will almost surely actually deploy, in his first term, additional types of theater missile defense (TMD) to counter shorter-range ballistic missiles. These programs are less contentious as a group, given the damage done by SCUD missiles in the 1991 Persian Gulf War and the growing prevalence of short-range missiles around the world. The main focus here, therefore, is on the question of defending U.S. national territory against ballistic missile attack. The argument advanced is straightforward: it makes sense to prepare to deploy national missile defense this decade—but the defense should be focused only on small, extremist states that may acquire such capabilities, with Iraq, Iran, or North Korea being the prime candidates.

Any effort to challenge the deterrents of Russia or China is bound to fail, given the natural advantages enjoyed by a potential attacker, and to cause serious harm to Washington's relations with Moscow and Beijing in the process. The defense should also emphasize technologies that would work in the boost phase of a threatening missile's flight, in the minutes just after missile launching (see figure 5-1).[1] Such systems are more promising technologically. They are also less likely to cause major strains with China and Russia, since they could only stop missiles launched within a few hundred miles of where they were based.

The Clinton administration's proposed defense system, by contrast, was a midcourse system that would seek to destroy an incoming warhead roughly halfway through its flight. It would use a combination of satellite sensors and radars to detect the launch of an enemy missile and then follow its trajectory, as well as the trajectories of any objects—including warheads and decoys—that it released. It would then send relatively large defensive missiles, launched from one or two sites in the United States, into space to intercept enemy warheads headed at U.S. territory. Once it reached high speed and left the atmosphere, the interceptor rocket would release a small "kill vehicle" to collide with the warhead. The kill vehicle would have its own sensors and numerous small thrusters to achieve the accuracy necessary to collide directly with the incoming threat. Given the tremendous speeds of both defensive and offensive objects, the sheer force of the collision would be enough to ensure the warhead's destruction.

Even if these technologies could be made to work as planned, however, the Clinton system would be vulnerable. It would likely be defeated by decoys capable of mimicking real warheads in the vacuum of outer space, fooling a defense designed to do its work in that region (that is, during the midcourse or exoatmospheric phase of a ballistic missile warhead's flight). Such a defense system still probably has value, since countries such as North Korea may not be able to develop the necessary decoys in short order and since it may provide a limited degree of protection against missiles launched from a wide range of locations that boost-phase defenses cannot stop. By itself, however, a midcourse defense is not enough. Thus a boost-phase system is also appropriate. If it can be made relatively invulnerable to attack, it could be deployed first

---

1. This chapter draws extensively on James M. Lindsay and Michael E. O'Hanlon, *Defending America: The Case for Limited National Missile Defense* (Brookings, 2001).

on barges in the Sea of Japan or on Russian soil near North Korea. Such a boost-phase system would probably be deployable before 2010—as soon, or nearly as soon, as the Clinton administration's proposed system would be.

As for the Clinton administration's proposed system, an Alaska deployment site might no longer be required under this proposal (its main advantage over a North Dakota site is its ability to defend the small populations of western Alaska). A more modest number of interceptors—probably twenty-five to fifty—deployed in North Dakota would suffice. The United States could limit its total number of interceptors, including midcourse and boost-phase varieties, to under two hundred. That would make it consistent with the original numerical restrictions—even if not the other stipulations, and not the subsequent reduction of that interceptor ceiling from two hundred to one hundred—of the 1972 Anti-Ballistic Missile Treaty.

Taking this approach, President Bush can afford to delay a decision on deploying NMD until at least 2003. That delay would provide time for further development of technology. Just as important, it would provide time for consultations with Russia and China, as well as with U.S. allies in Europe and East Asia. It is not that Beijing and Moscow deserve a veto over U.S. decisionmaking on matters of national security, or that the allies do. Rather, unless their concerns were at least partially addressed and their fears mitigated, Russia and China could take countervailing steps that would defeat much or all of the benefit of a national missile defense. For example, they could provide the technologies for countermeasures to extremist states such as Iraq that could defeat the U.S. defense, or they could slacken their efforts to tighten exports of missiles. Russia might also suspend collaborative efforts with the United States to reduce nuclear danger, ranging from offensive arms control and Nunn-Lugar cooperative threat-reduction programs to any consideration of the notion of taking nuclear weapons off hair-trigger alert.

Finally, a delay would synchronize NMD with major TMD development programs, the more advanced of which are not likely to have produced working capabilities before 2007 or 2008. The Clinton administration was trying to defend America by 2005 when it had little prospect of being able to offer protection to allies such as Japan or Britain before the end of the decade. That policy made little sense; there is little to be gained by defending this country while major treaty allies remain exposed and vulnerable. Since it will be at least seven or eight years before U.S.

Figure 5-1. *Trajectories of Ballistic Missiles (for standard, minimum-energy flight)*

Altitude, in kilometers

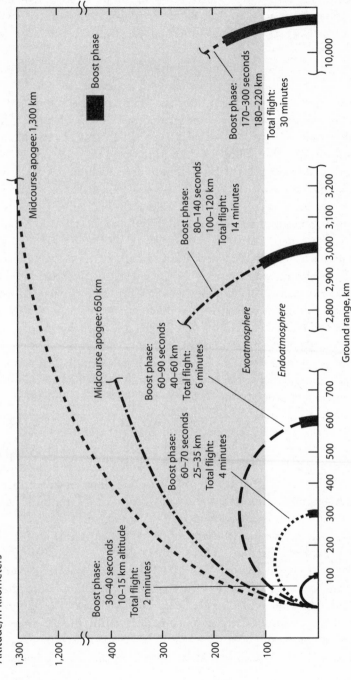

Ground range, km

Source: Ballistic Missile Defense Organization, "1993 Report to Congress on the Theater Missile Defense Initiative (TMDI)"; Union of Concerned Scientists.

allies abroad can be effectively defended, the United States will remain strategically vulnerable to missile attack for at least that long, whether its own territory is defended or not. An adversary could simply threaten a major U.S. ally with attack, rather than the United States itself, and thereby paralyze Washington almost as effectively as if it were pointing a missile at New York or Los Angeles. Rather than imagine that it really has the option of defeating the potential missile threat by 2006 or so, the United States would be wiser to work toward a more global solution for itself, its deployed forces, and its allies by 2008 or 2010.

While this chapter's main focus is missile defense, it also includes a short analysis of how offensive nuclear forces might be cut considerably more deeply than now planned in the years ahead—a process that could even be catalyzed by some U.S. unilateral cuts. The combined philosophy of more defense and less offense would have greater moral and political appeal than deploying missile defense while retaining a robust war-fighting nuclear posture. Keeping the latter capability would likely engender worries from countries such as Russia and China; working toward a new nuclear paradigm, by contrast, has a chance to be seen as a wise response to the times rather than an inherently competitive or aggressive act by the United States. In addition, cutting nuclear forces could help pay for the moderately high costs of even a limited national missile defense.

The Case for Limited National Missile Defense

Both proponents and critics of NMD marshal an impressive array of well-reasoned arguments to support their positions. The simple fact is that there are powerful rationales both for and against national missile defense, meaning that any wise policy must reflect a compromise between competing concerns. That translates into a case for a limited NMD, developed carefully, discussed diligently with allies and neutrals alike, and deployed patiently—unless the long-range missile threat to the United States suddenly becomes much more ominous and imminent than it now appears.[2]

Missile defense proponents are right that the global threat is growing. The club of nations with ballistic missiles now numbers about two dozen

2. This section draws heavily on Michael O'Hanlon, "Star Wars Strikes Back," *Foreign Affairs,* vol. 78, no. 6 (November/December 1999), pp. 68–82.

members.[3] Of equal concern is the increasing range of the missile forces possessed by many countries.

Exhibit A in this regard is North Korea. North Korea tested the Taepo Dong 1 in the summer of 1998, overflying Japan with the rocket. A three-stage rocket, as intercontinental ballistic missiles using standard fuel and materials must be, its first two stages worked successfully before the third failed, after having successfully separated from the second stage. Even though it failed, the overall accomplishment was nonetheless surprising and disconcerting to U.S. intelligence. North Korea also kept developing the Taepo Dong 2, a rocket four times as large and with a range of 4,000 to 6,000 kilometers.[4] A range of 4,000 kilometers would put the Aleutian Islands within reach; a range of 6,000 kilometers would put most of Alaska and the small western islands of Hawaii at risk.[5] The Taepo Dong 2 might even be able to deliver a nuclear-sized payload to parts of the continental United States if North Korea could succeed in adding a workable third stage to it, as in fact it tried with the Taepo Dong 1 in 1998.[6] (The nuclear weapon it carried would have to weigh no more than several hundred kilograms—not a demanding ceiling for U.S. bomb designers, but much less than the weight of the original U.S. atomic explosives in the 1940s, and not an easy weight to attain without the benefit of nuclear testing.)[7] Events in 2000, including a summit meeting between South Korean president Kim Dae Jung and North Korean president Kim Jong-Il, as well as Pyongyang's decision to impose a moratorium on long-range missile flight testing, improved the atmosphere on the peninsula somewhat, though the momentum of that détente process has since been largely lost. And it may not have slowed North Korea's Taepo Dong 2 program.[8]

3. Dov S. Zakheim, "Old Rivalries, New Arsenals: Should the United States Worry?" *IEEE Spectrum,* vol. 36 (March 1999), pp. 30–31.

4. Richard L. Garwin, "A Defense That Will Not Defend," *Washington Quarterly,* vol. 23, no. 3 (Summer 2000), pp. 213–24.

5. Zakheim, "Old Rivalries, New Arsenals," pp. 30–31.

6. "Current and Projected National Security Threats to the United States," Hearings before the Senate Select Committee on Intelligence, 106 Cong., 2 sess. (GPO, 2000), pp. 10–30; and Richard L. Garwin, "The Wrong Plan," *Bulletin of the Atomic Scientists,* vol. 56, no. 2 (March/April 2000), pp. 36–41.

7. Walter B. Slocombe, "U.S. Limited National Missile Defense Program," Briefing Slides (Harvard-CSIS Ballistic Missile Defense Conference, May 11, 2000); and Christopher E. Paine, "The U.S. Debate over a CTB," Working Paper NWD 93-5, rev. 2 (Washington: Natural Resources Defense Council, 1993), p. 30.

8. Steven Lee Myers and Eric Schmitt, "Korea Accord Fails to Stall Missile Plan," *New York Times,* June 18, 2000, p. 1.

Among their other effects, these North Korean missile developments helped persuade Japan to enter into a TMD research collaboration agreement with the United States in August of 1999.

The 1998 North Korean test also confirmed the findings of a task force led by Secretary of Defense Donald Rumsfeld. The task force report, published shortly before the Taepo Dong 1 overflew Japan, concluded unanimously and ominously that countries such as North Korea, Iran, or Iraq might develop a missile threat against American territory fairly quickly. Criticizing the U.S. intelligence community, which had argued that the United States would have a decade or more of clear notice before most countries could acquire credible missile threats against the United States, the report argued that we might have less than five years' warning—and perhaps virtually none at all. That is because would-be proliferators could do a good deal of their preliminary research in secret, conduct crash programs in missile testing (albeit at some price in missile capability and reliability), buy missiles or parts thereof from abroad, and possibly threaten the United States with medium-range missiles launched from ships or the territories of nearby countries.[9]

Missile defense supporters were also right to have profound doubts about the continued relevance, at least in its traditional form, of the ABM Treaty. Signed when the superpower arms race was essentially out of control, it was the product of a different day and age. Perceptions of nuclear advantage mattered so much then, and worst-case military analysis was so prevalent, that widespread deployment of even mediocre defenses might have provoked an unchecked offense-defense competition. Moreover, the technical challenge of missile defense was so daunting, given the magnitude of the potential threat, that it was implausible to believe meaningful protection could be provided (see table 5-1). In other words, NMD was prohibited not because it was believed to be inherently bad, but because of the specific political and technological circumstances of the day. Those circumstances have now changed.

Missile defense skeptics offer three very solid arguments in reply, however—which do not defeat the case for NMD, but do counsel a judicious, measured deployment that is cognizant of Russian and Chinese concerns to the extent possible. First, skeptics point out that even though the cold

9. The Commission to Assess the Ballistic Missile Threat to the United States, *Executive Summary of the Report of the Commission to Assess the Ballistic Missile Threat to the United States* (Washington, July 15, 1998), pp. 1–6, 11–13.

Table 5-1. Evolution of National Missile Defense (NMD) Programs, 1980s–Mid-2000s

Program	Mission	Threat size	Space-based laser	Space-based interceptors	Ground-based interceptors
SDI (1980s)	Counter massive Soviet ballistic missile strike	1000s	10s	4,000	1,500
GPALS (early 1990s)	Defeat ballistic missile accidental or unauthorized launch	200	No	1,000	750
Limited NMD (mid 2000s)	Defend against very small rogue state threat	A few to a few 10s	No	No	100 to 250

Source: Slocombe, "U.S. Limited National Missile Defense Program."

war is over, old arms race dynamics die hard. Both Russia and the United States maintain large and ready nuclear forces. One may argue that they should have shed cold war concepts about maintaining huge arsenals and pursuing strategic advantage by now—but in fact they have not. Russian president Vladimir Putin's acquiescence in President Bush's decision to withdraw from the ABM Treaty, while welcome, does not mean that all Russian policymakers have moved fully beyond cold war thinking.

A new superpower arms race is of course unlikely, However, if mistrust or rancor became bad between the countries in the future, they could even threaten the Nunn-Lugar cooperative threat reduction program, with which the United States helps Russia secure its frighteningly scattered nuclear arsenal, as well as U.S.-Russian cooperation in the war on terrorism.

These are powerful arguments, if not against NMD per se, then at least against a rapid, unilateralist, large-scale NMD deployment that amounts to sticking America's high-tech thumb in Russia's eye. Whatever threat countries like North Korea may pose to the United States in the coming years, the potential danger from Russian "loose nukes" is orders of magnitude greater; it would be folly to address the first concern and in the process exacerbate the second.

The second argument frequently invoked against NMD is technological: good missile defense systems are very difficult to develop. Some progress is being made in TMD, but much still needs to be done, and national defenses against intercontinental missiles remain a good distance away. Indeed, another 1998 task force, this one led by retired general Larry Welch, argued that missile defense research programs were being pushed too rapidly, in what amounted to a "rush to failure." Chairman of the Joint Chiefs of Staff General Hugh Shelton, former director of the Ballistic Missile Defense Organization Lieutenant General Lester Lyles, and current BMDO director Lieutenant General Ronald Kadish have repeatedly acknowledged that the NMD development schedule is very ambitious. Unwisely, the Clinton administration originally planned to reach an initial decision on whether to deploy a national missile defense after completing only three of nineteen planned intercept tests of the candidate system.[10] Thankfully, when the time came in the summer of 2000,

---

10. General Larry Welch and others, "Report of the Panel on Reducing Risk in Ballistic Missile Defense Flight Test Programs" (Department of Defense, February 27, 1998), pp. 7–27; Jeffrey A. Merkley, "Trident II Missile Test Program," Staff Working Paper

President Clinton recognized that three tests—two of which had failed to hit their target—could not justify committing to an NMD deployment.

Third, even missile defenses that work on the test range may be defeated by countermeasures thrown at them by a real enemy. The United States may be able to learn to hit a bullet with a bullet under controlled conditions; indeed, two flight tests in 2001 and another in 2002 succeeded, albeit under somewhat staged conditions. However, what if that incoming bullet is accompanied by dozens of decoys, or launched as part of a multi-missile saturation attack designed to overwhelm defenses in a given zone? Against a sophisticated foe, such countermeasures are to be expected. Even a less sophisticated foe might devise reasonably effective ones, or it could acquire them from Russia or China, should those countries prove willing to transfer countermeasures in order to gain hard currency or to complicate U.S. defense planning that they perceived as aggressive and threatening to their interests.[11] Concern about countermeasures is most serious for midcourse systems like that proposed by the Clinton administration (and for the Navy Theater Wide TMD program, which is designed to intercept threatening objects outside the atmosphere), as discussed further below.

Missile defense opponents make two additional arguments that stand up less well to scrutiny. On the issue of budgetary cost, opponents point out that the United States has spent some $3.5 billion a year on missile defense programs since Ronald Reagan announced the Strategic Defense Initiative in 1983, making for a total of more than $100 billion spent on missile defense since the early 1960s (in constant 2001 dollars). Since then spending has accelerated; plans call for spending $8 billion a year into the future. A multilayer missile defense could cost around $200 billion to deploy, moreover, according to a recent CBO study. Missile defense proponents respond that, given the stakes involved, these numbers are not so big—less than 3 percent of defense spending at present.[12]

(Washington: Congressional Budget Office, February 1986), p. 7; and Statement of Lieutenant General Ronald T. Kadish, Director, Ballistic Missile Defense Organization, before the Senate Armed Services Committee, February 28, 2000, p. 6.

11. Sherman Frankel, "Defeating Theater Missile Defense Radars with Active Decoys," *Science and Global Security,* vol. 6 (1997), pp. 333–55.

12. John E. Pike, Bruce G. Blair, and Stephen I. Schwartz, "Defending against the Bomb," in Stephen I. Schwartz, ed., *Atomic Audit: The Costs and Consequences of U.S. Nuclear Weapons since 1940* (Brookings, 1998), p. 296.

If we can spend 10 percent of the defense budget defending Persian Gulf oil or South Korean security, they argue, we can devote a couple of percent to protect our own territory—not an unreasonable position to take, assuming that the defenses really work and solve more problems than they create or exacerbate.

NMD skeptics also question why missile defenses are needed if the country remains vulnerable to "suitcase bombs," ships carrying nuclear weapons in their cargo bays, cruise missiles launched from ships or submarines off U.S. shores, and other means of delivery—not to mention attacks like that of September 11. They suggest that the United States instead continue to rely on the time-tested technique of deterrence. NMD advocates object fundamentally to placing all eggs in the deterrence basket, even if skeptics are right that deterrence is an appropriate first line of protection—and that it tends to work against even extremist states.[13] Advocates also argue persuasively that it makes no sense to throw in the towel on NMD just because missile defenses are not a panacea against all threats. They also point out that the country does have a Coast Guard and a customs service that offer at least some protection against these other means of delivery, whereas the United States is strategically naked against the missile threat.[14] Finally, it is worth noting that missile threats are fundamentally different from truck-delivered bombs or ship-delivered bombs in that they can be delivered very quickly—making them especially dangerous to the United States in crisis or wartime conditions, as Brookings scholar James Lindsay has observed.

The arguments against NMD, and particularly large-scale, unconstrained NMD, have enough merit to strongly influence the way the United States goes about deploying a national missile defense. Most of all, while Russia and China should not be given a veto over deployment, the United States should recognize that those countries probably have it within their power to counter a U.S. NMD with measures that could defeat the system and perhaps even lessen overall American security as a result.

---

13. For a persuasive argument along these lines, see Janne Nolan and Mark Strauss, "The Rogues' Gallery," *Brown Journal of World Affairs*, vol. 4, no. 1 (Winter/Spring 1997), pp. 21–38.

14. That is not to say that Customs efforts are adequate today; notably, only about one in twenty containers reaching the United States is inspected at the border. It is also possible that intelligence leads, and further improvements in Customs, can improve the odds. See Anthony Lake, *Six Nightmares* (Little, Brown, 2000), p. xii; Stephen E. Flynn, "Beyond Border Control," *Foreign Affairs*, vol. 79, no. 6 (November/December 2000), pp. 57–68.

China's most natural counterreaction might be to build up its offensive nuclear forces. The initial Clinton system would have one hundred interceptors, with a purported capability of intercepting perhaps twenty warheads—exactly China's current strategic inventory. Therefore, the PRC would probably build up its missile force to ensure that its offensive capability exceeded the defensive capability of the United States. (In fact, China is already upgrading and expanding its strategic forces somewhat, but it might be expected to expand them further in response to any U.S. NMD, especially since the Clinton proposal envisioned a total of 250 interceptors eventually.)

Such a Chinese reaction might not by itself be particularly disquieting. The United States would still enjoy a considerable strategic advantage over China. More to the point, the exact strategic balance between these two countries is probably of limited significance, since it could hardly make nuclear war a thinkable or winnable proposition in any event. However, Beijing might take other, more harmful steps. If it reacted to a U.S. NMD deployment by selling countermeasures to North Korea—perhaps simply out of pique, or perhaps in the hope that if it did so, the United States would have to spend more NMD dollars countering the North Korean threat and would be less able to devote resources to building defenses capable against those of the PRC—the basic purpose of the deployment could be defeated. The U.S. intelligence community, for one, takes this concern quite seriously.[15] In this sense, a large defense might buy the United States *less* protection against ballistic missile attack than would a small one limited in size and scope to deal with the North Korean, Iraqi, and Iranian threats.

A hasty, unilateral deployment could also lessen the security of U.S. allies. If such a U.S. NMD deployment led to rifts in NATO, for example, Europe might remain undefended—or a Saddam Hussein or a Kim Jong-Il might respond to the reality of a U.S. NMD by increasing threats against major U.S. allies in time of crisis or war. U.S. allies might find themselves less secure than they were before the United States deployed its defenses. If, in the end, major U.S. allies are undefended, the strategic benefits of a U.S. missile defense capability will be very limited. Moreover, for the European allies, simply buying U.S. TMD systems will not suffice as a complete solution. The relevant distances are too great. Britain, for

---

15. See Bob Drogin and Tyler Marshall, "Missile Shield's Destabilizing Potential Cited," *Los Angeles Times*, May 19, 2000, p. A1.

example, is 7,000 kilometers away from some points in southeastern Iran, or twice the range limit that applies to testing TMD systems under the 1997 U.S.-Russian demarcation agreement. Even Italy is more than 3,500 kilometers away from the most distant parts of Iran. If the European allies are to be safe against a future Iraqi or Iranian long-range missile force, some of them at least will need to buy a system that the United States has defined as NMD—be it the Clinton administration's program, a boost-phase concept, or something else.

The right solution is to take time, consult with not only Moscow and Beijing, but also major European, Mideast, and Asian allies, and move toward a moderate defense deployment that allows the opportunity for these allies to develop or purchase defenses as well. Indefinite procrastination is not in order, but one to two more years of negotiations and further technology development very much are. As noted, two types of defense systems are of principal interest for constructing a limited nationwide defense in the next decade: the Clinton administration's proposed exoatmospheric intercept approach, and a boost-phase approach using fast missiles near a potential threat country. Each has its limitations, so in the end a combination of a relatively small-scale version of each defense is probably the best approach.

The Clinton Administration's NMD Program

In 1997 the Clinton administration decided to commit to development of a light national missile defense system, to be based at a single site in North Dakota or Alaska, and to make at least a provisional decision about whether to deploy the system in 2000. It originally hoped to have such a defense system deployed by 2003, but later recognized that the earliest practical date for initial deployment would be 2005. The Clinton administration's initial NMD capability was designed to be enough to shoot down about five warheads from North Korea, with a full one hundred interceptors capable of downing up to twenty or so warheads deployed by 2007. The Bush administration has a broader agenda for missile defense (see table 5-2). But the Clinton system, or something based on it, remains the most advanced technology option available to the Bush administration at present.

The one-hundred-interceptor Clinton system would be able to intercept only a few warheads from the Middle East because its radar coverage in that direction is to be mediocre. Since the interceptor missiles are

Table 5-2. *Comparison of Clinton and Bush Administration Missile Defense Budgets*
Millions of dollars

Item	Fiscal year 2001	Clinton plan for 2002	Bush request for 2002
Overall system (design, testing)[a]	742	662	934
Theater missile defense systems			
Patriot advanced capability 3 (PAC-3)	442	534	784
Medium Extended Air Defense System (MEADS)	52	74	74
Navy areawide	270	297	395
Theater High-Altitude Area Defense (THAAD)	531	699	923
Arrow	94	46	66
National missile defense systems[b]			
Clinton midcourse system	2,029	2,458	3,285
Navy Theater Wide	456	246	656
Airborne laser	231	214	410
Space-based laser	73	137	165
Sea-based boost-phase missile	0	0	about 50
Space-based boost-phase missile	0	0	about 60
Satellites and sensors			
SBIRS-low sensor	239	308	420
U.S.-Russian satellites	35[a]	75	75
Total	5,194[a]	5,751	8,298[c]

Source: Pentagon briefing, July 2001.

a. Because budget documents for 2001 use different categories, these figures may be slightly inaccurate.

b. Systems explicitly designed for long-range missile defense or potentially usable for that mission; the Bush administration plans to investigate the potential of all of these technologies for long-range or national missile defense.

c. Congress eventually appropriated $7.8 billion.

to be based in Alaska, moreover, they are a long way from the trajectories of Mideast missiles aimed at East Coast cities. The so-called C2 and C3 capabilities (see table 5-3) would provide more thorough coverage against Mideast threats, the latter including a second base of interceptors in North Dakota.

After 1999 the Clinton administration explicitly allocated money in its future years' defense program to deploy NMD. It added $6.6 billion to its defense plan for the years 2000 through 2005 for that purpose (making for a grand total of $10.5 billion for NMD over that period, including research and development costs as well).[16] Even so, Congress continued to add more money to the missile defense development effort—and usefully so, based on statements from Pentagon officials responsible for the TMD and NMD programs.[17]

Estimated total acquisition costs later rose to $12.7 billion through 2005.[18] The Pentagon concluded in 2000 that total acquisition costs were likely to reach about $25 billion (in constant 2001 dollars).[19] Even if costs increase by 50 percent in the end, as is normal for high-technology weaponry, they would hardly be enormous by comparison with Pentagon fighter, submarine, and destroyer programs expected to cost several tens of billions of dollars each. Nonetheless, they would be significant.

In addition to the interceptor missiles, plans called for a new "x-band" radar (with relatively high frequency and thus relatively high accuracy), as well as upgrades to various U.S. early-warning radars around the world, to detect incoming threats and guide interceptors to them. The x-band radar was to be on Shemya Island, one of the westernmost Aleutians in Alaska. (The Bush administration may drop this feature of the Clinton midcourse system.) That is a hard place to do construction work and also potentially a difficult site to defend against enemy attack, especially in light of the heavy volume of shipping traffic in the vicinity (though security would surely be enhanced in any crisis or wartime situation, mitigating the latter concern substantially during such periods).[20] Altogether, this deployment plan is deemed "C1" by the Pentagon.

The C2 capability would retain one hundred deployed interceptor missiles, but add three more x-band radars, interceptor missile upgrades, and expanded communications infrastructure to share data among various sensors. It might also include the space-based infrared sensor for low

16. William S. Cohen, "FY 2000 Defense Budget: Briefing Slides" (Department of Defense, February 1999).

17. See Gopal Ratnam, "BMDO Deployment Pace Rests on $1 Billion Bonus," *Defense News,* March 20, 2000, p. A1.

18. Roberto Suro, "Missile Sensor Failed in Test's Final Seconds, Data Indicate," *Washington Post,* January 20, 2000, p. A4.

19. Tony Capaccio, "National Missile Defense Cost Estimate Rises Nearly 20 Percent," *Defense Week,* September 11, 2000, p. 2.

20. Roberto Suro, "Key Missile Defense Radar Planned for Remote Island," *Washington Post,* May 7, 2000, p. A6.

Table 5-3. Preliminary Architecture for the Clinton Administration's C1, C2, and C3 National Missile Defense Systems

Item	C1 configuration	C2 configuration	C3 configuration
Number of interceptors deployed in Alaska	100	100	125
Number of interceptors deployed in North Dakota	0	0	125
Upgraded early-warning radars	Beale (Marysville, Calif.) Clear (Alaska) Cape Cod (Mass.) Fylingdales (England) Thule (Greenland)	Beale Clear Cape Cod Fylingdales Thule	Beale Clear Cape Cod Fylingdales Thule South Korea
x-band radars	Shemya (Alaska)	Shemya Clear Fylingdales Thule	Shemya Clear Fylingdales Thule Beale Cape Cod Grand Forks (N.D.) Hawaii South Korea
In-flight interceptor communications systems	Central Alaska Caribou (Maine) Shemya	Central Alaska Caribou Shemya Munising (Mich.)	Central Alaska Caribou Shemya Munising Hawaii
Early-warning satellites (SBIRS-high)	4[a]	5	5
Warhead-tracking satellites (SBIRS-low)	6[b]	24	24

Sources: Ballistic Missile Defense Organization, "C1/C2/C3 Architecture—Preliminary," briefing slide TRSR 99-082 25, Washington, March 3, 1999; Michael C. Sirak, "BMDO: NMD 'C3' Architecture Could Feature up to Nine x-Band Radars," *Inside Missile Defense*, May 19, 1999, pp. 13–14; and Congressional Budget Office, *Budgetary and Technical Implications of the Administration's Plan for National Missile Defense*, April 2000, table 1, p. 8.

a. Existing defense support program satellites will also be used for national missile defense.

b. These satellites are planned engineering prototypes.

altitude (SBIRS-Low) satellite constellation to the ground-based radars used with the C1 capability. The basic goal would be to make the system more robust against Mideast threats, considered likely around 2010 (particularly from Iran), and to make it more capable against decoys and other countermeasures. It would be deployable by 2010 and would cost an additional $5 billion for radar and communications upgrades, plus another $10 billion for SBIRS-Low.[21] C3 would contribute additional radars, as well as a second base of interceptor missiles in North Dakota, for a further cost of about $10 billion.

The C1 and C2 systems would fall within ABM Treaty guidelines allowing as many as one hundred long-range interceptors to be based at a single site. However, the ABM Treaty does not permit a territorial missile defense of any kind or size; the single base of interceptors is supposed to defend only the nation's capital or an ICBM missile field. The ABM Treaty would need to be revised or abandoned to permit deployment of the proposed NMD system.[22]

Are Development Schedules Realistic? Is the Clinton administration plan sound, in light of statements even from Pentagon officials that its NMD program is "ambitious," "risky," and perhaps even rushed?

It seems likely that, some day, hit-to-kill technology against an incoming reentry vehicle flying a clear trajectory will work. Successful tests of the Patriot PAC-3, Theater High Altitude Area Defense (THAAD), and the national missile defense system were conducted in 1999—a notable accomplishment even if the NMD test was somewhat jury-rigged and somewhat lucky. An NMD test failure occurred in January 2000, when infrared sensors on the kill vehicle lost the target in the last few seconds before anticipated intercept because water droplets frozen in the kill vehicle's sensors blocked the flow of coolant to the sensor and thus prevented it from reaching the low temperatures necessary for operation. A second failure occurred in July 2000, when the booster rocket being used to place the NMD kill vehicle on a high-speed trajectory failed to separate from the kill vehicle. That failure, the result of a rather sloppy mistake, largely

21. Geoffrey Forden, *Budgetary and Technical Implications of the Administration's Plan for National Missile Defense* (Washington: Congressional Budget Office, April 2000), pp. 5–17; Slocombe, "U.S. Limited National Missile Defense Program."

22. Testimony of Walter B. Slocombe to the House Armed Services Committee, October 13, 1999.

wasted the $100 million spent on the test and meant that it provided little useful data while delaying the program by several months.[23]

Problems are to be expected in high-technology development programs. They do not suggest that the technology itself is unworkable.[24] They do, however, add further evidence to the contention that the testing program is imprudently rushed. In light of the July 2000 failure, they have delayed the time at which the technology could be ready for actual deployment until at least 2006 in all likelihood, though successes in 2001 and 2002 have put the program partly back on track.

Perhaps 2007 or 2008 will prove more realistic in the end. Leaving aside the issue of the two failures in 2000, the development and testing program remains rushed even for a 2006 deployment. The total number of flight tests planned is modest for a major missile system; although the MX was tested only 19 times in the R&D phase, all other major strategic missile programs were each tested at least 25 times, the Tomahawk cruise missile was tested 74 times, and the Patriot—perhaps the most comparable, given its mission and its integration of missiles with an advanced radar—was tested 114 times.[25] As of this writing, the actual booster rocket to be used in the final system is still under development (tests to date have used stand-in missiles). That fact is significant, because the actual booster will have a greater acceleration than those rockets used in earlier tests—meaning that it will subject the kinetic kill vehicle to greater stresses than they have experienced so far. It is hardly inconceivable that the kill vehicle, with its multitude of sensors and small thrusters, could be damaged under high-g flight conditions, necessitating some redesign.[26] Making matters more complicated, the development of the booster has itself been delayed, potentially postponing flight tests using that technology.[27]

23. Elaine Sciolino, "Key Missile Parts Are Left Untested as Booster Fails," *New York Times*, July 9, 2000, p. 1; and Roberto Suro, "Failure of Booster Foiled Missile Test," *Washington Post*, July 9, 2000, p. A1.

24. Suro, "Missile Sensor Failed in Test's Final Seconds," p. A4; Bradley Graham, "U.S. Anti-Missile Test Is Latest in String of Successes," *Washington Post*, October 4, 1999, p. A1; and Garwin, "A Defense That Will Not Defend."

25. Statement of Kadish before the Senate Armed Services Committee, February 28, 2000, p. 6; and Forden, *Budgetary and Technical Implications*, p. 25.

26. William J. Broad, "A Missile Defense with Limits: The ABC's of the Clinton Plan," *New York Times*, June 30, 2000, p. A1.

27. Michael C. Sirak, "NMD Booster Schedule Delayed; First Flight May Be Pushed to Mid-2001," *Inside the Pentagon*, June 22, 2000, p. 3.

The Decoy Question. An even greater challenge, and one that will not be easily solved by a simple scheduling change in the NMD program, is to distinguish advanced countermeasures from actual warheads. This may not always be easy even within the atmosphere, but it is particularly difficult in the exoatmosphere, where NMD systems now under development would have to work.[28] In such regions of outer space, air resistance will not have had a chance to separate the generally lighter decoys from the heavier warheads (as it would be able to do for the Patriot and most other TMD systems, which operate within the atmosphere).[29] In outer space, even extremely light decoys would fly the same trajectory as true warheads, so speed could not be used to distinguish the real from the fake. To mimic the infrared heat signature of a warhead, thereby fooling sensors that measure temperature, decoys could be equipped with small heat generators, perhaps weighing only a pound. To fool radars or imaging infrared sensors, warheads and decoys alike could be placed inside radar-reflective balloons that would make it impossible to see their interiors.[30] Decoys could also be spun by small motors so that the balloons surrounding them rotated at the same speed as real warheads, in case the defense's radar was sensitive enough to pick up such motion.

Such countermeasures would almost surely doom a national missile defense of the type now under consideration and development in the United States. Although the Ballistic Missile Defense Organization claims to know how to defeat them, its argument is unpersuasive for those decoys with the characteristics mentioned above. For example, it cites radars that can resolve the details of an object's shape and the polarization of its radar return.[31] However, such radars are physically incapable of distinguishing a radar-reflective balloon enclosing a spinning warhead from one containing a spinning decoy, since both objects give the same

28. George N. Lewis and Theodore A. Postol, "Future Challenges to Ballistic Missile Defense," *IEEE Spectrum*, vol. 34 (September 1997), pp. 60–68.

29. See Welch and others, "Report of the Panel on Reducing Risk in Ballistic Missile Defense Flight Test Programs," p. 56; and Elaine M. Grossman, "Rumsfeld Commission Member Sticks to Guns on Opposing Defenses," *Inside the Pentagon*, July 30, 1998, pp. 19–20.

30. Testimony of David C. Wright on the technical readiness of national missile defenses before the U.S. Senate Committee on Foreign Relations, May 4, 1999; and testimony of Richard L. Garwin before same committee on same date.

31. See Lieutenant General Ron Kadish, "Clearing the Fog: Eliminating Misconceptions in the Debate about Deploying a Limited National Missile Defense System," *Armed Forces Journal International* (June 2000), p. 59.

radar returns. They would also doom other exoatmospheric interceptors such as the Navy Theater Wide TMD system, a point not sufficiently appreciated by advocates of that program.[32]

Defenders of the Clinton administration's system often note that Britain had considerable difficulty in developing ballistic-missile countermeasures with its so-called Chevaline system. However, that system, designed to help warheads penetrate an endoatmospheric or terminal defense, was far more complex than what North Korea, Iran, Iraq, or some other country would need to defeat the planned U.S. system. Simple decoys are just fine in outer space; far more complex decoys are needed to mimic heavy warheads within the Earth's atmosphere. Unfortunately for the United States, it is in outer space where its planned system would have to detect, discriminate, and destroy enemy missile warheads.

Nonetheless, the news is not entirely bleak. It is not trivial to develop even relatively simple decoy technology, as well as the means to dispense decoys in space. After all, the superpowers did not develop MIRV technology for releasing several independently targeted warheads from a single missile until they had had long-range ICBMs for a decade or so. (MIRV technology is more complex than decoy technology, since it must send warheads on more accurate trajectories than are necessary for decoys, but there are important parallels.) Thus it could take a country such as North Korea quite a while to perfect the needed countermeasures. Specifically, an adversary may need realistic flight testing to make sure its decoys would work, and a state without the resources or diplomatic space to test very much may not succeed in any limited period of time.[33] In its July 2000 NMD test, even a country with the technological sophistication and missile testing experience of the United States failed to get its countermeasure to work properly. Specifically, the balloon decoy failed to inflate, making it straightforward for radar to distinguish it from the real warhead.[34]

Another point in defense of the Pentagon's current program: even though it could not intercept bomblets filled with chemical or biological agents, as critics have often pointed out, such attacks would probably be

32. Andrew M. Sessler and others, *Countermeasures: A Technical Evaluation of the Operational Effectiveness of the Planned U.S. National Missile Defense System* (Cambridge, Mass: Union of Concerned Scientists, April 2000).

33. Ibid., pp. 145–48.

34. Sciolino, "Key Missile Parts Are Left Untested as Booster Fails," p. 1; and Suro, "Failure of Booster Foiled Missile Test," p. A1.

Table 5-4. *Lethality of Biological Agents*

Disease	Incubation time (days)	Fatalities (percent)
Anthrax	1–5	20–80
Plague	1–5	90
Tularemia	10–14	5–20
Cholera	2–5	25–50
Venezuelan equine encephalitis	2–5	Less than 1
Q fever	12–21	Less than 1
Botulism	3	30
Staphylococcal enterotoxemia (food poisoning)	1–6	Less than 1
Multiple organ toxicity	Dose dependent	Dose dependent

Source: Institute for National Strategic Studies, National Defense University, *Strategic Assessment 1998: Engaging Power for Peace* (Government Printing Office, 1998), p. 174.

less dangerous than those with nuclear warheads. Chemical weapons are intrinsically less lethal than nuclear or biological agents. Biological agents are most lethal when distributed over a wide area by a device like a crop duster. They also tend to be most effective when the targeted country does not realize it has been attacked with biological agents until victims begin to show symptoms of disease, at which point it is already too late to treat most of them effectively for a number of agents (see table 5-4). Ballistic missiles are therefore less than ideal means of delivering such agents.[35]

All in all, a light nationwide missile defense using exoatmospheric missiles will have serious limitations. But it may still provide some capability against the type of threat a North Korea, Iraq, or Iran could develop in the next decade or so—assuming that China and Russia do not retaliate against a U.S. NMD deployment by transferring countermeasure technology to such states.[36] It also has the advantage of providing some type of defense capability against both Mideast and Korean threats, and it has the political reliability and physical security of being based on U.S. soil. For these reasons, the Clinton administration's plan to build such a defense was not entirely without merit—even if its exclusive reliance on

35. Defense Science Board 1998 Summer Study Task Force, *Joint Operations Superiority in the 21st Century* (Department of Defense, 1998), pp. 97–100; and Office of Technology Assessment, *Proliferation of Weapons of Mass Destruction* (GPO, 1993), p. 52.

36. Drogin and Marshall, "Missile Shield's Destabilizing Potential Cited," p. A1.

this system and its preference to rush to build it in Alaska were probably mistaken. Up to fifty such interceptors based in North Dakota make sense, however.

Boost-Phase Endoatmospheric Intercept

To make it much tougher for an enemy to defeat NMD with fairly simple countermeasures, and to provide defense for regions outside of North America as well, the United States could develop interceptor missiles for boost-phase defense. It might also consider using the airborne laser, originally being developed for TMD, in an NMD mode.

Boost-phase interceptors would be medium-sized, extremely fast-burn rockets that would be fired very quickly after an enemy launch was detected, catching up with the enemy ICBM while it was still in its burn or boost phase, either within the atmosphere or just outside it.[37] At that point, the enemy ICBM—essentially a large, burning gas tank—would be highly vulnerable and easy to see and hit. It would also not have had the chance to deploy decoys or countermeasures, since they would not yet be up to the speeds needed for intercontinental trajectories. While an advanced enemy could build fast-burn ICBMs to counter such a defense system, these types of ICBMs are much harder to develop than current missiles owned by countries such as North Korea, Iraq, and Iran.[38]

One drawback to the boost-phase defense concept is that hitting the rocket rather than the (nuclear) warhead would not necessarily destroy the warhead. The warhead could then continue onward, possibly detonating—and, most likely, at least scattering radioactive material where it landed. However, since the rocket would have been hit before completing its boost phase, the warhead would almost certainly not have enough speed to reach densely populated parts of North America, most likely landing instead in arctic waters or the tundra of Alaska, Canada, or Russia, if launched from North Korea. While far from ideal, chances are

37. See Richard L. Garwin, "The Wrong Plan," *Bulletin of the Atomic Scientists,* vol. 56, no. 2 (March/April 2000), pp. 36–41; and Garwin, "A Defense That Will Not Defend." Garwin estimates the weight of such a boost-phase interceptor, which need not carry a heavy payload, at fourteen tons; by contrast, existing U.S. ICBMs and SLBMs generally weigh thirty to one hundred tons.

38. Theodore A. Postol, "A Russian-U.S. Boost-Phase Defense to Defend Russia and the US from Postulated Rogue-State ICBMs," Briefing paper presented at Carnegie Endowment for International Peace, Washington, D.C., October 12, 1999.

low that anyone would be killed as a result, and chances are almost zero that any appreciable number of individuals would lose their lives. The risks would be greater for a missile launched from the Middle East, since its warhead could wind up landing in Europe, but even there the chances that the warhead would land near a heavily populated area would be only a few percent.

Such defense systems could be deployed near the Korean peninsula, the Middle East, and other potential trouble spots, provided appropriate basing on land or at sea were available. Otherwise, airborne boost-phase defenses might be deployed at a time when the United States had established air superiority, but that option would probably exist only after a major crisis or war had begun.

Because the U.S. intelligence community considers a potential North Korean threat most imminent—a judgment reaffirmed by the 1998 Taepo Dong I launch—a boost-phase defense might first be based in Northeast Asia, either on barges in the Sea of Japan or on land in the general vicinity of Vladivostok, Russia (missiles optimized for boost-phase defense would probably be too large to place in the vertical launch tubes of existing warships).

Deployments focused on the Middle East could follow, if necessary. Iraq is the easier case here. Iraqi missiles might be countered by a base in eastern Turkey, which could also defend the United States (and large parts of Europe) against launches from certain parts of Iran.[39] On the whole, however, Iran would be a tougher case. Given the country's size, defending against a missile launch by that country would require two boost-phase interceptor bases. One might be north of Iran—in the Caspian Sea, Turkmenistan, or possibly Kazakhstan or Uzbekistan. The other would be south of it—in the Persian Gulf or the Sea of Oman, or possibly on land in Oman, Saudi Arabia, or the United Arab Emirates. If the base north of Iran were not available, the only remaining option (short of the longer-term option of space-based boost-phase defense) might be to deploy airborne interceptors or airborne lasers. Those options would be practical only if the United States had established air superiority, meaning that they would probably become practical only during the course of a war.

Such boost-phase systems do, however, appear within reach technologically—quite possibly on roughly the time horizon of the Clinton

39. Presentation by Richard L. Garwin, Harvard-CSIS Ballistic Missile Defense Conference, Cambridge, Mass., May 11, 2000.

administration's planned C1 capability. Land-based and sea-based concepts would require a new interceptor of extremely high speed, but that could be built without radically new types of technologies. Missiles like the Trident II or D5 were built within a decade, and this boost-phase missile likely could be as well (though the challenges would admittedly be different in its case, relating more to speed than to precise guidance).[40] In fact, as early as the early 1980s, a major U.S. defense contractor was proposing a missile that could reach ICBM-range speeds of seven kilometers per second in just fifty seconds of boosting, in contrast to the boost times of seventy to one hundred seconds commonly foreseen for the slightly faster boost-phase interceptors.[41]

A boost-phase defense would not require a sophisticated sensor network on a par with what is required for the Clinton administration's program. In fact, its main infrared seeker would have such a hot target to home on that it could use relatively inexpensive, simple, short-wavelength devices rather than the long-wavelength infrared (IR) seeker needed on the exoatmospheric interceptor system (to say nothing of the long-range radars needed by the latter system).[42] Depending on the clarity of the IR sensor, however, it might need a small radar for final homing in order to differentiate the missile body from the booster plume.

Nor would a boost-phase defense likely be as expensive as the current NMD program now in the works. The interceptor rockets would probably be more expensive than those envisioned for the Clinton administration's planned system (about $18 million apiece, according to the latest estimates of the Congressional Budget Office), but they would probably not be on a par with expensive intercontinental ballistic missiles (ICBMs) and submarine launched ballistic missiles (SLBMs), which are much larger systems. (The MX, for example, cost more than $100 million per copy.)[43]

40. See, for example, Thomas B. Cochran, William M. Arkin, and Milton M. Hoenig, *Nuclear Weapons Databook, Volume I: U.S. Nuclear Forces and Capabilities* (Cambridge, Mass.: Ballinger, 1984), p. 145.

41. The Martin-Marietta Corporation (now part of Lockheed Martin) prepared such a study for the Fletcher Panel, an official advisory group evaluating technologies for national missile defense for the Pentagon. See John Tirman, ed., *The Fallacy of Star Wars* (Vintage, 1984), p. 62.

42. Theodore Postol, "Hitting Them Where It Works," *Foreign Policy*, no. 117 (Winter 1999–2000), pp. 132–33.

43. Congressional Budget Office, *The START Treaty and Beyond* (October 1991), p. 139; and Forden, *Budgetary and Technical Implications of the Administration's Plan for National Missile Defense*, p. 12.

But the rest of the NMD technology—which accounted for about two-thirds of the costs of the Clinton administration's C1 proposal and three-fourths of the cost of the C3[44]—would be far simpler for boost-phase defense.

The limited geographic scope of boost-phase defenses is at once one of the concept's greatest strengths and its greatest weakness. Basing a defense on foreign territory, especially that of a non-ally, raises questions about its dependability in wartime. Land-based boost-phase systems in particular would be difficult to move if new threats developed. Sea-based boost-phase systems would not be useful against missiles from all potential threats, since not all are near international or friendly waters. However, these characteristics should also make boost-phase defenses less troubling to Moscow (and Beijing) than the planned Clinton administration system, since boost-phase defenses would not work against missiles launched from the interior of Asia. Even though they could in theory be reconfigured to work against a missile after it had stopped burning, they would need new sensors as well as testing to gain such capabilities.[45] Missile defense barges would also have a hard time avoiding attack by cruise missile or submarine if deployed near a large, militarily advanced country. Russian president Vladimir Putin appears to agree with these arguments, if his proposals shortly after his June 2000 Moscow summit with President Clinton are a fair and sincere indication.[46]

The coverage zone of the boost-phase defense would be about 1,000 kilometers beyond where interceptors were based, since the interceptors would have only two to three minutes to destroy their targets. (They might be launched a minute or a minute and a half after the enemy ICBM was fired and would accelerate for seventy to one hundred seconds before cruising at roughly eight to nine kilometers per second thereafter.)[47] ICBMs launched from central, western, and southern China or most of Russia and headed over the North Pole would thus be beyond the range of interceptors based near the Korean peninsula, since

---

44. Forden, *Budgetary and Technical Implications of the Administration's Plan for National Missile Defense,* p. 10.

45. Richard L. Garwin, "Effectiveness of Proposed National Missile Defense against ICBMs from North Korea," March 17, 1999 [http://sun00781.dn.net/rlg/990317-nmd.htm (December 27, 2000)].

46. Alessandra Stanley, "Putin Goes to Rome to Promote Russian Arms Control Alternative," *New York Times,* June 6, 2000, p. A1.

47. Postol, "Hitting Them Where It Works," pp. 132–33.

the ICBMs would have completed their boost phase before interceptors could reach them.

In theory, these boost-phase defenses could be used to shoot down some Chinese missiles headed at Taiwan. They would be very expensive devices to use in such missions, however, and they would almost certainly not be produced or deployed in sufficient numbers to constitute a serious counter to a PRC missile force numbering in the several hundreds of weapons. In addition, short-range missiles based near the Taiwan Strait would not have long enough boost phases to provide time for these types of defenses to work in any case.

As noted, boost-phase defenses could hypothetically also be based on unmanned, long-endurance aircraft and flown in orbits over enemy territory. This approach would presumably only work during wartime, when the United States could establish air supremacy. Although the interceptors could be flown at high altitude, even countries like North Korea and Iraq could probably find ways to threaten them unless U.S. fighters provided cover for the planes hosting the interceptors. This approach could add an extra element of redundancy and could use slower, smaller, cheaper interceptors than boost-phase defenses operating from sea level.[48]

Offensive Nuclear Weapons

The subject of national missile defense should not be considered without tying it to the question of offensive nuclear weapons. Even if a limited NMD system does not impinge seriously on the implementation of the START II accords, it may eventually have implications for the negotiation of START III and any follow-on accords.

This section proposes a limit on U.S. and Russian nuclear stockpiles of one thousand warheads of all types per country—including strategic and short-range warheads, as well as deployed and reserve warheads. These numbers would represent not only at least a threefold reduction in strategic arsenals relative to START II, and at least a twofold cut relative to the Bush administration's plans as revealed in its recent nuclear posture

---

48. See Dean Wilkening, "Airborne Boost-Phase Ballistic Missile Defense," Briefing Slides (Stanford University, Center for International Security and Cooperation, May 9, 2000).

review, but also more than a tenfold overall reduction in superpower nuclear stockpiles.[49]

Limits on Strategic Arsenals

As of early 2000, prevailing wisdom in the U.S. government still embraced the need for enormous numbers of nuclear warheads. Official strategic inventories were estimated at about 8,000 warheads for the United States and 6,500 for Russia, in addition to many thousands more tactical and reserve warheads on both sides. The strategic numbers should be cut at least in half by a future U.S.-Russian accord; Russia will have to reduce its inventory to some extent in any event, given its budgetary situation and its aging strategic systems. However, discussion of reductions below about 2,000 to 2,500 strategic warheads has met resistance within the U.S. defense establishment.[50]

Nevertheless, it is eminently reasonable to consider cuts to a total of one thousand nuclear warheads of all types during the tenure of the new administration. In strategic terms, cutting U.S. and Russian arsenals to one thousand warheads on each side has a simple and compelling logic. It is a high enough number to allow the two countries to retain their numerical superiority for now—allowing these cuts to proceed without involving China, Britain, France, and other nuclear powers. These countries, as well as Israel, each have nuclear arsenals comprising up to a few hundred nuclear weapons. Representing at least a threefold cut in deployed strategic forces from START II levels, and at least a tenfold overall cut in each country's nuclear arsenal, a level of one thousand warheads is nonetheless significantly higher than that of any of the other powers.

Such deep cuts could elicit major objections from the American and perhaps the Russian defense establishments. Some would argue that this one-thousand-warhead ceiling would leave the United States unable to cover targets adequately, thus weakening deterrence. Such an argument needs to be attacked head-on. There is much to debate in the post–cold

---

49. This section draws heavily on Janne Nolan and Michael O'Hanlon, "Reducing Nuclear Arms in the Next Administration," *National Security Studies Quarterly*, vol. 6, no. 3 (Summer 2000), pp. 91–102.

50. See "Factfile: U.S. and Soviet/Russian Strategic Nuclear Forces," *Arms Control Today*, vol. 30, no. 4 (May 2000), p. 50.

war world about what nuclear weapons are for, the types of scenarios in which they might be useful, and whether their actual use could ever be moral. However, there is no serious argument for nuclear strikes involving thousands of warheads under any circumstances. Some Pentagon planners have allowed themselves to subscribe to a nuclear theology that gains its support from bureaucratic momentum rather than from sound political-military analysis.

Cutting to one thousand warheads on a side would hardly force the United States to resort to a strategy of targeting only population centers in its deterrence doctrine. Any enemy's major industrial centers could be attacked with at most dozens of warheads; its key petroleum and metals industries with a similar number; virtually all of its fixed conventional military infrastructure with hundreds.[51] Some such targets would probably be avoided in any attack, given their proximity to cities, but even if the entirety of these target sets were to be destroyed, warhead totals in the dozens or at most the low hundreds would more than suffice.

To put it differently, imagine a conflict scenario against the type of country the United States might really go to war with in the years ahead. If North Korea or Iraq attacked the United States or its allies with biological or nuclear arms, for example, the United States might consider nuclear retaliation under some circumstances. But a morally proportionate, or strategically savvy, response could not cause the obliteration of an enemy's society and population, let alone cause collateral harm (such as radiation effects) on a proximate ally like South Korea. Even severe reprisals would have to be judicious and careful. In theory a few nuclear weapons might be detonated over North Korea's invasion corridors around the demilitarized zone (DMZ), where DPRK troops would be concentrated (using airbursts so as to reduce the risk of fallout). Or the United States could attack those Iraqi military airfields, depots, and rail and road lines where civilian casualties could perhaps be minimized, again using airbursts. Even in the dreadful scenario of a nuclear war against China growing out of a conflict over Taiwan, nothing more than very limited strikes—together with retention of a capacity to target Chinese cities as a deterrent against PRC attacks against U.S. cities—could ever possibly make any sense.

51. See Frederic S. Nyland, "Exemplary Industrial Targets for Controlled Conflict," in Desmond Ball and Jeffrey Richelson, eds., *Strategic Nuclear Targeting* (Cornell University Press, 1986), p. 215; Joshua M. Epstein, *Measuring Military Power: The Soviet Air Threat to Europe* (Princeton University Press, 1984), p. 174; and Congressional Budget Office, *The START Treaty and Beyond,* pp. 8–26.

This line of reasoning is not meant to prejudge the desirability of U.S. nuclear retaliation in any circumstance. Even granting the possibility of a nuclear retaliatory blow, however, there is no credible scenario that would involve thousands of warheads or more. Indeed, there is no credible scenario that would require anything close to one thousand. It is worth considering the sobering perspective of the late McGeorge Bundy, who experienced the Cuban and Berlin nuclear crises firsthand as President John F. Kennedy's national security adviser:

> Given the warheads currently deployed, just one incoming strategic warhead on just one strictly military target—a missile silo perhaps, or a submarine base—would be the worst event for either government since World War II. Ten warheads on ten such targets would be much more than ten times worse, presenting not only immediate and hideous devastation, but questions of the utmost urgency and foreboding about the next decisions of both sides. A hundred warheads, on no-matter-what targets, would be an instant disaster still more terrible. A thousand warheads would be a catastrophe beyond all human experience. . . . As I put it twenty years ago, "There is no level of superiority which will make a strategic first strike between the two great states anything but an act of utter folly."[52]

Possible Force Postures

A one-thousand-warhead nuclear posture should be guided by the main goal of ensuring stability and the secondary goal of saving money. Although the allocation of forces could occur in any number of ways—and rightfully should be decided on within the context of a full review of nuclear posture involving senior political and military authorities and spearheaded by the president—these two criteria seem paramount.

One possible posture would consist of the following. On the U.S. side, the bulk of the force would probably be deployed at sea, given the survivability of American ballistic-missile submarines. For example, six Trident submarines might each carry 120 warheads—or five warheads per missile, as envisioned under START II—for a total of 720 warheads at sea. That number of submarines would ensure that at least two could be maintained

---

52. McGeorge Bundy, *Danger and Survival* (Random House, 1988), p. 589.

at sea at a time, one in the Atlantic Fleet and one in the Pacific Fleet (two U.S. ballistic-missile submarine bases could be retained as a hedge against terrorist attack). Some 150 single-warhead Minuteman III missiles could be kept as well, providing warheads for limited-attack options and constituting a second independent basing mechanism that would be reasonably survivable against any missiles but Russia's best (even against those, at least 10 to 20 of the 150 would likely survive an all-out first strike). Finally, some one hundred warheads could be retained for the bomber and tactical aircraft force—though new bomber "counting rules" would be needed in any formal treaty so that the United States would not have to eliminate aircraft that it will need for conventional military missions as well.

Alternatively, there is no compelling reason why the nuclear triad—of ICBMs, SLBMs, and long-range bombers—absolutely must be retained into the future. Unlike the situation in the cold war, there is little reason to think that any leg of the existing triad will be fundamentally threatened by adversarial capabilities in the foreseeable future, much less two of them at a time. Certainly the submarine force should be kept under any circumstances, given its inherent survivability. One might argue that ICBMs should be the other element of a possible two-leg U.S. nuclear force posture, since they are secure, reliable, always ready, and at this point rather inexpensive (since they have been purchased). However, air-delivered warheads probably offer greater advantages. For one thing, they can be delivered precisely in a tactical setting. For another, they may someday become the weapon of choice, if future arms control agreements ban ballistic missiles because of their rapid speed and their inability to be recalled once launched. If the United States is to consider giving up its nuclear triad, therefore, it should probably eliminate its ICBMs. But the costs of maintaining a small ICBM force may be modest enough for the foreseeable future that this issue need not be raised for a number of years.

On the Russian side, more weapons would probably be kept in the land-based missile force, given the rather poor state of its missile submarine (SSBN) fleet. A modest inventory of weapons might be retained that could be used by bombers and tactical fighter jets as well, given Moscow's concerns about the need to defend its borders using nuclear deterrence and the "first use" doctrine. While one would prefer that Russia reduce its reliance on nuclear forces over time, its conventional military forces are currently in such poor condition that it may be unrealistic to expect

Moscow to forgo nuclear options in planning for its territorial defense in the near term.[53]

Several points should be made concerning nuclear warheads themselves. First, they almost certainly do not require testing to ensure reliability. As former bomb designer Richard Garwin has argued, rather than rely exclusively on science-based stockpile stewardship, the United States should also rely on the simpler concept of engineering-based stewardship in which a certain percentage of the arsenal is simply rebuilt every year, to original specifications and with original materials. This approach should make it possible to keep the arsenal fully reliable. If absolutely necessary, backup could be provided by building a modest number of lower-yield, simple, rugged designs (such as gun-assembled uranium weapons) that can be confidently built without further testing, as Los Alamos physicist Stephen Younger has argued. Finally, such weapons might also be modified without testing for attacking underground targets (as the B-61 already was), should more such capability be considered necessary. Admittedly, some new types of warheads—such as those creating certain specialized electromagnetic effects or x-ray beams—could probably not be developed without testing. However, the United States does not need to test to retain a credible nuclear arsenal of some basic type.

U.S. nuclear weapons could also be maintained with a smaller nuclear warhead production complex if the arsenal were reduced to 1,000 warheads.[54] The arsenal proposed here would not require nuclear testing. In addition, it could be maintained at a savings of at least several hundred million dollars a year in Department of Energy accounts, on top of savings of roughly $2 billion to $3 billion in the Department of Defense budget.[55]

Any proposal for an ambitious arms control regime naturally raises the question of verification. It would be good, though naturally not perfect, for this type of proposal. The challenge of verifying limits on numbers of strategic weapons launchers would be straightforward and build directly on provisions in the existing START treaties. Some potential for rapid

53. On Russia's current defense doctrine, see "Russia's Military Doctrine," *Arms Control Today*, vol. 30, no. 4 (May 2000), pp. 29–38.

54. Stephen M. Younger, *Nuclear Weapons in the Twenty-First Century* (Los Alamos, N.M.: Los Alamos National Laboratory, 2000).

55. Michael O'Hanlon, *The Bomb's Custodians* (Washington: Congressional Budget Office, 1994), p. xiv.

breakout would remain, given the downloading of missile warheads and redefining of many bombers as non-nuclear platforms that the proposed framework requires. However, monitored limits on actual warhead inventories, a precedent in arms control agreements, would provide an additional, independent basis for ensuring compliance.

There are caveats to this positive assessment. Given uncertainties about the present size of Russia's nuclear arsenal, for example, it is hard to believe that monitoring of warheads and fissile material can be particularly effective until an accurate accounting has taken place. At the same time, given the increased openness of Russian society and the years of collaborative effort between the United States and Russia in securing nuclear warheads and materials, monitoring would make it very hard for either side to cheat significantly.[56] The need for tritium for advanced thermonuclear weapons may provide an additional source of reassurance, as its production can be monitored too.

In the end, it is possible that some small-scale cheating would fail to be detected, but it would not be militarily significant. The United States would retain invulnerable ballistic missile submarines, on which it would most likely base the majority of its total nuclear arsenal, denying Russia any meaningful military advantage from cheating.

In addition, the superpower relationship is not what it once was. Nuclear coercion based on perceptions of superiority, never particularly plausible even in the past, is entirely implausible today. When Russia briefly rattled its nuclear saber over NATO's decision to go to war against Serbia in 1999, for example, the threat was not taken seriously, and no one consulted the precise state of the nuclear balance for guidance on whether to take it seriously. For the types of security challenges that the United States and Russia will face in the post–cold war world, the details of their nuclear relationship will be unimportant—assuming that each side retains survivable second-strike forces.

Conclusion

In this decade, the United States should probably deploy a thin, two-layered national missile defense, while also making various missile

---

56. See Frank von Hippel and Roald Z. Sagdeev, eds., *Reversing the Arms Race* (New York: Gordon and Breach, 1990).

defense technologies available for sale to its allies (and perhaps even to Russia). It should base a defense of the type now envisioned for deployment in Alaska in North Dakota instead and consider deploying only twenty-five to fifty interceptors there, given the small size of the foreseeable North Korean, Iranian, and Iraqi threats. Meanwhile, and most important, it should also build boost-phase interceptor missiles and deploy a modest number near North Korea, unless diplomacy resolves the Northeast Asian confrontation. Ultimately, others might also be deployed in the Mideast region, making for a global total of up to 150 interceptors, as James Lindsay and I argue in *Defending America* (Brookings, 2001).

To show its good faith, save money, and move away from the dangerous nuclear war-fighting philosophies of the cold war, the United States should couple its efforts to deploy NMD with proposals for deep cuts in offensive nuclear forces. Ideally, it would also take nuclear forces off high alert and ratify the Comprehensive Test Ban Treaty.

SIX

Helping Taiwan Defeat a Chinese Blockade

Possible war between Taiwan and the People's Republic of China (PRC) has been grossly understudied in defense circles in the United States. In the past decade, American war planners devoted the overwhelming majority of their attention to Korea and the Persian Gulf, even though war in the Taiwan Strait may now be just as likely—and at least as foreboding.[1]

1. The two-war framework began with the Bush administration's 1991 "Base Force" concept. It envisioned a number of scenarios—including a Russian attack on a Baltic state—but ultimately highlighted simultaneous conflicts in the Persian Gulf and Korea as the most demanding likely challenge to U.S. military forces. The Clinton administration's 1993 Bottom-Up Review focused even more narrowly on the two-war scenario, optimizing U.S. military force structure to address possible overlapping conflicts in Korea and the Persian Gulf region. Capabilities for peace operations and other small contingencies were viewed simply as lesser requirements to be handled by the same force structure. Finally, the Clinton administration's 1997 Quadrennial Defense Review paid lip service to a broader range of missions, but ultimately fell back on the two-war framework as well for most planning purposes. See Chairman of the Joint Chiefs of Staff Colin L. Powell, "The Base Force: A Total Force," briefing paper presented to the House Appropriations Committee's Subcommittee on Defense, September 25, 1991; Patrick E. Tyler, "Seven Hypothetical Conflicts Foreseen by the Pentagon," *New York Times,* February 17, 1992, p. A8; Barton Gellman, "Pentagon War Scenario Spotlights Russia," *Washington Post,* February 20, 1992, p. A1; William W. Kaufmann, *Assessing the Base Force: How Much Is Too Much?* (Brookings, 1992), pp. 48–51; Les Aspin, *Report on the Bottom-Up Review* (Department of Defense, September 1993), pp. 7–23; and William S. Cohen, *Report of the Quadrennial Defense Review* (Department of Defense, May 1997), pp. 11–13.

This chapter analyzes both an attempted Chinese invasion of Taiwan and a Chinese naval blockade against Taiwan. It shows that while the PRC does not have a plausible invasion capability, Taiwan might need U.S. help to break a naval blockade. A missile attack would cause panic, and tragic loss of life, on Taiwan; massive cyberwarfare strikes could also cause great disruption. Unless missiles were equipped with weapons of mass destruction, however, such attacks would be unlikely to put Taiwan's basic survival or even its long-term economic well-being at risk. The blockade scenario, by contrast, may be more serious.

The overall message of this analysis is reassuring for force-planning and defense-budget purposes: U.S. armed forces are already adequately postured to intercede decisively in a war between Taiwan and China for those types of plausible conflicts in which U.S. military help might be needed. Specifically, a subset of those American forces that would normally be allocated for a major theater war—primarily naval components—should be adequate to break a PRC blockade rapidly and with only modest risk of substantial numbers of American casualties. Nevertheless, this issue is important enough, and understudied enough, that the arguments should be made explicit so that others can assess them for themselves.

Moreover, there is hardly any cause for complacency in broader strategic terms. Even if the United States, working with Taiwan, could break a Chinese blockade, sink much of the PRC naval fleet near Taiwan, and at least temporarily disable Chinese airfields and ports in the vicinity of the Strait, it could not plausibly eliminate all PRC means of waging lower-level war against Taiwan thereafter. Nor, on the other extreme, could it prevent China from taking steps that risked escalation, perhaps even to nuclear levels. As unlikely as the latter concerns may be, they cannot simply be dismissed, especially given the importance of Taiwan to China. These considerations argue for a U.S. war plan that is assertive enough to achieve victory decisively, yet restrained enough to minimize China's incentives either to carry on the war at a low level indefinitely or to escalate. Specifically, the United States and Taiwan would be well advised to limit any strikes against the Chinese homeland to coastal regions near Taiwan and to those assets directly involved in the blockade effort. These considerations also suggest that, even if war were to begin, it might not be wise to insist on Taiwanese independence as the essential end state of the battle. Such an extremist war aim could encourage extremist responses from Beijing, at either the low end (such as conventional missiles fired sporadically) or the high end (nuclear threats or worse) of the conflict spectrum. Washington and Taipei might have to settle for the political status quo ante, even if they could win a decisive conventional military victory.[2]

The Strategic Backdrop

The basic situation between China and Taiwan is delicate to say the least. China insists that Taiwan is a part of its territory, yet Taiwan refuses to be ruled by Beijing, and neither side shows any signs of changing these core views. Taiwan's president, Chen Shui-bian, was elected principally on a domestic-reform agenda. Although he has stated that he will avoid declaring independence from the PRC unless Taiwan is attacked, nonetheless his Democratic Progressive Party has long called for just such a declaration of independence—and Chen is willing to abstain from making one only on the grounds that it is unnecessary, given that Taiwan is already sovereign in his eyes.[3] This attempt to have it both ways may or may not prove sustainable indefinitely.

Beijing has offered a sweet-and-sour policy of its own. It has welcomed President Chen's restraint on the one hand, and even offered to view Taiwan as an equal partner in negotiations rather than as a local, renegade government. On the other hand, it has also issued a white paper declaring that it will not patiently wait for reunification indefinitely; it has stated that Chen must publicly renounce his party's stand on independence and explicitly reaffirm the "one China" principle; and it has reminded the international community that it reserves the right to use force against Taiwan to "safeguard its own sovereignty and territorial integrity."[4] Chinese officials recognize that their military will not excel until their economy develops further—a conclusion that would seem to

2. Richard K. Betts and Thomas J. Christensen, "China: Getting the Questions Right," *National Interest*, vol. 62 (Winter 2000/01), pp. 25–28.

3. Chas. W. Freeman Jr., "Preventing War in the Taiwan Strait: Restraining Taiwan—and Beijing," *Foreign Affairs*, vol. 77, no. 4 (July/August 1998), pp. 7–9; and John Pomfret, "Taiwan Takes Goodwill Steps toward China," *Washington Post*, March 22, 2000, p. 22.

4. Information Office of the State Council of the People's Republic of China, "The One-China Principle and the Taiwan Issue" (http://chinadaily.com/cn/net/highlights/taiwan/whitepaper.html [Beijing, China, March 2000]); Information Office of the State Council of the People's Republic of China, "China's National Defense" (Beijing, China, July 1998); and John Pomfret, "Beijing Stresses 'One China' to Taiwan," *Washington Post*, April 28, 2000, p. A24.

counsel strategic patience on Beijing's part.[5] However, they also understand that Taiwan is improving its own technology base and its armed forces, and they note pro-independence trends among the Taiwanese population. These latter concerns argue against patience.[6]

One might hope leaders in Beijing would be deterred from any attack on Taiwan out of fear of the enormous political and economic consequences that would follow. Surely, global trade and investment with China would suffer for years to come, regardless of the outcome of the battle. However, China may believe that western countries are so focused on making money that they would soon forgive and forget any war that had only limited direct effect on them. Failing that, they might feel that they had no choice but to attack Taiwan under certain circumstances, given the emotions that surround the Taiwan issue in China and the fear among some in Beijing that letting Taiwan go could encourage other separatist movements in their country.

Any war between China and Taiwan could easily involve the United States. Under the 1979 Taiwan Relations Act, official U.S. law stipulates that the United States would view any conflict over Taiwan with "grave concern"—and suggests a possible U.S. military response, even if neither that act nor any other U.S. law or treaty actually requires such a response.[7] In fact, the ambiguity is deliberate: Washington wishes to convey to Beijing that it might well respond to any attack against Taiwan, but simultaneously to signal Taipei that U.S. military support should not be taken for granted since, if it were, Taipei might be more tempted to declare independence. The goal is to maximize deterrence of China while minimizing any risk of emboldening Taiwan to take provocative actions. If war in the Taiwan Strait did occur, some U.S. military role would be more likely than not. In addition to the U.S. interest in Taiwan itself, there would be a broader strategic rationale for opposing any Chinese attack. If the United States stood by while a long-standing friend was in peril, the credibility of other American alliance commitments around the region, and indeed the world, would be called into question. That could possibly

5. See, for example, Major General Yang Chengyu, "Logistics Support for Regional Warfare," in Michael Pillsbury, ed., *Chinese Views of Future Warfare* (National Defense University Press, 1997), p. 184.

6. Wo-Lap Lam, "Act Soon if Force Is Needed, Says Jiang."

7. Harry Harding, *A Fragile Relationship: The United States and China since 1972* (Brookings, 1992), pp. 13–16, 82–87.

spur some allies to embark on undesirable military buildups as well as to develop nuclear weapons to ensure their own security; it could perhaps also embolden potential aggressors to attack U.S. interests overseas.

The 1995–96 Taiwan Strait crisis showed that, indeed, the United States does not take its interest in Taiwan's security lightly. A 1995 visit by former Taiwanese president Lee Teng-hui to his American alma mater, Cornell University, provoked China to conduct military exercises and fire missiles near Taiwan, leading the United States to send an aircraft carrier through the Strait that same December for the first time in seventeen years. In March 1996 the PRC launched more missiles near Taiwan; in response, the United States deployed two carriers in the vicinity as a show of strength.[8] Largely as a result of the 1995–96 crisis, many in the U.S. Congress have lost patience with the existing U.S. policy of strategic ambiguity and instead prefer a concrete commitment to aid Taiwan in the event of war. President Bush lent his voice to this trend when he stated early in 2001 that the United States would do "whatever it takes" to protect Taiwan. Taiwanese are aware of these dynamics in American politics, which may further embolden their pro-independence forces.[9]

War over Taiwan could theoretically take a number of forms. A PRC invasion scenario is the most dire possibility; it is the only way that China could physically seize the island, depose its government, and subjugate its people. However, it is not the most important scenario to consider for U.S. force planning purposes. China cannot conquer Taiwan even if the United States stays out of the conflict.

China's options would not end with invasion, however, especially if it were prepared to accept something short of Taiwan's unconditional surrender in any future war. If China caused Taiwan sufficient pain or economic loss, it might persuade Taipei to renounce aspirations for independence, accept some sort of confederal arrangement, and possibly

---

8. See William J. Perry, "Dealing with a Rising China," in Ashton B. Carter and William J. Perry, eds., *Preventive Defense: A New Security Strategy for America* (Brookings, 1999), pp. 92–99; and Richard D. Fisher Jr., "China's Missiles over the Taiwan Strait: A Political and Military Assessment," in James R. Lilley and Chuck Downs, eds., *Crisis in the Taiwan Strait* (National Defense University Press, 1997), pp. 167–75.

9. Owen Harries, "A Year of Debating China," *National Interest*, vol. 58 (Winter 1999/2000), pp. 145–47; Jonathan S. Landay, "How Far Would U.S. Go to Protect Taiwan?" *Christian Science Monitor*, September 3, 1999, p. 3; Freeman, "Preventing War in the Taiwan Strait," pp. 7–9; and Robert S. Ross, "Beijing as a Conservative Power," *Foreign Affairs*, vol. 76, no. 2 (March/April 1997), p. 39.

even accept certain limits on its domestic politics and its foreign policy. Such an outcome might or might not be particularly grievous; much would depend on the precise terms China demanded and the amount of damage Taiwan incurred before reaching a deal. Even if scenarios of this sort are of less concern than an invasion, they are nonetheless quite worrisome.

As one means of attempting to coerce Taiwan, China could undertake missile attacks. Missile strikes would be difficult to stop. If the United States had proper military assets in place in advance—most notably, Aegis ships with ballistic missile defense—it could help limit the number of PRC missiles able to strike Taiwanese targets. However, those defense capabilities are not expected to be available for several years. Some PRC missiles would still get through defenses even thereafter. Despite this vulnerability, missiles would probably not cause great harm unless they were carrying weapons of mass destruction. They could cause temporary shock, and perhaps hundreds or even a few thousands of civilian casualties—but then China would have spent its capability, and the tables would probably begin to turn in Taiwan's favor.

More worrisome would be even a limited, partially effective blockade. If carried out by China's best submarines alone, such an action could sink a few commercial ships, intimidate large numbers of others into not making the voyage to Taiwan, and force up shipping insurance rates for any ships that were still willing to risk the journey. The combination of these effects would quite probably cause a serious and prolonged economic downturn on the island. U.S. help would likely be needed to end it promptly.

The China-Taiwan Military Balance

China has the world's largest military by far. It is roughly tied with Russia, Japan, the United Kingdom, and France for the claim to second greatest level of military spending in the world, based on the most widely accepted estimates of its actual expenditures (as opposed to its misleadingly low official figures).[10] Taiwan has a much smaller and considerably

10. U.S. government estimates of China's military spending are typically about twice as great as those of the International Institute for Strategic Studies. See Arms Control and Disarmament Agency, *World Military Expenditures and Arms Transfers 1996* (Government Printing Office, 1997), p. 65; for an explanation of the methodologies involved, see

Table 6-1. *Basic Military Data, Late 1990s*

Type of military capability	China	Taiwan	United States
Population	1.24 billion	22 million	273 million
Active-duty military personnel	2.5 million	376,000	1.37 million
Reserve personnel	1.2 million	1.66 million	1.3 million
Active Army/Marines	1.8 million	240,000	640,000
Active Air Force	420,000	68,000	361,000
Active Navy	230,000	68,000	370,000
Annual defense spending, 1998	$38 billion	$14 billion	$270 billion
Heavy armor, including tanks, armored personnel carriers, large artillery	30,000	4,000	35,000
Combat jets (number of advanced jets)	4,000 (50)	600 (340)	4,000 (4,000)
Major ships (number of aircraft carriers)	53 (0)	37 (0)	130 (12)
Attack submarines (number of advanced subs)	69 (9)	4 (0)	55 (55)
Nuclear weapons	300	0	10,000

Sources: Bates Gill, "Chinese Defense Procurement Spending: Determining Intentions and Capabilities," in James R. Lilley and David Shambaugh, eds., *China's Military Faces the Future* (Armonk, N.Y.: M. E. Sharpe, 1999), pp. 197–211; International Institute for Strategic Studies, *The Military Balance 1999/2000* (Oxford: Oxford University Press, 1999), pp. 186–89, 202–09; Lane Pierrot, *Planning for Defense: Affordability and Capability of the Administration's Program* (Washington: Congressional Budget Office, 1994), p. 22; Office of Naval Intelligence, *Worldwide Challenges to Naval Strike Warfare* (Washington: U.S. Navy, 1996), p. 29.

less expensive military—but it still ranks about tenth in the world in total defense spending, and its reserve forces are actually larger than those of China (see table 6-1, which also includes corresponding U.S. data, for the sake of comparison). Taiwan's troops are generally better educated and better trained than China's, even though they fall short by some standards themselves. Finally, while Taiwan's defense technology is of uneven quality, it certainly surpasses that of the PRC. For example, its foreign arms purchases in the 1990s exceeded the value of those of China by a factor of about 7:1.[11]

---

pp. 186–92, as well as International Institute for Strategic Studies, *The Military Balance 1995/96* (London: Oxford University Press, 1995), pp. 270–75.

11. Bates Gill and Michael O'Hanlon, "China's Military, Take 3," *National Interest*, vol. 58 (Winter 1999/2000), p. 118.

Figure 6-1. *China and Taiwan*

China's military has traditionally focused on internal and border security much more than foreign operations. Of China's nearly two million ground troops, only about 20 percent are considered by the Pentagon to be mobile even within mainland China itself. Considerably fewer could deploy abroad, given their dearth of logistics assets (trucks, construction and engineering equipment, and mobile depots, hospitals, and fuel-storage infrastructure).[12] Even though Taiwan is only about one hundred miles away from mainland China (see figure 6-1), the fact that it is

12. William S. Cohen, "The Security Situation in the Taiwan Strait," Report to Congress pursuant to the FY99 Appropriations Bill (Department of Defense, 1999), p. 11.

separated by water further constrains the PRC's ability to project military power there. Few PRC troops could deploy over water, given China's very limited amounts of military airlift and sealift. Its seventy or so amphibious ships could move about 10,000 to 15,000 troops with their equipment, including perhaps 400 armored vehicles; airlift could move another 6,000 troops, or perhaps somewhat more counting the possibility of helicopter transport as well.[13]

These shortfalls in transport and logistics would be magnified by China's other military weaknesses. The training and the overall caliber of PRC armed forces leave much to be desired. Although Chinese military personnel are generally competent at basic infantry skills, the armed forces do not tend to attract China's best, nepotism is prevalent, party loyalty is of paramount importance, most soldiers are semiliterate peasants serving short tours of duty, and a strong professional noncommissioned officer corps is lacking. Combined-arms training, while somewhat enhanced of late for elite rapid-reaction forces, is infrequent, and joint-service training remains rare. Specialized assets such as aerial refueling, electronic jamming, and command aircraft are in short supply and of mediocre quality. The Chinese military's aspirations to conduct "local wars under high-technology conditions" remain aspirations, and its capabilities for taking advantage of the so-called revolution in military affairs, while much ballyhooed, are in all likelihood actually quite limited.[14] Furthermore, on the subject of a possible invasion of Taiwan, to quote the

13. International Institute for Strategic Studies, *The Military Balance 1999/2000* (London: Oxford University Press, 1999), pp. 187–88; Cohen, "The Security Situation in the Taiwan Strait," p. 9; William S. Cohen, "Future Military Capabilities and Strategy of the People's Republic of China," Report to Congress pursuant to the FY98 National Defense Authorization Act (Department of Defense, 1998), pp. 15–16; and Edward B. Atkeson, "The People's Republic of China in Transition: An Assessment of the People's Liberation Army," Land Warfare Paper 29 (Alexandria, Va.: Institute of Land Warfare, Association of the U.S. Army, 1998), p. 11.

14. Gao Heng, "Future Military Trends," in Michael Pillsbury, ed., *Chinese Views of Future Warfare* (National Defense University Press, 1997), pp. 85–94; Dennis J. Blasko, Philip T. Klapakis, and John F. Corbett Jr., "Training Tomorrow's PLA: A Mixed Bag of Tricks," in David Shambaugh and Richard H. Yang, eds., *China's Military in Transition* (Oxford, England: Clarendon Press, 1997), pp. 225–60; Cohen, "The Security Situation in the Taiwan Strait," pp. 6, 11, 13; Cohen, "Future Military Capabilities and Strategy of the People's Republic of China," p. 8; and Andrew N. D. Yang and Col. Milton Wen-Chung Liao, "PLA Rapid Reaction Forces: Concept, Training, and Preliminary Assessment," in James C. Mulvenon and Richard H. Yang, eds., *The People's Liberation Army in the Information Age* (Santa Monica, Calif.: RAND Corporation, 1999), pp. 56–57.

Pentagon, "China probably has never conducted a large-scale amphibious exercise which has been fully coordinated with air support and airborne operations."[15]

Taiwan's armed forces would have several built-in advantages against an invasion attempt. The conflict in question would be fought on their home island. In overall strategic terms that is hardly an advantage; Taiwan would stand the most to lose in the war, and it would surely suffer major material damage even in a successful defense. Taiwan would also face military disadvantages, such as the vulnerability of its early warning and command-and-control assets as well as airfields and ports. These vulnerabilities are exacerbated by the fact that Taiwan has not yet done enough to protect such assets against possible PRC attacks. Nor does it foster good cooperation or joint training between the different arms of its military or integrate communications systems adequately to make systematic use of early-warning data and other key information.[16] Among its other, generic military shortcomings, Taiwan like China continues to rely on conscription to fill out its force structure, meaning that there is a great deal of turnover in the ranks.[17]

Overall, however, Taiwan's location offers it a tremendous military advantage.[18] Taiwan is a small place, with limited numbers of beaches suitable for amphibious assault and only a small number of major ports and airfields to defend. It has had decades to prepare coastal defenses. Its numerous troops would not have to move far to reinforce each other at those places under concentrated Chinese attack. Many or most of Taiwan's reservists would be able to participate in the battle—a stark contrast from China's situation. Most of Taiwan's weaknesses are not as severe as China's in an absolute sense. Nor are they as crippling for a country that would be fighting on the tactical defensive. Defeating an

15. Cohen, "Future Military Capabilities and Strategy of the People's Republic of China," p. 15.

16. See Mark A. Stokes, *China's Strategic Modernization: Implications for the United States* (Carlisle, Pa.: Strategic Studies Institute, Army War College, 1999), pp. 79–108; Thomas E. Ricks, "Taiwan Seen as Vulnerable to Attack," *Washington Post,* March 31, 2000, p. A1; and Elizabeth Becker, "Problems Seen in Taiwan's Defenses," *New York Times,* April 1, 2000, p. A4.

17. Alexander Chieh-Cheng Huang, "Taiwan's View of Military Balance and the Challenge It Presents," in Lilley and Downs, *Crisis in the Taiwan Strait,* p. 291.

18. See David Shambaugh, "A Matter of Time: Taiwan's Eroding Military Advantage," *Washington Quarterly,* vol. 23 (Spring 2000), pp. 122–23.

amphibious and airborne assault, while not easy, poses a much less daunting problem of coordination than actually attempting the assault.[19] Taiwan's weaknesses are, however, more serious for maritime scenarios, which would be fought in effect on "neutral territory"—and which would directly harm Taiwan's economy much more than China's.

These overall realities are unlikely to change soon. China's indigenous defense industry is of mediocre caliber.[20] Much of its defense budget must be devoted to paying, training, and supplying its large numbers of troops.[21] For such reasons, and given the limited size of China's defense resources—especially when measured against such a large military—the Defense Intelligence Agency estimates that only 10 percent of China's armed forces will have "late–cold war" equivalent hardware even by 2010.[22] Its large attack submarine force includes only nine submarines that could be viewed as relatively modern—and five of those, the nuclear-powered Han vessels, are rather noisy and unreliable.[23] The People's Liberation Army Air Force (PLAAF) is projected to add only twenty to thirty top-notch fighter aircraft to its forces annually in the years ahead. It is having trouble completing the development of its indigenous F-10 fighter program and may not be able to produce such aircraft until after 2010, if the program succeeds at all. There are doubts about China's ability to maintain and effectively operate even whatever modest number of advanced fighter jets it is able to acquire.[24] These facts cast doubt on China's ability to establish air superiority in a hypothetical war against

19. See Michael D. Swaine, *Taiwan's National Security, Defense Policy, and Weapons Procurement Processes* (Santa Monica, Calif.: RAND Corporation, 1999), pp. 51–61.

20. Richard A. Bitzinger, "Going Places or Running in Place? China's Efforts to Leverage Advanced Technologies for Military Use," in Colonel Susan M. Puska, ed., *People's Liberation Army after Next* (Carlisle, Pa.: U.S. Army War College, 2000), pp. 9–54.

21. See Tim Huxley and Susan Willett, *Arming East Asia,* Adelphi Paper 329 (Oxford: Oxford University Press, 1999), pp. 75–77.

22. Lieutenant General Patrick M. Hughes, "Global Threats and Challenges: The Decades Ahead" (Defense Intelligence Agency, February 1999), p. 10; Avery Goldstein, "Great Expectations: Interpreting China's Arrival," *International Security,* vol. 22, no. 3 (Winter 1997/98), p. 46; and John Wilson Lewis and Xue Litai, "China's Search for a Modern Air Force," *International Security,* vol. 24, no.1 (Summer 1999), p. 87.

23. Eric McVadon, "PRC Exercises, Doctrine and Tactics toward Taiwan: The Naval Dimension," in Lilley and Downs, *Crisis in the Taiwan Strait,* p. 261.

24. Kenneth W. Allen, "PLAAF Modernization: An Assessment," in Lilley and Downs, *Crisis in the Taiwan Strait,* pp. 232–40; Jonathan Brodie, "China Moves to Buy More Russian Aircraft, Warships, and Submarines," *Jane's Defence Weekly,* December 22, 1999, p. 15; and Office of Naval Intelligence, *Worldwide Challenges to Naval Strike Warfare* (Washington: U.S. Navy, 1996), p. 29.

Taiwan even in five or ten years, or to compete favorably with Taiwanese ground forces should China ever manage to establish a toehold on a Taiwanese coast sometime in the future.

China may intend to increase its amphibious and airborne lift capabilities. However, it is not showing any major signs of doing so. On balance, it seems very unlikely to make major strides in these areas in the years ahead. Its current capabilities in these areas are quite modest, especially when compared with the size of Taiwan's armed forces.[25]

There are certainly important areas in which China could drastically improve its capabilities for attacking Taiwanese forces and infrastructure. For example, by improving the accuracy of missiles with global positioning system (GPS) guidance and developing submunitions that could be dispersed by cruise or ballistic missile, it could acquire the capacity to destroy exposed aircraft on most of Taiwan's airfields with as few as about one hundred cruise missiles or ten ballistic missiles. It could target ports and other key military and commercial infrastructure as well, trying to strangle Taiwan's economy without causing massive loss of life to its citizens. The PRC is developing, or attempting to develop, some of the requisite technologies. However, Taiwan would have recourses as well, many of them straightforward and relatively inexpensive. Building more hardened shelters for aircraft could deprive China of an area-effect attack capability against exposed fighters. Deploying jammers and missile defenses around airfields, ports, and key command, control, and communications facilities could degrade the accuracy of incoming missiles and reduce the number getting through. Taiwan could also consider operating aircraft off highways and otherwise dispersing them, albeit at some cost in the efficiency of aircraft operations and maintenance.[26]

Taiwan also needs to consider the possibility that, whatever Beijing's peacetime positions may be, China would use weapons of mass destruction against it, most likely in ways that maximized military effect while minimizing civilian casualties. Taiwan's armed forces need to continually improve their protective and decontaminating gear against chemical

25. Michael D. Swaine and Ashley J. Tellis, *Interpreting China's Grand Strategy: Past, Present, and Future* (Santa Monica, Calif: RAND Corporation, 2000), pp. 121–33; and Cohen, "Future Military Capabilities and Strategy of the People's Republic of China," pp. 15–16.

26. John Stillion and David T. Orletsky, *Airbase Vulnerability to Conventional Cruise-Missile and Ballistic-Missile Attacks* (Santa Monica, Calif.: RAND Corporation, 1999), pp. 8–45; and Stokes, *China's Strategic Modernization*, pp. 83–92.

weapons. In addition, key military infrastructure and equipment should be hardened against electromagnetic radiation. For example, if detonated high in the atmosphere to the east of Taiwan, a high-altitude nuclear burst might be capable of damaging unprotected electronics on the island while doing minimal direct damage to Taiwanese citizens—or to the PRC's own electronic systems. This threat is real, and it argues for further radiation hardening. However, it can be addressed, albeit again at some cost.[27] The required level of effort is probably in the hundreds of millions of dollars a year, though it is difficult to be more precise in the absence of detailed information about Taiwan's current vulnerabilities.[28]

Why China Could Not Seize Taiwan

Some analysts at the Pentagon, and a number of individuals on Capitol Hill, worry greatly about a possible Chinese invasion of Taiwan.[29] As a 1999 Department of Defense report puts it, "In order for an invasion to succeed . . . Beijing would have to possess the capability to conduct a multi-faceted campaign. . . . The PLA [People's Liberation Army] likely would encounter great difficulty conducting such a sophisticated campaign by 2005. Nevertheless, the campaign would likely succeed—barring third party intervention."[30] Not all Pentagon observers agree; for example, the director of the U.S. Defense Intelligence Agency does not believe China will have an invasion capability for many years.[31] However, the fact that some Pentagon analysts think China could conquer Taiwan,

27. Bruce G. Blair, *Strategic Command and Control: Redefining the Nuclear Threat* (Brookings, 1985), pp. 90–92, 132–37; and Denny Roy, "Tensions in the Taiwan Strait," *Survival*, vol. 42, no. 1 (Spring 2000), p. 85.

28. See Michael O'Hanlon, *Technological Change and the Future of Warfare* (Brookings, 2000), pp. 176–81.

29. For a longer version of the argument presented in this section, see Michael O'Hanlon, "Why China Cannot Conquer Taiwan," *International Security*, vol. 25, no. 2 (Fall 2000), pp. 51–86.

30. Cohen, "The Security Situation in the Taiwan Strait," p. 22.

31. Richard Lardner, "DoD Intelligence Chief Downplays China's Threats against Taiwan, U.S.," *Inside the Pentagon*, March 2, 2000, p. 2; Michael Pillsbury, "PLA Capabilities in the 21st Century: How Does China Assess Its Future Security Needs?" in Larry M. Wortzel, ed., *The Chinese Armed Forces in the 21st Century* (Carlisle, Pa.: Strategic Studies Institute, U.S. Army War College, 1999), pp. 137–38; and Swaine and Tellis, *Interpreting China's Grand Strategy*, pp. 132–33.

if not right away, then soon, is reason enough for the possibility to warrant some attention.

However, these latter analysts appear to be wrong. China does not have the basic key elements for a successful invasion, and it is unlikely to obtain them in the course of the decade. To succeed, an invader should first be able to achieve air superiority. Second, the attacker should try to use maneuver, surprise, and strength to land troops in a place where they locally outnumber defenders in troops and firepower. Third, it should be able to strengthen its initial lodgment faster than the defender can bring additional troops and equipment to bear at the same location. If an attacker can do most or all of these things, it has a good chance of establishing and then breaking out of an initial lodgment. As table 6-2 shows, attackers can succeed without enjoying all three advantages. However, in the cases considered here, they did not succeed without at least two of them. In all likelihood China could not attain any.

In modern times, amphibious assault forces have other problems too. They need to worry about antiship missiles that could be launched from the defender's airplanes, ships, or shore batteries and could hit approaching amphibious ships even when they were still miles off shore. Any helicopters or airplanes used in the assault must deal with the threats not just of antiaircraft artillery but also of surface-to-air missiles—which are now far more effective against low-flying aircraft than in previous eras of warfare. Given these trends in weaponry, amphibious assault against fixed defensive positions is if anything becoming harder—leading the U.S. Marine Corps now to place a premium on maneuver and speed rather than traditional frontal attack.[32]

For the present and the foreseeable future, China has only a small chance of meeting the first key criterion for success shown in table 6-1 and virtually no chance of satisfying either of the next two. In fact, it may fall short of the material requirements by as much as a factor of ten and the technology and military operational competence needed to invade Taiwan by half a generation.

Initial PRC Attacks with Missiles and Aircraft

China would almost surely have to try to surprise Taiwan with a major strike against ports and airfields. Otherwise, Taiwanese ships and airplanes

---

32. See U.S. Marine Corps, "Operational Maneuver from the Sea," *Marine Corps Gazette,* June 1996.

Table 6-2. *Ingredients in Successful Amphibious Assaults*

Case/attacker	Air superiority	Initial superiority in troops/firepower at point of attack	Reinforcement/ buildup advantage at point of attack
Historical successes			
Okinawa, 1944/U.S.	Yes	Yes	Yes
Normandy, 1944/U.S., allies	Yes	Yes	Yes
Inchon, Korea, 1950/U.S.	Yes	Yes	Yes
Falklands, 1982/UK	No	Yes	Yes[a]
Addendum: Failed attempts			
Anzio, 1943/U.S. and UK[a]	Yes	Yes	No
Gallipoli, 1915/UK, allies	No	Yes	No
Bay of Pigs, 1961/Cubans	No	Marginal	No
Possible Chinese attack on Taiwan			
Taiwan Straits, 2000/PRC	Doubtful	No	No
Taiwan Straits, 2010/PRC	Doubtful	No	No

a. Although British forces were outnumbered on East Falkland Island, they did manage to build up their lodgment successfully and move out from it without opposition, satisfying the requirement listed here. Although the forces at Anzio ultimately contributed to allied victory in Italy in the spring of 1944, their initial objective of making a quick and decisive difference in the war during the previous winter was clearly not met; thus the operation is classified here as a failure.

could turn the shores near Taiwan into a shooting gallery as PRC amphibious ships and transport aircraft tried to approach. If it used this tactic, China could not start loading and sailing most of its ships toward Taiwan until after the missile and air strikes began, for fear of tipping off Taiwanese and U.S. intelligence about its intentions. In fact, the PRC would do extremely well simply to prepare its air and missile forces for the attack without having those preparations noticed.

Consider first China's large ballistic-missile force. These missiles are numerous, perhaps now totaling 300 in southeastern China near Taiwan, with the PRC adding an estimated 50 missiles a year there, according to U.S. Pacific Commander Admiral Dennis Blair.[33] However,

33. Bill Gertz, "Admiral Says Taiwan Invasion Would Fail," *Washington Times*, March 8, 2000, p. A5; and Steven Mufson and Thomas E. Ricks, "Pentagon to Seek Delay on Ship Sale to Taiwan," *Washington Post*, April 17, 2000, p. A1.

China's ballistic missiles are rather inaccurate.[34] Until they are modernized, for example with more capable submunitions, they will have limited military purpose, and even as the PRC acquires such submunitions, Taiwan will be increasingly capable of dealing with them through hardened aircraft shelters and the like. Consider, for example, the notion that PRC ballistic missiles might be used to attack runways. In fact, this would not be a practical option. The missiles might achieve an occasional hit on a runway, but the missiles' accuracy—typically no better than 300 meters—would be too poor to make that happen more than every tenth shot or so.[35] Runways can absorb a number of hits before being seriously disabled; dozens of properly distributed craters could be needed to shut down operations at a single runway.[36] (China presently lacks advanced submunitions that could reduce the number of missiles required per base.)[37] To shut down a runway even temporarily using conventional munitions, therefore, literally hundreds of ballistic missiles might be required—virtually the entire PRC inventory. China's missiles may be good weapons of intimidation, but they are far less impressive in their military effectiveness.

Chinese attack aircraft could probably do better. If China could get several hundred of its 800 to 1,000 attack aircraft through to runways, it could shut some of them down at least temporarily and could perhaps destroy part of the Taiwanese combat air fleet on the ground as well.[38]

34. Bruce Dorminey, "Chinese Missiles Basic to New Strategy," *Aviation Week and Space Technology,* vol. 151 (March 8, 1999), p. 59.

35. International Institute for Strategic Studies, *The Military Balance 1999/2000,* p. 310; and Robert G. Nagler, *Ballistic Missile Proliferation: An Emerging Threat* (Arlington, Va.: System Planning Corporation, 1992), p. 15.

36. See the U.S. Marine Corps estimates cited in Joshua M. Epstein, *Measuring Military Power: The Soviet Air Threat to Europe* (Princeton University Press, 1984), pp. 198–201.

37. Ibid., p. 201; Stillion and Orletsky, *Airbase Vulnerability to Conventional Cruise-Missile and Ballistic-Missile Attacks,* pp. 9–15; and Stokes, *China's Strategic Modernization,* pp. 79–93.

38. There are now roughly thirteen Chinese airports within 450 kilometers of Taiwan. See Sean Boyne, "Taiwan's Troubles," *Jane's Intelligence Review,* September 1998, p. 27; and Richard A. Bitzinger and Bates Gill, *Gearing Up for High-Tech Warfare? Chinese and Taiwanese Defense Modernization and Implications for Military Confrontation across the Taiwan Strait, 1995–2005* (Washington: Center for Strategic and Budgetary Assessments, 1996), p. 45. On the size of China's attack aircraft fleets, see Cohen, "The Security Situation in the Taiwan Strait," p. 6; and International Institute for Strategic Studies, *The Military Balance 1999/2000,* pp. 186–88.

However, the difficulty of doing so should not be understated. First, it is not clear that all or even most of China's attack planes would be available against airfields. Moving the bulk of them to bases near Taiwan could tip off Taipei and Washington about a pending military action, allowing Taiwanese air defenses to be alerted, mines to be laid, and reservists to be mobilized. Even if China could move most attack aircraft within combat range of Taiwan clandestinely, it might have to use substantial numbers against Taiwan's air defenses and command-and-control assets, as well as Taiwan's thirty-seven surface combatants and fifty-nine smaller coastal combatants that carry antiship missiles. China has a large number of submarines it could try to use against these ships, but most are in poor condition, and a surging of the fleet to sea could tip off Taiwanese authorities about the likelihood of a pending attack. Nor is it clear that China has the organizational and operational proficiency to run large aerial operations; it has not demonstrated the capacity to fly more than a few hundred sorties a day in exercises or in previous operations.[39]

Assume nonetheless for the sake of conservatism that China could use the majority of its entire attack plane inventory against Taiwan's air bases. Most PRC attack aircraft could carry only a few unguided bombs; some might carry cruise missiles, though China does not have a sophisticated or large land-attack cruise-missile inventory and is not expected to obtain one for a number of years.[40] Making favorable assumptions about the accuracy and effectiveness of the Chinese munitions, it is likely that two to three dozen planes would be needed to shut down a given runway—meaning that thirty to fifty planes might have to be dedicated to each location, allowing for aircraft breakdowns, attrition, poor aiming, and other problems.[41]

The entire PRC air armada might thus incapacitate ten to twenty of Taiwan's airfields if virtually everything went right for it. More likely, China might shut down operations at the three or four bases where Taiwan keeps its most advanced fighters. However, Taiwan would immediately begin to repair its airfields. China could undertake subsequent attack sorties, of course, but Taiwan's antiaircraft artillery and SAMs would then be on a high state of vigilance. Since Chinese planes do not

39. Allen, "PLAAF Modernization: An Assessment," pp. 224–32.

40. Stokes, *China's Strategic Modernization*, pp. 79–86; Cohen, "Future Military Capabilities and Strategy of the People's Republic of China," p. 10.

41. Epstein, *Measuring Military Power*, pp. 208–09, 223.

carry precision munitions as a rule, they would have to fly low, leaving themselves very vulnerable. They might well lose 10 to 20 percent of their planes on each subsequent sortie. In addition, given their poor state of repair, and their lack of night-flying capabilities, it is implausible that most PLAAF and PLAN aircraft could fly more than two sorties before being grounded by darkness or maintenance requirements. Typically, PRC aircraft do not fly more than one sortie every two days or more, whether in training or even during major exercises; their mission-capable rates are poor, and repairs are frequent as well as time-consuming.[42] Since most PRC amphibious ships would need more than a day to reach Taiwan (most are not based near the Strait in peacetime, and moving them there prior to an attack, to say nothing of loading them up, would alert Taiwan), Taiwan could use the night to repair many runways. PRC attacks on subsequent days would be far less effective.[43]

China could try to directly attack Taiwanese aircraft on the ground. However, doing so is difficult for aircraft lacking precision-guided bombs, for pilots receiving only limited training in low-altitude flight, and against air defenses like those Taiwan deploys at its airfields. Cruise missiles or terminally guided ballistic missiles dispensing submunitions could be very lethal in this context; however, despite a number of research and development programs in the works, China's capabilities in the area of land-attack cruise missiles are fledgling at present.[44] Even if China could destroy some planes on the ground, Taiwan already has hardened shelters for many of its fighters and should soon be able to provide 60 percent of them with protection against anything but laser-guided bombs.[45] The costs of doing so are not insignificant—perhaps $4 million per plane—but are far less than the purchase costs of the aircraft themselves.[46]

42. Allen, "PLAAF Modernization: An Assessment," pp. 224–32.

43. China probably keeps only 20 to 40 percent of its amphibious forces within close range of Taiwan under normal circumstances; see International Institute for Strategic Studies, *The Military Balance 1999/2000*, p. 188. On this general subject, see also Epstein, *Measuring Military Power*, pp. 225–61; and L. Nordeen Jr., *Air Warfare in the Missile Age* (Smithsonian Institution Press, 1985), pp. 201–03.

44. Stillion and Orletsky, *Airbase Vulnerability*, pp. 9–15; and Stokes, *China's Strategic Modernization*, pp. 79–93.

45. Personal communication from Shuhfan Ding, Institute of International Relations, National Chengchi University, Taipei, Taiwan, April 14, 2000; see also David Shambaugh, "China's Military Views the World," *International Security*, vol. 24, no. 3 (Winter 1999/2000), p. 61.

46. Stillion and Orletsky, *Airbase Vulnerability*, pp. 30–32.

The Desert Storm experience is instructive here as an analogy. Coalition aircraft averaged dozens of strike sorties a day against Iraqi airfields during the war's first week, yet did not stop the Iraqi air force from flying about forty sorties a day.[47] That was at a time when coalition aircraft completely ruled the skies, moreover. In the airfield attacks, British planes were dropping advanced runway-penetrating weapons known as the JP-233, and doing so precisely and from low altitude. Those munitions carried some thirty bomblets apiece, each bomblet consisting of two charges: a primary explosive to create a small hole in the runway, and a second explosive to detonate below its surface, causing a crater of ten to twenty meters' width (depending largely on soil conditions). They also carried various sorts of antipersonnel mines designed to impede runway repair (Britain has now eliminated the JP-233 from its military as a result of signing the land mine convention).[48] A standard attack would have used eight aircraft, each dropping two weapons, to shut down a standard NATO-length runway of 9,000 feet by 150 feet—a difficult mission, given the need to drop the weapons at precise and quite low altitudes.[49] China does not have the excellent munitions, airplanes, and pilots that Britain and other elements of the U.S.-led coalition wielded against Iraq in 1991. It is entirely implausible that it could do nearly as well as the coalition in restricting its adversary's flight operations should it go to war against Taiwan.

There are caveats to these generally optimistic conclusions. Shelters may not be constructed for larger planes, such as airborne warning and control aircraft. Conservative planning should probably assume that Taiwan would not have such aircraft available for combat, having lost them to preemptive PRC attacks.

In addition, China could use chemical weapons against Taiwanese airfields, drastically complicating air operations. The standard assumption

---

47. Thomas A. Keaney and Eliot A. Cohen, *Gulf War Air Power Survey Summary Report* (Government Printing Office, 1993), pp. 56–65; General Accounting Office, *Operation Desert Storm: Evaluation of the Air Campaign*, GAO/NSIAD-97-134 (June 1997), pp. 209–12; and Christopher S. Parker, "New Weapons for Old Problems," *International Security*, vol. 23, no. 4 (Spring 1999), p. 147.

48. Duncan Lennox, ed., *Jane's Air-Launched Weapons* (Alexandria, Va.: Jane's Information Group, 1999); and Christopher M. Centner, "Ignorance Is Risk: The Big Lesson from Desert Storm Air Base Attacks," *Airpower Journal*, vol. 6, no. 4, (Winter 1992), pp. 25–35 (www.airpower.maxwell.af.mil/airchronicles/ apj/centner.html [December 27, 2000]).

49. Personal communication from Dave C. Fidler, Wing Commander Air 1, British Embassy, Washington, April 14, 2000.

is that operating in a chemical environment would reduce a military's flight operations in half. In other words, if an air force would otherwise fly two sorties per aircraft per day, it might manage only one if personnel needed to wear protective gear and frequently decontaminate equipment. China would need to weigh the potential military benefits of attacking Taiwanese airfields and other key military infrastructure with chemical weapons against the risks that doing so would only steel Taipei's resolve and persuade the United States to come to Taiwan's military aid regardless of which side Washington viewed as having provoked the conflict. In the end, however, it must be acknowledged that China's precise assessment of the pros and cons of such an attack cannot be predicted, and there is some chance that it would use chemical weapons.[50] (It seems highly unlikely that China would use nuclear weapons against the island. It has stated it would not do so, and the political repercussions—not to mention the risks of U.S. retaliation—would surely be enormous.)[51]

All told, China could not achieve clear air superiority and thus would fail to satisfy the first criterion for most successful amphibious assaults, as shown in table 6-2. Of Taiwan's 600 or so combat aircraft, at least half would likely survive even a well-coordinated, large-scale Chinese preemptive attack that caught them by surprise. Most of Taiwan's airborne control aircraft might be lost, and remaining combat jets might be reduced to flying only a sortie a day, at least in the war's first day or two, given damage to runways and the possible use of chemical weapons by the PRC. However, the surviving Taiwanese planes, at least one hundred of which would likely be capable of ground attack, would generally have little trouble finding Chinese ships as they approached Taiwanese shores. (Note that Chinese pilots would probably need clear skies to have a good chance of finding their targets, since they generally require visual identification of targets to attack them.[52] That same good weather would help Taiwanese pilots to find troop ships near Taiwan's coasts—though if need be, they could probably do so even in cloudy weather.) Assuming two munitions per aircraft, one hundred Taiwanese aircraft, each flying one

50. Victor A. Utgoff, *The Challenge of Chemical Weapons: An American Perspective* (St. Martin's Press, 1991), pp. 172–81.

51. Associated Press, "China Says It Will Not Use Nuclear Weapons against Taiwan," *New York Times*, September 3, 1999, p. A3.

52. Allen, "PLAAF Modernization: An Assessment," p. 232.

sortie, might sink five to twenty ships a day in the subsequent amphibious phase of the conflict.[53]

Taiwan would lose airplanes to Chinese fighters, but only gradually, given the poor quality of those PRC aircraft and their command and control support.[54] Even as China gradually obtains airborne control aircraft, perhaps from Russia, Taiwan should be able to obtain electronic-warfare capabilities that will limit their effectiveness. Since Taiwan's attack aircraft could fly low and concentrate their efforts in the eastern part of the Strait, near Taiwan's coasts, China's ground radars and control centers would contribute little to the battle. Thus many Taiwanese aircraft would sneak through PRC fighter cover and carry out attacks, using antiship missiles or even dumb bombs against the poorly defended Chinese ships. They could similarly use air-to-air missiles against transport aircraft.[55] They would probably suffer no more than 5 percent attrition per sortie, meaning that a given plane could fly many missions before being shot down.[56]

53. Typically, about two to six Harpoon-sized missiles would be needed to destroy a large surface vessel. See *Jane's Naval Review 1987* (London: Jane's Publishing, 1987), p. 124. In flying some three hundred sorties against British forces in the Falklands War, and attacking the U.K. ships on the open oceans where they are harder to spot than when approaching shore, Argentina sank four British ships with bombs and hit another six with bombs that did not detonate because they had been improperly fused. Argentina sank a total of six ships, including those hit by Exocets and other weapons. See Nordeen, *Air Warfare in the Missile Age,* pp. 201–03.

54. Kenneth W. Allen, Glenn Krumel, and Jonathan D. Pollack, *China's Air Force Enters the 21st Century* (Santa Monica, Calif.: RAND Corporation, 1995), pp. xiii–xxi; Cohen, "The Security Situation in the Taiwan Strait," p. 6; Allen, "PLAAF Modernization: An Assessment," pp. 224–33; and Peter Yu Kien-hong, "Taking Taiwan," *Jane's Intelligence Review* (September 1998), pp. 31–32.

55. McVadon, "PRC Exercises, Doctrine and Tactics toward Taiwan, pp. 262–65.

56. Most likely, aircraft attrition rates per sortie would be no more than 5 percent, actually quite high by historical standards. Higher rates are possible; for example, Argentina may have suffered attrition rates per sortie as high as 20 to 30 percent or so in the 1982 Falklands War. But the only aircraft likely to do this poorly in a China-Taiwan confrontation would be China's older planes, particularly if flying low-altitude missions near or over Taiwan, where Taiwanese air defenses would be most effective. See Nordeen, *Air Warfare in the Missile Age,* pp. 201–03; Edgar O'Balance, "The Falklands, 1982," in Lt. Col. Merrill L. Bartlett, *Assault from the Sea: Essays on the History of Amphibious Warfare* (Annapolis: Naval Institute Press, 1983), pp. 435–36; Epstein, *Measuring Military Power,* pp. 151–52; and Barry R. Posen, "Measuring the European Conventional Balance: Coping with Complexity in Threat Assessment," *International Security,* vol. 9, no. 3 (Winter 1984/85), p. 104.

A PRC Amphibious Assault

China has the capacity to transport 10,000 to 15,000 troops with some heavy armor by amphibious lift. Assume for the moment that it could deploy all of them to a single point on Taiwan's shores at once, and do so without losses (the second assumption will be revisited below). Even so, such a force would not be large given the defenses that the Taiwanese military could marshal in response. Taiwan, with about 200,000 available active-duty ground troops, 1.5 million more ground-force reservists, and a coastal perimeter of about 1,500 kilometers, could deploy roughly 1,000 defenders per kilometer of coastline along all of its shores if it wished. So over any given stretch of ten to fifteen kilometers, a fully mobilized Taiwanese defense force would be able to deploy as many troops as China could deploy there with all of its amphibious fleet. (An attacker would need to seize a shoreline of roughly that length to create areas safe from enemy artillery.)[57]

By contrast, on D-Day allied forces outnumbered German strength in Normandy by more than 2:1 within such tactical distances. As suggested in table 6-2, other successful invaders have generally managed to achieve initial force superiority at the point of attack as well.[58] China almost definitely could not.

The density of defenses assumed above presupposes no advance knowledge by Taiwan about where the PRC intended to come ashore. In reality, unless completely blinded and paralyzed by China's preemptive attacks against airfields, ships, shore-based radars, other monitoring assets, and command centers—most unlikely propositions—Taiwan would see where ships sailed and be able to react with at least some notice. (It is also likely that, if necessary, the United States would be willing to provide Taiwan with satellite or aircraft intelligence on the concentration of China's attack effort; it is very doubtful that Washington would refuse to provide such warning—even if the United States stayed out of combat operations.) Although the Strait is typically only one hundred miles wide, Taiwan itself is about three hundred miles long, so ships traveling twenty knots would need more than half a day to sail its full length and could not credibly threaten all parts of the island at once. In

57. See James F. Dunnigan, *How to Make War: A Comprehensive Guide to Modern Warfare for the Post–Cold War Era*, 3rd ed. (Morrow, 1993), pp. 284–292.

58. John Keegan, *The Second World War* (London: Hutchinson, 1989), pp. 376–85.

addition, amphibious assault troops cannot come ashore just anywhere. Only about 20 percent of the world's coastlines are considered suitable for amphibious assault; on Taiwan's shores, the percentage is even less, given the prevalence of mud flats on the west coast and cliffs on the east.

As a practical matter, then, Taiwan would not need to mobilize all of its reservists to achieve force parity in places most likely to suffer the initial PRC attack. If it could mobilize even 20 percent of its reservists in the twenty-four to forty-eight hours that China would require, at a bare minimum, to assemble and load its amphibious armada and then cross the Strait, it could achieve force parity along key beachlines while maintaining thinner defenses elsewhere.[59] Taiwan also has two airborne brigades that it could use for rapid reaction to any point experiencing amphibious or paratroop attack (and will also soon have an airborne cavalry brigade equipped with helicopters for that purpose).[60] China would thus be unlikely to establish even a local, temporary advantage along the section of beach where it elected to try coming ashore. Therefore it does not possess the ability to generate the second element of most successful amphibious attacks as shown in table 6-1.

Nor could China subsequently build up its initial force as quickly as Taiwan could. In other words, it also lacks the third crucial element of most successful invasions identified above. In fact, here its shortcomings are even more striking, and its prospects even worse. Whatever happened during the first day of conflict, Taiwan could almost surely use roads to reinforce its forces en masse on the first night of the war and thereafter. The Chinese air force has limited capacity for finding and attacking mobile ground targets and limited capacity to operate at night, so it could not seriously slow such reinforcements. China's naval gunfire would not be particularly effective either; its ship-based guns are relatively small and few.

China's inability to stop Taiwanese road traffic, particularly at night, would have dire consequences for the PRC, given the availability of Taiwanese reinforcements and the small distances at play on the island. Taiwan could probably move reinforcements at least fifty kilometers

59. Dunnigan, *How to Make War*, pp. 290–91; Swaine, *Taiwan's National Security, Defense Policy, and Weapons Procurement Processes*, p. 52; and McVadon, "PRC Exercises, Doctrine and Tactics toward Taiwan," p. 253.

60. Swaine, *Taiwan's National Security, Defense Policy, and Weapons Procurement Processes*, p. 60; and International Institute for Strategic Studies, *The Military Balance 1999/2000*, p. 205.

every twenty-four hours. Countries on the tactical offensive on foreign soil can often attain movement rates of twenty to thirty kilometers a day.[61] Faced with nothing more than Chinese aerial harassment, most of it only during the day, Taiwan could certainly move reinforcements at twice that speed on its own territory (if not even faster). That would make for more than 100,000 troops available in forty-eight hours on a typical part of the island.[62]

In fact, Taiwan would not have this same buildup capacity everywhere. Near major military bases and cities, its capacities would tend to be greater, whereas in some rural areas they would be less. That would not constitute a major vulnerability, however. For one thing, if China wished to attack a port and airfield, it would need to do so near a city. In addition, even if China chose a spot for amphibious assault where Taiwan's initial reinforcement capacity was limited, Taiwan could deploy initial holding forces by aircraft—and still bring overwhelming firepower to bear within a couple of days.

If it somehow established an initial lodgment ashore, China could try to reinforce it using its small amphibious fleet. But it would probably need at least two days for each round trip of its ships, and even that schedule would be highly contingent on encountering good seas in the notoriously foul-weathered Taiwan Strait.[63] Moreover, returning ships would need to resupply troops already ashore, limiting their ability to deliver reinforcements. After forty-eight hours, therefore, Taiwan would likely have more than 100,000 troops facing the PRC's total of perhaps 20,000 at Beijing's chosen point of attack—and the situation would continue to deteriorate from there for China.

Indeed, the likely force ratios are even worse than indicated for Beijing. The above analysis has ignored attrition to PRC forces as they approach land and come ashore. In reality, such losses would be enormous, both in the initial assault and in subsequent reinforcement operations. Many of the troops crossing the Strait in China's amphibious ships would never make it to land. As one way of getting a very rough quantitative grip on

61. Joshua M. Epstein, *Strategy and Force Planning: The Case of the Persian Gulf* (Brookings, 1987), p. 52.

62. Even in the highly implausible case that it could move no faster than German troops in France in 1944 after D-Day, when allied aircraft totally ruled the skies, Taiwan's forces would still move fifteen kilometers a day—bringing at least 25,000 troops to the battle every twenty-four hours. See Keegan, *The Second World War*, p. 389.

63. McVadon, "PRC Exercises, Doctrine and Tactics toward Taiwan," p. 251.

the problem, consider that the British lost five ships to missiles and air-craft and had another twelve damaged, out of a one-hundred-ship task force, in the Falklands War—and that they did not generally have to approach any closer than four hundred miles from the Argentine main-land during the conflict. That amounts to an effective attrition rate of 5 to 15 percent during blue-water operations—against an outclassed Argentine military that owned only about 250 aircraft.[64]

PRC losses would surely be greater against a foe whose airfields they would have to approach directly, whose air forces would likely retain at least 300 planes even after a highly effective Chinese preemptive attack against airfields (see above), and whose antiship missile capabilities sub-stantially exceed Argentina's in 1982. Taiwan possesses significant num-bers of antiship missiles such as Harpoon and its own Hsiung Feng. There are weaknesses in Taiwan's capabilities for resisting invasion; its air force has focused primarily on air-to-air attack, not antiship operations, and the United States has resisted providing Taiwan with certain attack capa-bilities out of fear that they might be used provocatively. Despite these limitations, however, Taiwan's panoply of capabilities is considerable, and would be potent even at night or in bad weather.[65]

All told, the PRC would likely lose at least 20 percent of its forces just in approaching Taiwan's coasts and fighting ashore.[66] It would continue to suffer high attrition rates during subsequent efforts to reinforce troops already ashore. On average, China could not hope to add more than about 5,000 troops per day to its initial beachhead—assuming that the beachhead could be established in the first place (see table 6-3 for esti-mates of reinforcement rates for an amphibious assault as well as other kinds of Chinese transport, which are further discussed below). More likely, given expected attrition, the PRC would do well to deploy 3,000 to 4,000 amphibious troops daily in the first few days after its initial assault.

What if the PRC used chemical weapons in this part of its attack? If it could fire chemical munitions from its ship-based guns, it might be able to deliver enough ordnance to cover a battlefield several kilometers on a

64. International Institute for Strategic Studies, *The Military Balance 1981/1982* (London, 1992), pp. 92–93.

65. Ronald Montaperto, "China," in Patrick Clawson, *1997 Strategic Assessment* (National Defense University, 1997), p. 52; Peter Yu Kien-hong, "Taking Taiwan," p. 31; and Swaine, *Taiwan's National Security, Defense Policy, and Weapons Procurement Processes*, p. 57.

66. Nordeen, *Air Warfare in the Missile Age*, pp. 201–03.

Table 6-3. *Estimated Daily Troop Reinforcement Rates, for Days 3–10 after "D-Day,"* at a Specific Site on Taiwan

Means of transport	China	Taiwan
Amphibious lift	4,000	0
Other sealift	3,000	0
Airlift	1,000	5,000
Internal land lines/roads	0	50,000
Daily total	8,000	55,000

dimension within several minutes. China would presumably want to use a nonpersistent agent, like sarin, so that its troops could occupy the area within a short time without having to wear protective gear. The effects of the weapons on Taiwan's defenders would depend heavily on whether they had gas masks handy, on the accuracy of Chinese naval gunfire, on weather conditions, and on the speed with which Taiwan could threaten the PRC ships doing the damage.[67] Historical experiences with chemical weapons suggest that China should not expect these weapons to radically change the course of battle in any event. Even in World War I, when protective gear was rudimentary, chemical weapons caused less than 10 percent of all deaths; in the Iran-Iraq war, the figure has been estimated at less than 5 percent.[68] China would need to worry that, if its timing and delivery were not good, its own mobile and exposed troops could suffer larger numbers of casualties than the dug-in defenders.[69] Using chemical weapons could also invite Taiwanese retaliation in kind against China's relatively concentrated and exposed forces on and near the island.[70] All told, this approach would improve China's odds of getting an initial foothold on Taiwan somewhat—upgrading the PRC's prospects from terrible to poor. However, it would not change the fact that Taiwan could subsequently build up reinforcements far faster than the PRC.

67. Office of Technology Assessment, *Proliferation of Weapons of Mass Destruction* (Washington, 1993), pp. 45–67.

68. Trevor N. Dupuy, *Attrition: Forecasting Battle Casualties and Equipment Losses in Modern War* (Fairfax, Va.: HERO Books, 1990), p. 58; and Anthony H. Cordesman and Abraham R. Wagner, *Lessons of Modern War, Volume 2: The Iran-Iraq War* (Boulder, Colo.: Westview Press, 1990), p. 518.

69. See Utgoff, *The Challenge of Chemical Weapons*, pp. 148–88; and Dupuy, *Attrition*, p. 58.

70. Nagler, *Ballistic Missile Proliferation*, p. 10.

Some have raised the possibility that the PRC could use its fishing fleet to put tens if not hundreds of thousands of troops quickly ashore on Taiwan. There are several important reasons not to take this threat particularly seriously, however. First, the ships could not carry heavy equipment. Second, shore-based coastal defense guns and artillery, as well as Taiwanese aircraft, small coastal patrol craft, and mines, might well make mincemeat of many of the unarmored ships, which would have to approach very close to shore in order for the soldiers not to drown after disembarking. (Taiwanese guns and artillery could be expected to be at least ten times as accurate per shot against a target several hundred yards off shore as against a ship several kilometers away—where amphibious ships would normally remain. They would also have time for more shots against ships that had to approach so close to land.)[71] Third, the fishing ships could not carry landing craft, leaving soldiers completely defenseless after they disembarked from the ships and trudged through mudflats or swam in the face of Taiwanese fire. Many soldiers would be killed by Taiwanese forces; many others would likely drown. Fourth, given the distances involved, it would be impossible to coordinate the assault very well; the ships would inevitably arrive on Taiwan's shores in ragged, staggered formations that would deny PRC troops the benefits of massed attack. The only factor in China's favor would be that, with so many vessels to shoot at, Taiwan could run out of precision munitions and be reduced to using less accurate shore gunnery and dumb bombs against many vessels. However, those vessels would need to approach shore so closely that even this advantage would be of limited benefit. On the whole, this scenario is simply not credible.[72]

A PRC Airborne Assault to Seize a Port and an Airfield

China might try, instead of or in addition to an amphibious assault, to seize a port, an airfield, or both through an airborne operation. If successful, it would then be able to use commercial airlift and sealift to bring in reinforcements as quickly as they could be loaded up, sent across the Strait, and unloaded. Reportedly, Taiwan's army has not devoted enough

71. See Dunnigan, *How to Make War,* pp. 284–92. The typical lateral inaccuracy of gunfire or artillery fire is proportional to the distance over which the round must travel, meaning that a shot to five hundred meters would be expected to have one-tenth the miss distance of a shot to five kilometers.

72. For a concurring view, see McVadon, "PRC Exercises, Doctrine, and Tactics toward Taiwan," pp. 254–55.

effort to providing protection for ports and airfields, perhaps offering a glimmer of hope to the PRC that it could pull off this type of operation.[73]

China has the capacity to airlift about two brigades' worth of paratroopers in a sortie of its entire military airlift fleet. That is possibly enough to establish at least temporary control of both a port and an airfield—but just barely, and only if PRC losses are quite modest during the initial airlift operation. When seizing such facilities, it is generally considered necessary to control the surrounding area for several miles in each direction to prevent enemy direct-fire weapons from shooting at ships, planes, runways, and piers. Doing so typically requires at least a brigade of troops per facility, according to U.S. military doctrine.[74]

However, PRC paratroopers (or troop-carrying helicopters) over Taiwan would be at great risk from Taiwanese fighters, surface-to-air missiles, and antiaircraft artillery. Paratroopers in fixed-wing transports are particularly vulnerable in situations in which the attacking force does not completely dominate the skies and in which the defender has good ground-based air defenses.[75] To mitigate these vulnerabilities, China would need to achieve surprise, attempting an airborne landing at nearly the same time it was launching initial attacks against airfields and other key infrastructure—further complicating an already very complex opening operation.

The United States has made good use of airdrops, even as recently as the 1989 invasion of Panama. It has done so by exploiting air dominance, night-combat capabilities, heavy air-to-ground fire support, and a careful choice of circumstances. For example, in the invasion of Panama, it was taking on a foe that lacked modern surface-to-air missiles and had a total active-duty military of less than 5,000 troops.[76] China would not have such luxuries in an attack on Taiwan.

---

73. Swaine, *Taiwan's National Security, Defense Policy, and Weapons Procurement Processes*, pp. 57–60.

74. See Headquarters, Department of the Army, *Field Manual 100-5: Operations* (Washington: U.S. Army, 1993), pp. 3-3 through 3-10; and Commandant, U.S. Army Infantry School, "The Application of Peace Enforcement Operations at Brigade and Battalion," Fort Benning, Georgia, August 1994, p. 9.

75. For historical perspective, see James A. Huston, "The Air Invasion of Holland," *Military Review* (September 1952), pp. 13–27; and Gerard M. Devlin, *Paratrooper! The Saga of U.S. Army and Marine Parachute and Glider Combat Troops during World War II* (St. Martin's Press, 1979).

76. Susan L. Marquis, *Unconventional Warfare: Rebuilding U.S. Special Operations Forces* (Brookings, 1997), pp. 196–98; and International Institute for Strategic Studies, *The Military Balance 1989–1990* (Oxford, England: Brassey's, 1989), pp. 198–99.

Even if China somehow managed tactical surprise with its first sortie of airlift, thus keeping initial losses to a minimum—a highly dubious proposition—it would only have about 6,000 to 8,000 soldiers on the ground as a result. Efforts to reinforce and resupply them would have to cope with alerted Taiwanese air defenses. The drop positions of subsequent paratroopers would be predictable; so would the ingress and egress corridors of aircraft actually trying to use a seized runway. Taiwan has well over one hundred surface-to-air missile batteries with ranges of tens of kilometers—more than enough to have some coverage near all of its twenty to thirty large airfields and five major ports. It also has 400 anti-aircraft guns and many smaller surface-to-air missile batteries that use high-quality modified Sidewinder and Sparrow missiles.[77]

Unless Taiwanese SAM batteries and antiaircraft artillery (AAA) sites were suppressed by Chinese attack aircraft, Taiwan would be able to detect and fire at most airplanes delivering reinforcing troops. It is doubtful that China could suppress Taiwanese air defenses. The PLAAF has mediocre electronic warfare and precision-strike capabilities. It might be able to find large runways and drop unguided bombs on them; it would not be likely to find and jam or destroy smaller, more easily camouflaged radars and missile launchers.[78]

Finally, as estimated before, Taiwan would retain a substantial fraction of its air force as well—perhaps 50 percent—even after a very successful Chinese preemptive strike against air bases.[79] Taiwanese air-superiority planes would be hard for PRC fighters to fend off, and many would get into position to fire at PRC troop transports.

Even if China gained temporary control of an airfield, it could not build up its initial lodgment very fast. It would be hard pressed to deliver more tonnage per day than what the United States could manage under secure airfield conditions at the peak of its Desert Storm buildup operation—a rate that averaged about 600 tons per airfield per day, which translates into equipment and initial supplies for fewer than 1,000 lightly

---

77. Cohen, "The Security Situation in the Taiwan Strait," p. 8.

78. See for example, Bernard Blake, ed., *Jane's Weapon Systems* (Alexandria, Va.: Jane's Information Group, 1988), pp. 187–90; and Duncan Lennox, ed., *Jane's Air-Launched Weapons* (Alexandria, Va.: Jane's Information Group, 1999).

79. Taiwan has twenty runways with runway length of at least 8,000 feet and a total of thirty with lengths of at least 3,000 feet; see Central Intelligence Agency, *The World Factbook 1999* (1999) (www.odci.gov/cia/publications/factbook [December 27, 2000]).

armed troops.[80] If China could somehow double or triple that rate, it would still amount to only a very modest reinforcement capacity.

China would probably not do much better by using a port. First, ships are hard to load and unload quickly even in harbors that are not under attack. Over the Operation Desert Shield/Storm experience, the United States averaged delivering about 8,000 tons of equipment per day to each of the two major Saudi ports it used.[81] Even under good conditions at the ports, backlogs developed due to shortages of cranes, elevator loaders, trucks, and the like.[82] China would do well to deliver 5,000 tons of equipment and initial supplies with port facilities under attack— enough for perhaps 2,000 to 3,000 troops a day (assuming that some would be heavy forces, which the PRC would want in order to fend off the inevitable counterattack by Taiwanese ground forces).[83] The entire operation could be virtually halted by destruction of major cranes and ship berths by Taiwanese air attack or by the sinking of a couple of ships near piers. China might be able to increase the rate of troop deployment severalfold if it were willing to forgo heavy equipment, simply sailing into port its fishing vessels and other troop transports, and turning loose large numbers of rifle-wielding infantrymen once it seized a port. It could try to do so even if major port infrastructure were destroyed. However, these individuals would come under severe artillery fire immediately and would have little in the way of defensive cover. They would also lack the firepower and armor needed to move out from their initial foothold to more secure positions.

In short, whether they tried to seize a port or an airfield or both, China's armed forces could not build up their strength very fast. Even after two days, they would probably have no more than 20,000 troops ashore, granting them the highly generous assumption that they could establish a foothold in the first place. Unfortunately for them, within that same time, Taiwan could concentrate well over 100,000 troops at the same site or sites and proceed to overrun China's forces. The PRC would have been able to seize an area of only a few kilometers' diameter with

80. Rachel Schmidt, *Moving U.S. Forces: Options for Strategic Mobility* (Washington: Congressional Budget Office, 1997), pp. 48, 54, 80–81.

81. Department of Defense, *Conduct of the Persian Gulf War: Final Report to Congress* (1992), p. F-26.

82. Schmidt, *Moving U.S. Forces*, pp. 30, 50, 54.

83. This tonnage would correspond to the equipment and supplies for only about 1,000 heavy U.S. Army soldiers (or 4,000 light soldiers); ibid., pp. 79–80.

such small, rather light, tactically rather immobile forces and to set up a hasty defense. Historically, attackers with the types of force advantages Taiwan would be able to generate can advance several kilometers per day against such weak defenses, and often ten kilometers per day. At that rate, the PRC forces would be defeated in twenty-four to forty-eight hours, even if they managed to establish initial lodgments.[84]

If China were able to concentrate amphibious and airborne forces all in one place, it could theoretically deploy up to 40,000 troops in one area within forty-eight to seventy-two hours, perhaps adding nearly 10,000 a day thereafter (see table 6-3). Taiwan would have more than 100,000 troops in the same place within roughly the first two days of war, and it would continue adding forces at the rough pace of 50,000 daily thereafter, gaining a huge advantage by the third or fourth day. (In addition, with its own forces approaching from several sides, China would be hard pressed to use chemical weapons against Taiwanese defenders at its chosen battle-field.) Relative buildup rates would work strongly to Taiwan's advantage, especially since such a battle would by definition occur in the proximity of a Taiwanese city, meaning numerous reservists would be nearby.

A somewhat less reassuring inference from these quantitative assessments is that China might be capable of seizing Matsu or Quemoy, the small islands near the PRC coast that were the object of Chinese artillery attacks in the 1950s and that remain under Taiwanese control to this day. Taiwan stations about 40,000 troops on Quemoy and 10,000 on Matsu. The latter number in particular is comparable to what China might be able to put ashore on such an island within hours. Moreover, Taiwan would have to traverse a greater distance to reinforce its garrisons on these islands than China would have to cover in building up any beach-head. Given geography, Taiwan might also concede the advantage in the air to China for such a scenario; in such a location PRC fighters could benefit from shore-based air controllers, and they would waste little fuel and time flying to the combat theater from their bases on the mainland.

If China managed to take one of these islands against the local Taiwanese defenders, what should Taipei and Washington do? Trying to seize the islands back seems imprudent, even if the United States were willing to join Taiwan in the fight. Even though the United States and Taiwan together wield much more military capability than the PRC, they

84. Trevor N. Dupuy, *Numbers, Predictions, and War*, rev. ed. (Fairfax, Va.: HERO Books, 1985), p. 213.

would face disadvantageous geographic conditions for an attempted amphibious assault if trying to approach within sight of the Chinese mainland to carry it out. Given China's improving antiship cruise missiles and mines, and the difficulty of conducting antisubmarine warfare in shallow waters, approaching so close to China would be very risky. To be sure, the scenario would not be trivial for the PRC either, since its small landing party could be vulnerable to a U.S.-Taiwanese quarantine of the island. Nevertheless, the conditions would be less than ideal for the United States and Taiwan.

Should China seize one of these islands, the proper responses might include expanding American arms sales to Taipei, formalizing and clarifying Washington's defense commitments to the island, perhaps basing some U.S. combat aircraft directly on Taiwan, and imposing severe economic sanctions on China. They would not include fighting a battle within visual range of the Chinese mainland over marginal pieces of rock, whatever the historical significance of those small islands may be.[85]

Taiwan is in a very good military position for defending the main island against invasion. It has large ground forces, good internal lines of communication, advanced munitions to use against an enemy that must expose itself to attack, and an enemy with limited technological excellence or operational proficiency. Were China to attempt an all-out invasion, it could suffer not just defeat, but one of the most staggering losses of modern military history. It would not be militarily necessary for U.S. combat forces to come to Taiwan's help in such a war. Whether it was deemed politically desirable or not would be a function largely of how the war began and of whether Washington considered it essential under the circumstances to demonstrate unimpeachable support for Taiwan. Regardless, any demands on U.S. combat forces would be modest.

Could China Coerce Taiwan's Capitulation?

Even if China could not seize Taiwan, it could try to use military force in a more limited way to pressure Taipei to accept terms for political association highly favorable to Beijing. Two scenarios are of particular interest: a missile attack designed to terrorize or coerce (rather than to achieve direct military effect) and a blockade. In the latter case, U.S. military

85. International Institute for Strategic Studies, *The Military Balance 1999/2000*, p. 205. For a view similar to my own, see Michael D. Swaine, *Taiwan's National Security*, p. 56.

forces would probably need to come to Taiwan's assistance in order to avoid a slow strangulation of the island.

Consider first a possible missile attack by China against Taiwan. The PRC has about 200 ballistic missiles deployed near Taiwan today, and it may double or even triple this package within five years. From their current positions, the M-9 and M-11 missiles can reach Taiwan. As shown above, however, neither possesses sufficient accuracy to effectively strike military assets using conventional explosives. Indeed, they would generally miss their targets by several football fields and almost always by the length of at least a single field. Granted, if Beijing unleashed a salvo of hundreds of missiles, it might register a few direct hits against lucrative military targets (as well as dozens of hits, with varying degrees of lethality, against population centers). Commercial sea traffic might diminish drastically for a period of time. But if China exhausted the bulk of its missile inventory to sink a grand total of two or three cargo vessels and temporarily slow operations at a port or an airfield, that might not be seen as such an intimidating or successful use of force.

Used against civilian populations, each conventionally armed missile might typically kill anywhere from a few to ten or twenty citizens, judging by the experiences of Operation Desert Storm and the Iran-Iraq "war of the cities."[86] Such terror tactics would be tragic for the well-being of the Taiwanese—but limited in overall magnitude, at least by the standards of war, and more likely to embitter and harden the Taiwanese than coerce their capitulation, if past experience with such terror tactics is any guide. In the end, using missile attacks in this way would say more about Chinese weakness than anything else—just as limited air and cruise missile attacks by the United States in recent years have often shown irresoluteness rather than strength or staying power and have achieved correspondingly poor results.[87]

The more troubling coercive scenario is a blockade. Rather than relying on sheer terror and intimidation, it would take aim at Taiwan's econ-

86. Cordesman and Wagner, *The Lessons of Modern War*, pp. 205–06; and Michael O'Hanlon, "Star Wars Strikes Back," *Foreign Affairs*, vol. 78, no. 6 (November/December 1999), p. 69.

87. Daniel L. Byman and Matthew C. Waxman, "Kosovo and the Great Air Power Debate," *International Security*, vol. 24, no. 4 (Spring 2000), pp. 37–38; and Richard N. Haass, "The Squandered Presidency: Demanding More from the Commander-in-Chief," *Foreign Affairs*, vol. 79, no. 3 (May/June 2000), p. 138.

omy and try to drag it down substantially for an indefinite period. It is doubtful that China could truly cut Taiwan off from the outside world with such a blockade. However, if it were willing to take losses, it could certainly exact attrition from commercial vessels trading with Taiwan as well as Taiwanese military forces trying to break the blockade. Even with an imperfect, "leaky" blockade, it could sink enough commercial ships to scare others off, and it could do so over an extended period. Should it convince most commercial shippers not to risk trips to Taiwan, it could effectively begin to strangle the island. If Beijing then offered Taiwan a compromise deal, Taipei might be coerced into capitulation. For example, Beijing might demand reaffirmation of the one-China principle and some degree of political fealty from Taiwan while permitting the island to retain autonomous rule and finances, and perhaps some armed forces. Moreover, whether Taipei could be coerced in this way or not, China might believe it could—and hence try such a coercive use of force in response to future behavior from Taipei that China finds unacceptable.[88]

A Chinese blockade could take a number of forms. For the PRC, the least risky and most natural approach would simply attempt to introduce a significant risk factor into all maritime voyages in and out of Taiwan by occasionally sinking a cargo ship with submarines or with mines it laid in Taiwan's harbors. Using airplanes and surface ships would put more of its own forces at risk, especially since it could not realistically hope to eliminate Taipei's air force with a preemptive attack. A blockade using planes and surface ships would also be rather straightforward for the United States to defeat quickly. China might couple such a blockade with a preemptive air and special-forces attack—but perhaps just a limited one focused on Taiwanese submarine-hunting ships and airplanes, which it might be able to attack effectively.

In conducting a blockade of Taiwan, China would be taking advantage of three main facts. First, Taiwan has only a small coastline—forcing ship traffic to take predictable routes into ports. Second, it is quite vulnerable to blockade because it has few natural resources, extreme energy dependence, and no other way to import or export than via sea or air. Taiwan's foreign trade accounts for two-thirds of its GDP.[89] Finally, Taiwan has

88. For a somewhat similar assessment, see Bitzinger and Gill, *Gearing Up for High-Tech Warfare?* pp. 44–45.

89. Central Intelligence Agency, *The World Factbook 1999*.

few submarines or long-range attack aircraft to conduct a countervailing blockade of its own. Ships headed to or from China could simply sail around Taiwan far enough to keep out of range of its weapons. China does not enjoy asymmetric advantages over Taiwan for much-ballyhooed scenarios such as computer virus warfare, so it seems more likely that Beijing would resort to a blockade to cause Taiwan economic harm.

Taiwan could take a number of steps to break a Chinese blockade and to mitigate any effects it might have. Ships could come and go from Taiwan's eastern shores as much as possible. They could avoid the Indonesian Straits and South China Sea and force the PRC to attempt attacks in the open oceans far from Chinese territory.[90] This approach would add a few thousand miles and modest cost to the merchant ships' journey, but such costs are not particularly onerous in modern ocean shipping. It would also permit any of Taiwan's surviving antisubmarine surface ships to operate either within cover of land-based Taiwanese air-power or out of range of both PRC and Taiwanese fighter bombers.[91] Similarly, Taiwanese airpower would be well positioned to defend ships to the east of the island from any PRC aircraft that might pursue them.[92]

Nonetheless, Taiwan would remain rather vulnerable. If it tried to route ships only to ports on its east coast, it would give up use of its Kaohsiung harbor, which is the third largest port in the world and accounts for more than half of all of Taiwan's trade, as well as harbor facilities near Taichung, which account for another quarter of Taiwan's total trade. Other ports could probably handle somewhat more traffic than they do today, but Taiwan's harbors are already busy, and it is implausible that they could sustain anything close to current levels of trade without Kaohsiung and Taichung. Taiwan could certainly mitigate the economic effects of its reduced trade by rationing use of fuel and certain foods, stockpiling manufactured goods with long shelf lives to export once the blockade was lifted, and giving preferential treatment to

90. Shambaugh, "A Matter of Time," pp. 130–31.

91. Paul H. B. Godwin, "The Use of Military Force against Taiwan: Potential PRC Scenarios," in Parris H. Chang and Martin L. Lasater, eds., *If China Crosses the Taiwan Strait: The International Response* (Lanham, Md.: University Press of America, 1993), pp. 22–25.

92. John Caldwell, *China's Conventional Military Capabilities, 1994–2004: An Assessment* (Washington: Center for Strategic and International Studies, 1994), p. 20.

its highest-revenue exports and most crucial imports. It could also offload some ships anchored near shore using small barges, easing the constraint posed by the limited harbor capacity on its eastern shore.[93] However, as with Britain in World War II, its ability to endure a long blockade is not certain.[94]

Most of China's submarines do not have antiship cruise missiles or great underwater endurance at present,[95] and their capacity to conduct a coordinated blockade operation in conjunction with surface and aerial assets is limited.[96] However, these shortcomings may not be particularly onerous when the submarines' targets are commercial ships approaching Taiwan. The submarines have adequate ranges on a single tank of fuel—typically almost 10,000 miles—to stay deployed east of Taiwan for substantial periods.[97] Although their ability to coordinate with each other and reconnaissance aircraft is limited, that might not matter greatly for the purposes of a "leaky" blockade. Carrying torpedoes with ranges of ten kilometers or more, and being able to pick up commercial ships by sonar or by sight, such submarines acting individually could maintain patrols over a large fraction of the sea approaches to Taiwan.[98] It could take Taiwan weeks to find the better PRC submarines (of which China has nine today, as shown in table 6-1), particularly if China used them in hit-and-run modes. Modern attack submarines are able to detect enemy warships at considerable distance and are fast when submerged (unlike, say, World War II submarines), giving them a chance to escape surface ships without running vulnerably on the surface.[99]

Taiwan could use its surface fleet to set up and accompany convoys of merchant ships. It could be harder to do this for ships approaching Taiwan

93. Godwin, "The Use of Military Force against Taiwan," pp. 21–22.

94. Republic of China, *Republic of China Yearbook 1999* (1999) (www.gio.gov.tw/info/yb97/html/content.htm [December 27, 2000]).

95. See E. R. Hooton, ed., *Jane's Naval Weapon Systems*, issue 30 (Alexandria, Va.: Jane's Information Group, August 1999).

96. Montaperto, "China," p. 52; and Cohen, "The Security Situation in the Taiwan Strait," pp. 9, 16–17.

97. Captain Richard Sharpe, ed., *Jane's Fighting Ships 1995–96* (Alexandria, Va.: Jane's Information Group, 1995), pp. 117–18.

98. Anthony J. Watts, *Jane's Underwater Warfare Systems, 1998–99*, 10th ed. (Alexandria, Va.: Jane's Information Group, 1998), pp. 215–16.

99. Karl Lautenschlager, "The Submarine in Naval Warfare, 1901–2001," *International Security*, vol. 11, no. 3 (Winter 1986/87), pp. 258–68.

than for those leaving, however, since those that approach come from many different places, and if they assembled east of Taiwan to wait for escorts, they would be vulnerable at that point. An additional complication is that Chinese submarines lucky enough to be lying quietly in wait in the right places would tend to hear approaching convoys before they were themselves detected, making it likely that they could often get off the first shot—if not the first couple—before being put at risk themselves.

The overall outcome of this struggle is very hard to predict. China's advanced submarine force is small, but Taiwan's advanced antisubmarine warfare capabilities are not much greater. In addition are the uncertainties over how many escort ships Taiwan would have lost in a preemptive Chinese attack and how proficiently the two sides would use their respective assets.[100]

Chinese mines would likely pose a problem, too. China's submarines usually each carry two to three dozen mines, so half of its entire submarine fleet would carry about 1,000. If half the fleet were able to deploy mines near Taiwan without being sunk, China would be able to deploy nearly as many mines as Iraq did—with considerable effect—against the U.S.-led coalition in 1990–91. China surely has, and will acquire, more sophisticated mines than Iraq possessed, moreover, including "smart mines" that would be difficult for minehunters to find or neutralize.[101] Moreover, Taiwan's minesweeping ships are limited in number and mediocre in quality and condition. It is likely that China could exact a price with its mines, perhaps causing attrition rates of a few percent each time ships tried to enter or leave Taiwan's ports, by analogy with the U.S. Persian Gulf experience and other previous conflicts.[102]

Force Planning Implications for the United States

Taiwan could defeat even a full-fledged Chinese invasion without help, but it might not be able to endure and finally break a blockade by itself. U.S. forces might therefore be quite important militarily as well as polit-

---

100. McVadon, "PRC Exercises, Doctrine and Tactics toward Taiwan, pp. 259–62.

101. See for example, Andrew F. Krepinevich Jr., *The Conflict Environment in 2016: A Scenario-Based Approach* (Washington: Center for Strategic and Budgetary Assessments, 1996), p. 7.

102. Yu Kien-hong, "Taking Taiwan," pp. 31–32; and Sharpe, *Jane's Fighting Ships 1995–96*, pp. 116–18, 700–01.

ically. The focus of the U.S. effort would be on antisubmarine warfare, air superiority, minehunting, and minesweeping. The United States might also choose to marshal, at least temporarily, capacity for offensive air strikes against PRC ships, ports, airfields, and air defenses in southeastern coastal China. Such attacks would not be absolutely necessary to break the blockade; the antisubmarine barriers, an air defense umbrella near Taiwan, and minesweeping assets could achieve that goal rather confidently. Offensive air strikes might be considered important to minimize risks to U.S. assets in the area, however, and perhaps to limit China's ability to immediately resume blockade efforts once American forces left the region in the aftermath of hostilities.

My estimates, developed below, are that a fairly large U.S. naval force package would be required to break the Chinese blockade quickly and at minimal risk to U.S. military personnel. Although significant, it would not be larger than the naval force package commonly associated with planning for a major theater war. Thus, provided that the blockade could be definitively broken within a few months, this contingency does not argue for a larger U.S. Navy. Even if the mission took a year, at or near its current size, the Navy could rotate in additional ships to replace the first group, provided that it was deemed possible to make do with considerably less naval presence elsewhere in the world during that period.

Specifically, to break a Chinese blockade of Taiwan, the United States might require the following capabilities, most of them naval. The majority would have to be deployed from the west coast of the United States (meaning that the armada would need about a month to deploy):

—four aircraft carrier battle groups (though several squadrons of U.S. Air Force aircraft might be based on Taiwan as a substitute for one or two carriers, and U.S. aircraft on Okinawa might also contribute if Tokyo assented);

—about two dozen additional surface combatants for escorting merchant-ship convoys and protecting minesweepers and minehunters;

—a half dozen minesweepers and/or minehunters (in addition to minehunting helicopters on surface ships and other mine warfare assets);

—ten to fifteen submarines;

—ten to twenty land-based P-3 aircraft;

—most of the dozen so-called surveillance towed array sonar system (SURTASS) sensors, pulled by tugboats known as T-AGOS, in the U.S. inventory (or possibly additional frigates instead);

—up to several dozen additional aircraft—perhaps including long-range bombers carrying Harpoon antiship missiles and JDAM GPS-guided bombs—for a limited time to assist in offensive strikes against Chinese ships, ports, and airfields directly involved in the conflict.

The given numbers of most types of U.S. military assets would be determined largely by the geography of the scenario, rather than the size of the Chinese submarine force. Specifically, setting up antisubmarine warfare (ASW) barriers and a certain number of convoy escort teams would determine many of the numbers, whether the Chinese advanced submarine threat of concern numbered five or nine or twenty (as it may someday). That said, these estimates are rough. One could imagine different ways of creating barriers and different locations for those ASW barriers.

By focusing on directly breaking the blockade and by attacking only those Chinese military instruments involved in it, the United States would be doing its utmost to avoid the unthinkable—the possibility of general war against the People's Republic of China. One could imagine many other military options for the United States, from general conventional bombing attacks on Chinese infrastructure (as in Operation Allied Force against Serbia in 1999), or general attacks against most or all of China's military power (as in Operation Desert Storm), to a counterblockade of China's coasts. However, these escalatory options would make little strategic sense, given their extreme risks—up to and including the possibility of nuclear war. Given the high confidence with which the United States could break a Chinese blockade of Taiwan by directly targeting those PRC assets carrying out the blockade, there would be little need to attempt more general and strategically dangerous attacks. Moreover, carrying them out would require more airpower than the United States could realistically expect to deploy in the region, except in the unlikely event that Japan opened up several of its major airfields to U.S. use for that purpose. Establishing air dominance throughout much of eastern China and attacking a wide range of target sets there would imply an operation at least comparable in scope to the air war of Operation Desert Storm—an operation for which the Pentagon now believes that some fifteen to twenty wings of combat aircraft would be needed.

Even a limited operation against PRC ships, airplanes, ports, airfields, and air defense assets in southeastern coastal China would be demanding and dangerous. It would hardly be something to undertake lightly. China could not realistically expect the United States to refrain from such attacks if it was using those assets to threaten not only merchant shipping into Taiwan, but U.S. ships and planes and submarines as well. Nevertheless, the United States would be well advised to limit the attacks in time and space. Otherwise it could find the force requirements excessive and could run far greater risks of provoking Chinese escalation than would be necessary or prudent.

The Basic Approach to Breaking the PRC Blockade

The basic concept for U.S. antisubmarine operations would be to set up a safe shipping lane east of Taiwan and to heavily protect ships during the most dangerous part of their journeys near the island. To carry that mission out, the United States, together with Taiwan, would need to establish air superiority, protect ships against Chinese submarine attack, and cope with the threat of mines.

One forward ASW barrier could be maintained by U.S. attack submarines operating in the Taiwan Strait, most probably near China's ports. This would be the first line of defense. These submarines would seek to destroy any Chinese submarines they found. Over time, they could annihilate the PRC submarine force, except perhaps those vessels that remained in port throughout the conflict.

The second ASW barrier would consist of ships, primarily ASW frigates, accompanying convoys of merchant ships as they sailed in from the open ocean waters east of Taiwan. These convoys might form a thousand miles or more east of Taiwan, and they would enjoy armed protection from that point onward as they traveled to the island and later as they departed. The frigates would listen for approaching submarines and for the sound of any torpedoes being fired.

Finally, additional assets would be dedicated to various special purposes. Some would protect U.S. aircraft carriers. Others would provide additional protection to ships, be they merchant ships or mine warfare vessels, as they operated near Taiwan's shores (and thus fairly close to China). Two main types of assets might be used. Surface ships—either additional frigates or SURTASS arrays towed by T-AGOS vessels—might be deployed near aircraft carrier battle groups to provide additional protection for those groups. In addition, P-3 aircraft could be kept on call, or airborne, to pursue any submarines that might be roughly localized by surface-ship or submarine sonar.

The U.S. minehunters and minesweepers would of course operate near Taiwan's ports and the main approaches to those ports. Land-based or ship-based helicopters might assist them, as might robotic submersibles deployed from ships near shore.

The U.S. aircraft carrier battle groups would operate east of Taiwan. They would probably function best as two pairs. One pair would be stationed relatively near the island to provide air superiority over and around Taiwan. Another pair would operate well east of the island, serving, in part, as a backup to those near Taiwan. In addition, it would provide control of the airspace over the open ocean east of Taiwan; doing so would help defend against any indirect Chinese attack (most likely by longer-range bombers) that managed to avoid the first pair of carriers and Taiwan's air force.

As an alternative to one or two of the carriers, several squadrons of U.S. Air Force or Navy aircraft might be deployed on Taiwan, provided that hardened shelters, effective air defense, and logistics support could be made available for them there. If most of Taiwan's air force survived initial Chinese attacks, that might not be deemed desirable, given concerns about overcrowding airfields and flight corridors. It would, however, be a sound option to consider in order to reduce strain on the Navy's carrier battle groups and to provide for shorter fighter flight paths to the waters of the Taiwan Strait. It could also be important for preparing any offensive options against nearby coastal regions of the PRC mainland (such as ports, ships, and airfields near Taiwan) that might be considered at some point in the conflict. Some surveillance and support aircraft, such as airborne warning and control system (AWACS) and joint surveillance target attack radar system (JSTARS) planes, as well as tankers, may also be useful to station on Taiwan. Finally, if Japan allowed it—hardly a given—U.S. aircraft at Kadena air base on Okinawa could contribute to the operation as well, securing the northern flank of the theater of operations. Overall, in any event, these missions would not tax Air Force capabilities nearly as much as this operation would tax the Navy.

The overall effect of this constellation of assets would mean that any Chinese submarine wishing to fire at a merchant ship or aircraft carrier would first have to evade submarine detection and then evade a second ASW barrier as it approached its target. To survive the overall engagement and return to port, it would of course then need to successfully negotiate through two barriers in the other direction. During the cold war, the effectiveness of ASW operations was commonly assessed at 5 to

15 percent per barrier. By those odds, the typical Chinese sub would do well to survive for two full missions from base.[103] Nevertheless, it might succeed in getting off several shots against valuable surface ships before meeting its own demise.

Calculating the Quantitative Force Requirements

So much for the broad-brush argument. How does one calculate, in more precise if still approximate terms, the numbers of U.S. forces needed for these missions? Desert Storm and major theater war (MTW) building blocks are not of much use; nor are ship rotation rules for naval forward presence in peacetime. Fortunately, some of the analytical techniques that were in frequent use during the cold war are applicable here.

Consider first U.S. submarines. The most efficient way to use them would probably be forward, near China, and preferably close to China's ports. If stationed some fifteen to twenty kilometers outside three major Chinese ports, for example, the total length of the perimeter they would defend would be around one hundred kilometers. Doing so would require operation under difficult sonar conditions, given the shallow water and boat traffic, so doing the job this way could require spacing submarines every ten kilometers apart or so. But even if they were that close, a total of ten submarines would suffice for the mission, with several in a backup mode to chase any Chinese submarines that made it through the barrier but were detected in the process.[104]

How much aircraft carrier cover would be needed? China has less than a hundred modern aircraft, so thinking in terms of establishing superiority with fourth-generation planes, and ensuring the ability for twenty-four-hour operations, two carrier battle groups might seem ample. Many of China's older planes do not have adequate range to fly very far east of

---

103. As points of reference, U.S. cold war forces were thought capable of setting up barriers that might each cause 5 to 15 percent attrition to passing submarines; submarines and surface combatants were thought to be relatively equally likely of destroying one another, meaning that on average roughly one submarine would be lost for each escort sunk. See Congressional Budget Office, *U.S. Naval Forces: The Sea Control Mission* (Washington, 1978).

104. If the force were aided by SOSUS arrays, which may still be deployed in that part of the western Pacific, the number of attack submarines could decline. See Tom Stefanick, *Strategic Antisubmarine Warfare and Naval Strategy* (Lexington, Mass.: Lexington Books, 1987), pp. 39–41; and Congressional Budget Office, *U.S. Naval Forces: The Peacetime Presence Mission* (Washington, 1978), p. 60.

Taiwan and back to the mainland. However, if they were used in a quasi-kamikaze mode, or if they were able to attack ships that were fairly close to Taiwan (and thus China), up to several hundred Chinese jets might be able to participate in such an effort. Such a saturation attack might also be used against any U.S. mine warfare ships that were needed to open up Taiwanese ports, particularly those on the western side of the island facing China. The U.S. carrier battle groups would be aided in countering PRC fighters by perhaps 300 surviving Taiwanese aircraft. However, operating on the principle that the carrier fighter fleet should have largely autonomous capability to take on such an attack, in case other assets were otherwise in use or disabled, the United States would probably want more than two aircraft carriers.

In fact, four carrier battle groups would make sense, comprising two pairs, each of which would have the capacity for continuous flight operations. That would allow one pair to operate near Taiwan, and one pair farther east, with the ability to aid the first group as well as to provide air cover several hundred miles east of Taiwan (in case China tried to route bombers there indirectly). Assuming the need to get off an average of two shots per PRC aircraft, and assuming four to six air-to-air missiles on each of forty to fifty airplanes per carrier, the four carriers could literally take on 300 to 400 Chinese attack aircraft—a number the PRC might be able to put in the air simultaneously, if it wanted to risk all on a single all-out assault against the carrier task forces.

Even this number of U.S. aircraft, aided by ship-borne warning and control aircraft, could not hope to shoot down all PRC planes. Ship-based air defenses would be needed, too. However, in rough quantitative terms, that number of carriers would appear roughly correct. For one thing, it would deny China the option of attempting to simply overwhelm U.S. air defenses by saturating them. Second, it would discourage China from having any illusions about compensating through numbers for what it could not hope to achieve through quality.

As noted before, land-based U.S. Air Force fighters on Okinawa or Taiwan could be substituted for some carrier aircraft, in roughly one-for-one proportions, if that were deemed practical. If it were practical, it would probably be desirable, given the shorter distances to the Taiwan Strait and the relief it would provide to the Navy.

Additional aircraft might be needed, at least temporarily, for any strikes against Chinese assets on the PRC homeland. The purposes of any such attacks should be limited: minimizing risks to U.S. military forces operating in the region and reducing China's capabilities for reinstating a naval blockade once U.S. forces had completed their mission and left the region. The United States and Taiwan should harbor no illusions about fully eliminating China's airpower, missile capabilities, or similar assets during such air strikes. Any damage done to Chinese ports and airfields would be rather quickly repaired after a conflict, so there would be little point in conducting anything more than suppressive attacks against such infrastructure. If they were to be conducted at all, most U.S. attacks should presumably be against ships and submarines in port, and perhaps against some PRC aircraft on bases near the coast. Given the implausibility that the United States and Taiwan could achieve air dominance over Chinese territory, U.S. attacks should generally be limited to targets that could be struck by aircraft situated over the East China Sea, South China Sea, or Taiwan Strait. If the goal were to destroy a dozen or so ships, several dozen sorties of attack aircraft could be needed; if the goal were to suppress air operations at several airfields, a comparable number of sorties could be needed daily to crater runways and suppress air defense sites. All told, these operations could require up to an additional wing of U.S. aircraft—perhaps seventy fighters, or a smaller number of aircraft if the contingent included both fighters and large bombers—for whatever period of time they were conducted.

As for escorting convoys, during the cold war the United States maintained enough surface combatants to accompany about seven convoys at a time, allocating one destroyer and nine frigates per convoy for a total of seventy ships. That was to help carry provisions to a NATO military structure of some five million troops and an allied civilian population of well over 200 million in Europe. In Taiwan, corresponding numbers would be a factor of five to ten less, and the magnitude of the enemy submarine threat would also be far less—though the island's overall dependence on sea trade would clearly be greater than was NATO Europe's. Roughly speaking, then, a capability to accompany two convoys at a time would probably be appropriate, translating into twenty U.S. surface combatants (above and beyond those associated with the carrier battle groups).[105]

105. Congressional Budget Office, *Building a 600-Ship Navy: Costs, Timing, and Alternative Approaches* (Washington, 1982), p. 8; and Congressional Budget Office, *Future Budget Requirements for the 600-Ship Navy* (Washington, 1985), pp. 5–6, 13–15.

SURTASS ships, any additional frigates protecting carriers, and P-3s would be needed in only modest numbers. As for P-3s, two to three aircraft on continuous patrol relatively near Taiwan should suffice, making for a total requirement of no more than ten planes. Several ships could be maintained around each key port; several could also contribute (along with escort vessels) to an outer layer of protection for the two aircraft carrier task forces.

U.S. mine warfare ships would face a difficult challenge. They would surely be vulnerable, primarily to surprise air attack and possibly also to submarine attack. For that reason, they would receive extra protection in the form of aircraft cover and ASW barriers. The more positive aspect of the situation is that there would not be a great deal of water to clear, since Taiwan has only a few major ports. Mine warfare ships travel at five to ten knots when searching for or neutralizing mines, and they can detect even relatively sophisticated mines at up to a kilometer's distance. At that pace, the waters within twenty miles of a port could be cleared of mines in several days' time by a single ship. Allowing for the possibility that several harbors could require clearing of mines, and that a mine warfare ship or two could be damaged in the process, the United States might wish to deploy up to a half dozen vessels for this purpose.[106] As noted, other assets such as helicopters and robotics might contribute to the mission as well, for redundancy and for their special advantages in certain types of mine-detection technologies. However, the necessary numbers of such assets would probably not be great.

The United States could suffer significant casualties in this type of conflict, even if its ability to prevail would not be in serious doubt. Creating several ASW barriers does not guarantee immediate success, especially against China's modest number of good submarines. They would eventually be sunk, but perhaps not before sinking a few merchant vessels—and possibly even a U.S. Navy ship. A lucky Chinese aircraft might also penetrate a carrier's air defenses and manage a strike against it. The United States would also be likely to lose some pilots, and quite possibly a mine warfare vessel or two. Its losses would likely number at least in the dozens, and quite possibly in the hundreds, of troops killed in action during the

---

106. See Colonel Timothy M. Laur and Steven L. Llanso, *Encyclopedia of Modern U.S. Military Weapons* (New York: Berkley Books, 1995), pp. 439–40; Department of Defense, *Conduct of the Persian Gulf War* (Washington, 1992), pp. T-212–T-213.

conflict. In the remote event of a catastrophic attack against a carrier, losses could even reach into the low thousands.

The United States may also have vulnerabilities that cannot be easily deduced from my unclassified analysis. Top on the list of candidates is the possible vulnerability of electronics to electromagnetic pulse from a high-altitude nuclear detonation. China would not need to kill many people to carry out such an attack. This type of attack could disable many ships and aircraft (though not U.S. attack submarines). If, as reported, the United States has reduced its investment in the hardening of electronics, it would be wise to restore funding in this area to levels like those of the cold war; otherwise it would be unwisely allowing its forces to retain an Achilles' heel.[107]

Arms Sales

The implications of this analysis for U.S. arms sales policy are complex. In early 2000 the Clinton administration announced a decision to sell Taiwan several types of precision-guided air-to-air and air-to-ground missiles and to provide a land-based radar for warning of any missile attacks by the PRC as well. These ideas make sense, as do further efforts to help Taiwan harden its airfields, fuel and ammunition storage facilities, and command and control infrastructure.[108] The Clinton administration chose, however, not to sell Taiwan large naval weaponry, including P-3 surveillance aircraft, attack submarines, and Aegis-class destroyer ships. The Bush administration later approved sales of P-3 aircraft, attack submarines, and second-hand destroyer ships lacking Aegis capabilities.

That balanced approach to arms sales makes sense as a matter of principle. The military benefit of possible arms sales to Taiwan must always be evaluated against the likely political fallout, including the chance that, should Taipei ever feel either invulnerable or automatically assured of U.S. military aid in a crisis, it might be more inclined to pursue its independence aspirations provocatively.[109]

107. See O'Hanlon, *Technological Change and the Future of Warfare*, pp. 174–75.

108. See, for example, the comments of James Mulvenon, quoted in Steven Mufson, "Warship Sale Could Fuel China Tensions," *Washington Post*, April 14, 2000, p. A1.

109. For a similar view, see Thomas J. Christensen, "Correspondence: Spirals, Security, and Stability in East Asia," *International Security*, vol. 24, no. 4 (Spring 2000), p. 196.

Congressional Republicans tended to ignore this concern in crafting their Taiwan Security Enhancement Act, approved by the House in February of 2000.[110] It would have been a bad idea—formalizing links between U.S. and Taiwanese militaries, stating a U.S. predisposition to sell Taiwan any arms Taipei requested, and otherwise changing the tone of American involvement in the Taiwan problem without directly addressing Taiwan's defense needs.[111] Nonetheless, Congressional Republicans were correct in saying the Clinton administration's arms-sales package for Taiwan denied the island weapons it should have. Their argument is strongest not for the four Aegis destroyers Taipei has requested for missile defense—which have taken on a greater symbolic significance than their military capabilities warrant—but for antisubmarine warfare capabilities.[112] In particular, there is little reason not to consider replacing most of Taiwan's current S-2 fleet of 31 aircraft with faster, longer-range, better-equipped P-3s, as the Bush administration agrees. In addition, hardened shelters should be built for these aircraft if possible.

Given China's missile firings near Taiwan in 1995 and 1996, as well as its recent buildup of short-range missiles along its coast near Taiwan, Taipei's request for the Aegis vessels seems understandable. China's protestations notwithstanding,[113] it cannot expect the United States to refuse all theater missile defense (TMD) sales to Taiwan under such circumstances. However, Chinese ballistic missiles armed with conventional warheads are less of a threat to Taiwan than meets the eye. Even if they could cause some damage, they are too inaccurate to threaten Taiwan's military bases seriously. Under these circumstances, Aegis-based TMD, and particularly the advanced Navy Theater Wide system, may not be the right answer.

In addition, the Aegis technology is immature—even the versions the U.S. military uses will not provide reliable defenses against ballistic missiles until 2007 or thereafter. The Navy Theater Wide defense only works in the vacuum of space, beyond the Earth's atmosphere, meaning that it could not

110. Christopher Marquis, "GOP Criticizes White House on Taiwan Aid Plan," *New York Times*, April 19, 2000, p. A14.

111. Thomas E. Ricks, "Admiral Takes Stand against Pro-Taiwan Legislation," *Washington Post*, March 8, 2000, p. A32; and Steven Mufson and Helen Dewar, "Taiwan Bill Tabled as Island's Leaders Urge Delay," *Washington Post*, April 27, 2000, p. A24.

112. Mufson, "Warship Sale Could Fuel China Tensions," p. A1.

113. Information Office of the State Council of the People's Republic of China, *China's National Defense in 2000* (Beijing, October 2000), pp. 62–63.

intercept missiles China launched from near its coast (since such short-range missiles never leave the atmosphere) and also could not intercept somewhat longer-range missiles that were directed to fly on low or "depressed" trajectories. Finally, Navy Theater Wide could also be defeated by simple, light decoys that mimicked warheads in the vacuum of outer space.

Other measures to improve Taiwan's air and missile defenses—measures that would be more timely, less costly, and less politically provocative—do make sense. They include not only further hardening of key infrastructure, but also sale of more advanced Patriot missile defense batteries. Someday, THAAD TMD may also make sense, with its limited endoatmospheric capability (which also provides a partial antidote to PRC decoys). However, THAAD is not yet ready for use or overseas sales and will not be available until 2007 or so. Moreover, it should probably only be sold if the situation further deteriorates by then. China's major ballistic-missile buildup near Taiwan merits a response, but the response should be calibrated to the nature of the military threat, lest it either embolden Taiwan to take dangerous steps toward independence or lead to a hostile Chinese reaction that might leave Taiwan in a worse military situation than before.

Aegis destroyers, designed for air defense, do have some antisubmarine warfare capability.[114] However, they would be no antidote to a blockade—particularly if they were constrained to remain near Taiwan's shores to provide missile defense for the island. More useful is the P-3 Orion aircraft, which can drop buoys with sonar devices and fire torpedoes at any submarines the buoys detect. They possess ultra-low-frequency sonar capable of detecting Kilo-class submarines that Taiwan cannot now easily find with its existing ASW assets.[115] If Taiwan had these, it might be able to break a PRC blockade on its own, or at least reduce the need for the United States to deploy P-3s in any future combat operations near the Strait. Taiwan would also benefit from more warships optimized for antisubmarine warfare, such as frigates.

114. Erik Eckholm and Steven Lee Myers, "Taiwan Asks U.S. to Let It Obtain Top-Flight Arms," *New York Times*, March 1, 2000, p. A1.

115. June Teufel Dreyer, "Taiwan's Military: A View from Afar," in Larry M. Wortzel, ed., *The Chinese Armed Forces in the 21st Century* (Carlisle, Pa.: Strategic Studies Institute, Army War College, 1999), p. 307.

The United States is also right to help Taiwan upgrade its decaying submarine fleet. However, given the difficulty of finding a willing manufacturer, this could take some time.

Conclusion

China's most promising way to threaten Taiwan militarily over the next decade is with a blockade using its submarine force. Such a blockade, if effective, might not be enough to ensure Taiwan's capitulation, but it could put China in a good position to coerce Taipei into accepting terms for a confederation of two autonomous entities, possibly on political and economic terms highly favorable to Beijing. Other types of Chinese attacks seem less worrisome. Conventionally armed missile attacks would be of limited military effectiveness, given the poor accuracy of China's present ballistic-missile inventory, and cannot be reliably prevented in any case. An invasion is beyond China's capacity, even if the United States plays no combat role in any conflict.

Were the PRC to undertake a blockade, U.S. help might be needed to break it. A U.S. naval force of the size generally assumed for a standard major theater war could be needed to decisively break the blockade. To decisively defeat the Chinese operation, the following assets, in particular, could be needed: four aircraft carrier battle groups; two dozen additional surface combatants for convoy escort; about fifteen attack submarines; ten to twenty P-3 aircraft, as well as several additional ships (such as T-AGOS) for ASW operations; and half a dozen mine warfare vessels. They would establish local air superiority; maintain ASW barriers; escort commercial ship convoys on their voyages; clear harbors of mines; and provide various options for attacking Chinese ships as well as key ports and airfields in southeastern coastal China. Several Air Force fighter squadrons on Taiwan and/or Okinawa might replace one or two of the carrier battle groups, political and military circumstances permitting.

The United States need not increase the size of its Navy to cope with this scenario. It is, however, a scenario that would tax its naval force structure roughly as much as a conflict in the Persian Gulf or Korea—and probably pose greater risks of casualties to its crews. Moreover, it would almost surely require temporary reductions in other U.S. naval activities around the world—though some presence could be sustained in the Persian Gulf and Arabian Sea, and an armada could be generated for a second major war if absolutely necessary.

To limit demands on American forces and the risks of U.S. casualties, some additional arms sales to Taiwan may make sense. Most appropriate are ASW assets; less important are advanced TMD systems, particularly Navy Theater Wide. The former respond to the most worrisome potential combat scenario in the Strait that could do the greatest real harm to Taiwan's population; the latter, by contrast, have little chance of stopping a concerted Chinese attack in any case. As always, however, the issue of arms sales to Taiwan must be handled extremely carefully; given its certain political implications, it is far more than a matter of military planning.

SEVEN

Summary and Conclusion

Defense spending does need to increase further in the years ahead, but the Bush administration's plans are excessively expensive at a time of federal deficits and competing national and international needs. Moreover, most of the administration's planned increases from 2003 until 2007 have little to do with the war on terror. No more than 20 percent of the planned increase can be attributed to the demands imposed by that war and the new challenge of homeland security. But how can spending increases be contained?

Less Expensive Weaponry

The military services do need to replace aging equipment, but they need not spend as much as current plans would require. Rather than retain what is essentially a cold war–lite approach to weapons modernization, the guiding philosophy should be somewhat more restrained and selective. Three principles should guide future procurement: making sure enough equipment is bought to keep the military's weapons inventory reliable and safe; profiting from the electronics revolution to purchase adequate numbers of new sensors, computers, communications capabilities, and munitions, which provide substantially improved capabilities for generally modest costs; and purchasing relatively small numbers of next-generation major weaponry as "silver bullet" forces.

In practice, this philosophy means that while large numbers of weapons will need to be purchased in the years ahead, and procurement spending will need to rise somewhat, the military services should generally purchase cost-effective technology rather than ultra-expensive new capabilities. For example, rather than buying large numbers of advanced fighter aircraft that cost twice as much as today's, they could purchase more modest numbers—and otherwise buy more of existing aircraft like F-16s to replace aging planes. If they are equipped with advanced munitions, sensors, computers, and communications systems—all of which are improving greatly due to the ongoing electronics revolution—they will be more capable than current fighters in any event. They will also be far better than anything adversaries could muster. Similar silver-bullet philosophies might be applied to the Marine Corps V-22 Osprey, the Army's Comanche helicopter, and the Navy's submarine force. With this approach, and selective additional economies in areas such as nuclear weapons procurement and the Army's transformation program, procurement spending might be held to $75 billion to $80 billion a year rather than the $90 billion or more that could otherwise be necessary.

A Different Two-War Capability

The military should continue preparing for two nearly simultaneous conflicts. It is important for the United States to be able to robustly deter, and possibly even undertake, war in a second theater even when engaged in large-scale combat elsewhere. Rather than plan for two overlapping Desert Storm–like wars, as it did during the 1990s, however, the military should adopt something akin to a one and one-half major theater war capability—or a force structure based on a scenario of Desert Storm plus Desert Shield plus Bosnia/IFOR. The Bush administration has reached a similar conclusion. However, it did not recommend any resulting cuts in forces or personnel. My analysis suggests that this alternative strategic framework would allow modest reductions in U.S. military end-strength, with active-duty forces declining in number to about 1.3 million from their current target of 1.36 million. More important, it would allow forces to be reshaped and reconfigured, augmenting the types of units that are frequently deployed and making other changes to reduce the strain of frequent deployments on U.S. military personnel.

With this approach, the United States would plan on only a single all-out war that included a prompt massive ground offensive to overthrow an enemy government and occupy its territory. In a second possible war, it would rely more heavily on airpower in the early going and factor in the likely contributions of major allies (most important, South Korea or Britain, depending on where the war occurred). In the extremely unlikely event that a large-scale ground counteroffensive was needed in two theaters, the United States would still have recourses: either to use substantial numbers of U.S. reserve forces, or to await the conclusion of one war before prosecuting the second to completion. These are admittedly less than ideal options, but they are only insurance policies against an extraordinarily unlikely event. In that sense, they are sound concepts.

A Desert Storm plus Desert Shield plus Bosnia/IFOR framework would give the U.S. military the capability for an all-out effort that might involve half a million or more troops and for a second overlapping conflict requiring 200,000 to 300,000 personnel. The latter number is comparable to what the United States deployed in the fall of 1990 for Operation Desert Shield, and much less than what was later deemed necessary for Desert Storm, but it would represent far more than a "hold" capability. As NATO showed in Operation Allied Force, when only 50,000 uniformed personnel ultimately bombed Slobodan Milosevic into submission, modern militaries can do far more than establish a defensive perimeter with roughly a quarter-million troops. A force of 200,000 to 300,000 would be capable not only of establishing a robust defense, but also of carrying out extensive aerial bombardment operations and limited ground counteroffensives. Depending on where it fought, and on the strength of neighboring allies, it might even have enough capability to contribute to the overthrow of an enemy regime without reinforcement.

A Desert-Shield equivalent of forces, emphasizing naval elements (and minus the associated ground-force package), would also be more than adequate for the U.S. role in any China-Taiwan conflict. Specifically, it would allow the United States to decisively break any attempt by China to impose a naval blockade on Taiwan—the type of military scenario most likely to challenge, and perhaps overwhelm, Taiwan's own defense capabilities. Such a scenario would have to be handled extremely carefully to avoid escalatory risks. In particular, any U.S. attacks against targets on the PRC mainland, if needed at all, would wisely be limited to Chinese military assets in southeastern coastal China. Nevertheless, the U.S. armed forces would retain the necessary capabilities to break such a blockade of Taiwan, if sized to a Desert Storm plus Desert Shield plus Bosnia/IFOR framework.

Selective Reductions in Overseas Deployments

It would be desirable that the United States scale back some overseas military deployments, but any reductions need to be made very strategically and selectively. They should not weaken deterrence, hamstring military effectiveness if deterrence should fail, or deprive the United States of an ability to participate in important peace and humanitarian missions.

Although U.S. military forces in the Balkans received primary attention during the 2000 presidential race, it is in other theaters that substantial reductions may be possible. Most notable are the Marine Corps deployment on Okinawa, Navy deployments in the Mediterranean Sea, and Air Force deployments for Southern Watch over Iraq. Neither of the first two missions serves its original purposes any longer; both could be sharply curtailed without harming core American interests, though in the case of Okinawa, equipment would need to be stockpiled in Japan to compensate for the departure of most of the Marines and to allow for their rapid return in the event of war in Korea. The Iraq operations, at their present scale, are not needed to achieve the core U.S. goals in the Persian Gulf of preventing Saddam Hussein from attacking his neighbors or his own people and pressuring him not to develop weapons of mass destruction. Nor do they seriously threaten his hold on power. By stocking more advanced air-to-ground munitions in the region and making preparations for rapid deployments in a crisis, it should be possible to cut back Air Force airpower in that theater by nearly 50 percent. Clearly, however, this proposal cannot be seriously entertained until the United States has decided whether to overthrow Saddam Hussein.

More Defense and Less (Nuclear) Offense

After decades of maintaining a huge offensive nuclear arsenal while forgoing any missile defense, the United States can now profit from the end of the cold war and other trends in international politics and technology to adopt a new nuclear strategy. It should shift away from exclusive reliance on overwhelming retaliation and deterrence—moving toward a more mixed policy that still emphasizes deterrence, but does so at dramatically lower offensive force levels, and that complements deterrence with a modest missile defense designed to handle small threats from small extremist states.

It makes sense to complement continuing national missile defense efforts, as pursued by the Clinton administration, with a new program to investigate technologies for boost-phase intercept. A large missile defense with multiple tiers is not needed, but a modest two-tier system for the United States and its allies is a sound notion.

It should also be possible to move to a U.S. nuclear arsenal of 1,000 total warheads, including strategic as well as tactical and reserve weapons, negotiated in a bilateral agreement with Russia. This policy should include U.S. ratification of the Comprehensive Test Ban Treaty. Even if it did not, it should save at least $2 billion a year relative to existing plans; depending on how the remaining force posture was designed, savings might even be twice as much.

Modest Increases in the Defense Budget

The United States does not need to increase defense spending to well over $400 billion a year, as the Pentagon's current plans suggest. Even after making the above changes, however, the military will probably still need more money. The steady-state defense budget might be $390 billion or so, as expressed in constant 2002 dollars. Defense spending as a fraction of GDP would rise modestly, to about 3.2 percent—less than half the cold war norm, even though actual dollar budgets would exceed average real dollar levels during the cold war.

While much of Rumsfeld's proposed budget plan can be defended, it goes too far. In times of war, it is often militarily necessary, and politically natural, for defense spending to rise. But the nation presently runs the risk of spending too much on defense. Many members of Congress are fearful of challenging a popular president over his proposed defense requests during such a time of national crisis.

This dynamic puts the nation's fiscal health and domestic agenda at risk and may not even be good for national security. Defense budgets may decline in the years ahead, especially as September 11 no longer dominates the national debate to the extent it has in recent months. If that happens, the Bush administration may then regret that it sacrificed its opportunity to promote the kind of defense reform it championed on the campaign trail and during its first few months in office. The country could be left with a defense program that is too large and expensive for the resources at hand.

Some defense spending increases, beyond those already put in place since 1999, are needed. But most of those proposed by the Bush administration have only limited relevance to the war on terrorism. They should not be justified on the grounds of fighting al-Qaida, other terrorist organizations, or state sponsors of terrorism. And many are not needed on other grounds, either.

President Bush, Vice President Cheney, and Secretary Rumsfeld all have considerable experience in the private sector. Yet they seem to be ignoring an important principle of corporate management—institutions need incentives to become more efficient. Give an organization all it wants and it will fail to prioritize; impose some financial discipline and it will innovate and reform.

Index

ABM Treaty. *See* Anti-Ballistic Missile
Treaty
Abrams tanks, 113–14
Acquisition, military: current major
programs, 102; definition of, 86;
innovation in, 94–99; procurement
spending, 21–23, 86–87, 88,
94–99, 204–05; RDT&E budget,
21, 86, 87, 88, 95, 120; Selected
Acquisition Report program, 102,
103–04. *See also* Defense spending;
Equipment, military; Joint-service
experimentation; Revolution in
military affairs
Aegis-class destroyer ships, 159, 199,
200, 201
Afghanistan: U.S. military commitment, 7, 8, 32, 45. *See also*
Operation Enduring Freedom
Air Force, U.S.: AWACS crews, 43,
194; combat role, 97, 99, 102;
deployment over Iraq, 32, 59–61;
"Link 16" data links, 100;
mission-capable rates, 37; in
Operation Enduring Freedom, 101;
overseas deployment, 42, 84, 85,

207; overseas munitions stocks, 72;
PRC/Taiwan conflict, 194, 202;
recruitment, 36; strategic role,
26–27; structure, 11; two-war
framework, 67, 80; unit reduction
recommendations, 26–27. *See also*
Joint strike fighter aircraft; Raptor
fighter aircraft; *specific bombers*
Aircraft carriers, 22, 202
Aircraft, military: AWACS, 106, 107;
boost-phase missile defenses, 146;
Gulf War, 71–72; long-range
bombers, 115–16, 150, 152;
Operation Enduring Freedom, 99;
potential PRC/Taiwan conflict,
162, 164–65, 169–74, 180–85,
191–92, 193, 195–97, 198, 200;
procurement recommendations,
97, 102–19; spending projections,
102, 107, 108; technological
advances, 90, 102; U.S. dominance, 105–06, 107. *See also specific aircraft and bombers*
Alaska deployment site, 123, 133,
134, 135, 142, 153
Almeida, Pedro, 81